1971

CATHOLIC INFLUENCE ON AMERICAN COLONIAL POLICIES, 1898–1904

CATHOLIC INFLUENCE ON AMERICAN COLONIAL POLICIES 1898–1904

by Frank T. Reuter

UNIVERSITY OF TEXAS PRESS, AUSTIN & LONDON

Library of Congress Catalog Card No. 66–15701

Type set by G&S Typesetters, Austin
Printed by The Steck Company, Austin
Bound by Universal Bookbindery, Inc., San Antonio

To my wife, Kathleen

ACKNOWLEDGMENTS

The completion of this study would have been impossible without the generous assistance of many people. I was given unlimited access to the official archives of the Roman Catholic Diocese of Richmond and those of the Archdioceses of Baltimore and New Orleans. I also benefited from the facilities of the libraries of the University of Illinois and Catholic University, the Manuscripts Division of the Library of Congress, and the National Archives. Quotations from *The Letters of Theodore Roosevelt,* Elting E. Morison, editor, are reprinted by permission of the publishers, Harvard University Press. Material from the Gibbons Correspondence is reproduced by permission of the Archives of the Archdiocese of Baltimore, and that from the O'Connell Correspondence, by permission of the Chancery Office of the Catholic Diocese of Richmond. I am grateful for research grants from the University of Illinois and Texas Christian University, and am particularly grateful to the latter for release from my teaching duties during the summer of 1964. I wish also to acknowledge special debts of gratitude to Professor Arthur E. Bestor for guidance and inspiration, and to my wife, Kathleen, for her patience and encouragement.

FRANK T. REUTER

Texas Christian University

INTRODUCTION

Much has been written about the role of the Roman Catholic Church in the political affairs of states. In most of these discussions the Church has been considered a monolithic organization that on occasion could exert unusual pressure against civil organizations to gain policies favorable to its own. Examples are frequently cited of the powerful influences the Church enjoys in Spain, in Italy, or in the Latin American republics. But what of the Catholic Church in the United States? Is it, or has it been, a powerful influence in American political affairs?

In order to answer this question adequately it is necessary first to isolate a particular historic church-state conflict in American history. There have been many individual problems of conflict since the Catholic Church was formally organized in the United States in 1790. But these difficulties were local or statewide in character and never really involved the entire Church organization or the government of the United States. Not until the end of the nineteenth century can the historian find a basic clash of interest between the policies of the Catholic Church in the United States and those of the federal government.

War with Spain provided the cause for this first basic clash of interests. Actually there were two separate but closely related situations that brought anxiety to American Catholics. The first was the Spanish-American War itself. Catholic loyalty to the United States was challenged. This had never been a serious question before; but Spain was a Catholic country. Would American Catholic loyalties be divided in such a war? The unfortunate, eleventh-hour attempt by Pope Leo XIII to preserve peace simply underscored the Protestant sentiments of distrust of Catholics. Fortunately the brevity of the War, the outspoken pronouncements of loyalty by the hierarchy, and the heroism of Catholics in the armed forces caused these fears to subside.

However, the second situation was more complex than the first and brought about more subtle but nonetheless more important issues between church and state. These resulted from the establishment of the American overseas colonial empire. The new territories, brought under American jurisdiction after the War, had been Spanish for over three centuries. During all this time, and within the limits of Spanish colonial policy, the Catholic Church was given a free hand. It converted the natives, built churches, convents, and monasteries, and provided all of the educational and charitable services for the populace. For more than three hundred years the roles of the colonial administration and the Church became increasingly entwined. By the 1890's each was dependent on the other. Yet by the stroke of a pen this interdependence was brought to an end. The Treaty of Paris, signed in December, 1898, provided that the government of the United States was to assume all of Spain's privileges, properties, and responsibilities in Puerto Rico, Guam, the Philippine Islands, and, temporarily, in Cuba. America's traditional policy of the separation of church and state would go into effect immediately.

If the United States was to assume the responsibility for governing more than ten million people resident in these dependencies, the Catholic Church in the United States had to assume the responsibility of maintaining their religious organization. Practically all of this native population was at least nominally Roman Catholic. They had looked to Spain as the center of their religious organization and the source of most of their priests. Now that Spain's influence was gone, they must have another source of religious leadership. Catholics in the United States felt that it was their responsibility to provide this leadership until a native Catholic hierarchy and clergy could be established.

Here, then, was the source of the real conflict of interest resulting from the War. In assuming jurisdiction over these former Spanish colonies the United States government immediately became a partner with the Catholic Church in the islands in practically every organization for educational and charitable services as well as in the ownership of an extensive variety and amount of real estate, including buildings used for worship. When the American government began its policy of disestablishment the entire fiscal structure of the Church in the islands was endangered, and with it the religious fidelity of its members. Catholic opinion in the United States increasingly feared and distrusted the colonial policies of the American government. Yet it was not distrust of disestablishment itself, for Catholics were well satisfied with the American tradition of the separation of church and state. But many American Catholics sensed a deliberate anti-Catholic direction in the policies set down by the government, policies that they felt might destroy the Catholicism of the natives and turn them over to Protestant missionaries.

The problems of colonial administration confronting the inexperienced, naive American government were enormous. And the Catholic-Church–state controversy was only one of many. But the solution of the controversy was important to both the American government and the American Catholic Church. The government developed a new respect for Catholic opinion that had never before existed. It cooperated with Catholic desires when it had never before cooperated. In so doing it helped begin the process of minimizing the anti-Catholic prejudice that had existed in the United States for so long.

The greatest significance of the Church-state controversy was its effect on the Catholic Church in the United States itself. Representing one sixth of the total U.S. population by 1898, this Church was weak, divided, and fraught with internal dissension. But the War and the subsequent colonial difficulties seemed to be a turning point in Catholic development. By 1904 the Church appeared more united and certainly more aware of the fact that it was the largest single religious body in the United States. Although issues other than the colonial questions helped bring about this greater unity in Catholic activity, the problems in the colonies were the catalyst that tended to produce a crystallization of nationwide Catholic opinion. The Church in the United States prior to 1898 was not a monolithic organization, nor was it about to become one. But by 1904 it was more conscious of itself as a national organization than it had ever been before.

This study endeavors to examine some of the Church-state problems in the new American empire, to observe the Catholic reaction in the United States to these problems, and then to determine what influence, if any, the Catholic Church in the United States had on the formulation or direction of American colonial policies. It is not intended as a discussion of the constitutional questions involved in the separation of church and state in the dependencies nor an account of the laborious litigation inherent to that separation. But rather it is a search for the existence of a particular pressure group within the United States and an attempt at measuring the effectiveness of that pressure group as it endeavored to preserve or extend its own basic interests.

"Pressure group" is a poor term for historians to use, as are "public opinion" and "voting bloc." One must ask: Was the Catholic Church in the United States a pressure group? But before this can be answered another question must be posed: What was the Catholic Church in the United States? The hierarchy? The millions of Catholic laymen throughout the country? The multitude of Catholic organizations? The Catholic press? Or all of these put together? And another term, too, must be considered: What is "Catholic opinion"? And still another question: Is there a Catholic vote? What issues determine it? Where is it located?

All of these questions are tremendous problems for the historian. They can not be ignored, although none of them can be answered adequately. The reader can only recognize that the Catholic Church, comprising one sixth of the total population, was the largest single religious body in the United States. But attempts by the writer to find any kind of voting pattern among these Catholics in the national elections of 1898, 1900, 1902, and 1904 were most disappointing. The number of Catholic members of Congress was insignificant in relation to the total number of Catholics in the country. There was, of course, the organization of the Church itself, headed by a hierarchy of bishops, archbishops, and one cardinal. But these men were often inarticulate on secular affairs; only a few expressed themselves on political matters. There existed also a widely distributed and fairly outspoken Catholic press. Yet these journals were not all official organs of the Church nor did they all maintain consistent or united positions on specific issues.

Despite all of these limitations an observable segment of the Catholic minority claimed to be speaking for the entire Catholic community. What is more important, however, is that the Administrations of Presidents William McKinley and Theodore Roosevelt became increasingly more sensitive to the statements and requests of these particular Catholics. This group consisted primarily of a few members of the hierarchy, who were willing to speak to members of the government, and several major Catholic journals that were located in such politically important areas as Boston and New York. Using these spokesmen as a basis, the writer has attempted to locate a particular Catholic viewpoint as it was expressed to members of the Administration, and to trace the government's reaction accordingly. The following study, therefore, is not necessarily an examination of American Catholic opinion, per se. It is, nonetheless, an attempt to observe a Catholic position on a particularly important issue and the federal government's reaction to that position.

The time period under consideration fits logically into the history of American colonialism. Obviously the victories of the war of 1898 began the colonial period. But 1904, the terminal date of this study, perhaps requires an explanation. The tensions incident to the Church-state problems reached a climax during the administration of the first Philippine civil governor, William Howard Taft. The Philippine problems were the principal problems during the entire controversy, and most of these had been solved by the time Taft returned to the United States in early 1904 to become Secretary of War. The Catholic press actually praised his activities in the Islands, and for the most part the entire controversy then subsided in the public's interest. To be sure, there were still some unsolved difficulties, especially the Aglipayan dispute, which concerned the rise of the Independent Philippine Catholic Church. The writer has deliberately avoided discussing this problem. It was a distinct situation in itself which basically concerned the upsurge of Philippine nationalism rather than an application of American colonial policies that were of interest to most American Catholics. As a whole the issue that aroused American Catholics had disappeared when Taft left Manila.

CONTENTS

CATHOLIC INFLUENCE ON AMERICAN COLONIAL POLICIES, 1898–1904

CHAPTER ONE

BACKGROUND TO CONFLICT: CATHOLICS AND THE SPANISH-AMERICAN WAR

For Catholics in the United States the genesis of their future problems over colonial matters was the Cuban insurrection that began in 1895. American interest in the cause of a free Cuba would present these Catholics with a conflict between Church and state that many of their Protestant contemporaries considered insurmountable. As press dispatches increasingly reported the barbarities of Spanish colonial misrule American traditional distrust of Spain conjured up unpleasant memories of the Black Legend and the Inquisition. Unfortunately this historic fear of anything Spanish was closely related to an equally historic dislike of Spanish Catholicism. If the Cubans were being sacrificed to Spanish greed, the sacrifice was taking place on a Roman altar. For most Americans, Catholicism in Cuba was an integral part of the callous Spanish colonialism that had to be destroyed. In a sense, then, American intervention on behalf of the Cubans must also be a war against the Catholicism of Spain.

Whether they realized it or not, these Americans were also participating in the birth of a new America. A new spirit of growth and change was pervading the country, shaking off the lethargy left in the wake of the Civil War. A demand for greater industrial expansion, overseas markets, and international commerce was a part of this spirit. A war against the decaying empire of Spain might fulfill this demand and set the United States on the road toward future greatness. To the expansionist-minded American, Spain stood in the way of this future. The destruction of Spanish power would mean new American opportunities in Cuba, in the long-desired isthmian canal, and perhaps even in the Philippines. In this context, too, the Spanish-American War would become a holy crusade.[1]

Interest in these enticing opportunities was heightened by the newborn sensationalist presses of William Randolph Hearst and Joseph Pulitzer. The circulation rivalries between these two newspaper empires found the Cuban issue far too palatable to American popular tastes to be ignored. Despite jarring inaccuracies and deliberate falsifications the press whipped up an enthusiasm for war that has no equal in the history of the republic. A brief, glorious war with Spain would not only give the impetus to expansion but it would also accomplish the twin aims of freeing Cuba and destroying the Spanish empire.[2]

Some of the less responsible elements of the press and a few Protestant clergymen found in the exaggerated reports of Spanish atrocities enough evidence for continuing the attack on the Roman Catholic Church that had been recently unleashed by the American Protective Association.[3] Among these attacks were resolutions adopted by several different religious bodies condemning Spain's rule in Cuba and demanding an end to the "ecclesiastical dominion

[1] Recent scholarship has challenged some of the more traditional interpretations of the causes of American expansion as advanced by Julius Pratt in *Expansionists of 1898,* and in the somewhat cynical *The Martial Spirit* by Walter Millis. See Margaret Leech, *In the Days of McKinley;* H. Wayne Morgan, *William McKinley and His America;* and Ernest R. May's excellent *Imperial Democracy: The Emergence of America as a Great Power,* especially Parts Three and Four.

[2] A perusal of contemporary issues of journals such as *Forum, Harper's,* and *North American Review* indicates that the daily press was not the sole inspiration for American jingoism. The impact of the Hearst-Pulitzer rivalry, however, is discussed in N. M. Wilkerson, *Public Opinion and the Spanish-American War,* and in the more recent Frank Freidel, *The Splendid Little War.*

[3] See Chapter 2 for a more detailed account of the American Protective Association.

and inquisitorial persecution" of the Cubans.[4] Such comments made American Catholics uneasy and presented them with their dilemma. Although they were naturally sympathetic to the Cubans, as were most Americans, they could not let this sympathy be construed as a condemnation of the Catholic Church in the island. The number of these comments was sufficient to bring other members of the Protestant clergy to the defense of the American Catholics. One such defense, a letter published in the *New York Times,* was typical. Written by William Croswell Doane, Protestant Episcopal bishop of Albany, the letter condemned a resolution adopted by the New York Conference of the Methodist Episcopal Church as being based "plainly on the ground of their hatred of the Roman Catholic faith."[5]

The Catholic press, of course, could not avoid discussing such a momentous issue as potential American intervention on behalf of the Cubans. But the exaggeration in the news dispatches and the subtle inferences that Catholics could not be loyal citizens if the United States entered the war against Spain naturally threw the Catholic writers on the defensive. Catholic press opinion became increasingly divided. Some writers immediately recognized elements of anti-Catholicism in the almost universal condemnations of Spanish policies. As a result their journals sought a broader view of the entire Cuban problem and tended to defend the Spaniards.

Ave Maria, published at Notre Dame, typified this more conservative position among some Catholic writers. Its editor commented: "If Spain were not a Catholic country, sentiment would at least be divided."[6] Accepting the idea that there must be two sides to every question, *Ave Maria* attempted an objective analysis:

> We have carefully examined the documents lately issued by the Spanish Legation in Washington, and are fairly persuaded of two points: first that Cuba has no valid and irremediable grievance against the mother country; and second, that if Spain were not a Catholic country misrepresentation of her government would not be so general, and there would be less enthusiasm for Cuba in both pulpit and press.[7]

Many of the other Catholic journals took this stand too, attempting to look at the Spanish side of the problem and to minimize the reli-

[4] *New York Herald,* April 6, 1898, p. 7.
[5] *New York Times,* April 9, 1898, p. 6.
[6] *Ave Maria,* LXII (June 6, 1896), 636.
[7] *Ibid.*

gious connotations implied in press dispatches. Most of them considered the Cuban insurrection a family affair which could best be solved without American interference.[8] Still other Catholic writers went one step further and even defended the Spanish, often drawing comparisons between English and Spanish colonialism, always giving the benefit of the doubt to the Spaniard. One author asked, "O, Englishman of New England, yes, and Dutchman of New Amsterdam, so distinguished for your humanity that even the domesticated negro dare not sit in the same car with you, what has become of the poor savage Indians?"[9]

While the more intellectual conservative Catholic journals were endeavoring to minimize America's interest in the Cuban situation, the popular Catholic weekly papers were becoming as jingoistic as the press of the rest of the country. The Boston *Pilot,* one of the oldest Catholic newspapers in the country, appealed to a large Irish-American readership. It compared Cuba's relation to Spain with Ireland's relation to England. The United States, as a former colony, should take the side of the downtrodden, be they Armenians, Irish, or Cubans, against the colonial powers.[10] The *Pilot* even suggested that as France interfered on behalf of the American colonies in 1778, the United States should serve the cause of humanity by interfering in Cuba and rescuing the Cubans from utter extinction, and thus freeing "the gallant people of Spain from their incompetent rulers that were leading Spain to financial ruin."[11] Despite these sentiments, as late as February, 1898, the *Pilot* nevertheless commended the patience of the United States government in trying to respect the rights of nations instead of pleading military necessity and abruptly seizing the island.[12]

When the *U.S.S. Maine* was sunk on February 15, 1898, in Havana harbor, Catholic opinion was as confused as that of the rest of the country. Previously the American Catholic hierarchy said little publicly about the Cuban question. But the incident of the *Maine*

[8] Bryan J. Clinch, "Spain and Cuba," *American Catholic Quarterly Review,* XXII (October, 1897), 809–819.

[9] Thomas A. Hughes, "Catholic Spain—Its Politics and Liberalism," *American Catholic Quarterly Review,* XXII (July, 1897), 515.

[10] Boston *Pilot,* June 22, 1895, p. 4, *et seq.* The *Pilot,* considering itself the spokesman for Bostonian Catholics, was an independent newspaper at this time and had no official relationship to the Archdiocese of Boston.

[11] *Ibid.,* December 26, 1896, p. 1.

[12] *Ibid.,* February 5, 1898, p. 1.

meant that American intervention on behalf of the Cubans was a very real possibility and would require public comment. This was especially true when the *Catholic Telegraph* claimed that 190 crewmen of the *Maine* were Roman Catholics and thus Catholics were among the first to die in this latest defense of the rights of humanity.[13] After the first flush of anger over the tragedy had subsided, most of the religious leaders of the country cautioned patience until the President's fact-finding commission could return from the scene of the disaster. James Cardinal Gibbons, archbishop of Baltimore, was the first of the Catholic prelates to speak publicly on the issue. In a sermon delivered at the Requiem Mass sung in honor of the *Maine's* dead the Cardinal commended the statesmanlike patience of President McKinley in the face of the "mischievous and intemperate" sensationalist press. In reference to Spain he said, "I do not believe, and no sane man can believe, that a chivalric nation would be guilty of such inhumanity."[14] Archbishop John Ireland, of St. Paul, a close friend of the President, warning against making hasty conclusions, commented that "in my opinion nothing has yet come to light that would in my judgment call for a rupture between the United States and Spain."[15]

Other Catholics, however, were more sensitive to the drift of popular indignation. Some of the more bellicose elements of the press refused to accept the Cardinal's admonition to exercise patience. Shortly after the sinking of the *Maine* the Boston *Pilot* demanded that "Mr. McKinley display a tithe of the resolution which Andrew Jackson would have shown in a similar crisis."[16] Several weeks later, still agitating for a free Cuba, the same newspaper gave considerable space to an unconfirmed letter claiming that an English manufacturer of land and sea mines had sold under-

[13] William A. Karracker, "The American Churches and the Spanish-American War" (Ph.D. Dissertation, University of Chicago, 1940), p. 38.

[14] *New York Times,* March 1, 1898, p. 1. As the only American cardinal at this time and also as archbishop of the primatial see of Baltimore, Gibbons was the senior member of the American hierarchy. His actions and public statements were therefore significant. For a thorough biography see John Tracy Ellis, *The Life of James Cardinal Gibbons, Archbishop of Baltimore, 1838–1921.*

[15] *New York Freeman's Journal,* March 5, 1898, p. 1. Ireland was the most outspoken member of the "liberal" faction among the hierarchy. See also James H. Moynihan, *The Life of Archbishop Ireland.*

[16] Boston *Pilot,* February 26, 1898, p. 4.

water mines which were loaded aboard a ship bound for Havana.[17] The implication was obvious to the editor of the *Pilot.* As more and more Catholic papers took up the "Remember the *Maine*" slogan, a few members of the hierarchy began to echo the same sentiment. Among these was Bishop John S. Foley, of Detroit, whose speech of March 19 was widely circulated in the Catholic press. Bishop Foley compared the Cuban cause with that of the American colonists in 1776; he insisted that Americans had a duty to perform in Cuba.[18] Even Archbishop Ireland succumbed to the mounting pressure against Spain. During a press interview in Chicago on March 11 he stated that "no true American Catholic will think of espousing the cause of Spain against that of this country because the former is a Catholic nation."[19]

Archbishop Ireland was in an unusually delicate situation for an American Catholic clergyman when he made this statement. While most of the Catholic prelates leaned more toward the Democrats, the Archbishop was an outspoken supporter of the Republicans. During the entire Cuban crisis he defended the policies of the McKinley Administration whenever possible. He developed a close personal contact with the President and was frequently called to the White House to give advice on religious matters or to offer the cooperation of American Catholics. Because of this friendship with McKinley he became the object of frequent interviews by the press, which considered him the unofficial religious spokesman of the party. This unique relationship to the expansionist-minded Republican Administration led him to undertake one of the most significant ventures of his career.

Archbishop Ireland was charged with the responsibility of attempting a last-minute mediation between the United States and Spain. At the request of Pope Leo XIII he traveled to Washington to confer with the President and congressional leaders in order to find the means to preserve peace between the two nations.[20] This request was the result of a frantic appeal to the Pope by the Spanish queen-regent, who feared that a war with the United States would cause an overthrow of her dynasty. She had already relied on

[17] *Ibid.,* April 16, 1898, p. 1.

[18] San Francisco *Monitor,* April 16, 1898, p. 6.

[19] Boston *Pilot,* March 19, 1898, p. 4.

[20] John Ireland, Washington, April 6, 1898, to James Cardinal Gibbons, Gibbons Correspondence, Box 96.

a potential alliance of European Great Powers for assistance, but they had failed her. The appeal to the Pope was an unwise eleventh-hour attempt to stem the tide of American public opinion.[21] The best that Ireland and the Pope could hope to accomplish was that war might be averted if the Spanish government could legitimately accede to American demands and still save face. The armistice that Spain offered the Cuban insurrectionists was due primarily to the pressure that Ireland applied on Spain through the Pope.[22]

At first the Archbishop expected success. The Pope's efforts to maintain peace were well received by the President.[23] But the pressure on McKinley for war was irresistible. Time, the most important element for quiet, intelligent negotiations, was needed and there was no time. The lateness of the Pope's offer and the mounting indignation of popular opinion doomed Ireland's mediation before it started. Somewhat embittered by his failure to maintain peace, Archbishop Ireland admitted that he had gambled for time—and had lost. Had the Pope asked his assistance two months earlier, he claimed, he might have succeeded.[24]

Papal intervention in the foreign affairs of the United States was not accepted by most Americans.[25] The press made too much of Ireland's visit to Washington, claiming that he had come "through the good offices of the Pope."[26] To avoid so much publicity the Archbishop deliberately avoided direct contact with the White House, and instead worked through his friend Senator Stephen B. Elkins.[27] Unfortunately the press had exaggerated his commission and the public misconstrued his purposes. Speaking before a meeting of Methodists in New York, the Reverend James M. King voiced a characteristically Protestant sentiment: "We want no overtures

[21] For details of a possible European coalition against the United States and the Pope's relation to it consult Orestes Ferrara, *The Last Spanish War,* May, *Imperial Democracy,* Chapter XII, and Morgan, *William McKinley,* pp. 372–374; Stewart Woodford, Madrid, April 9, 1898, to Secretary Day, *Foreign Relations of the United States, 1898* (Publication of the Department of State), p. 746.

[22] *New York Herald,* April 11, 1898, p. 7.

[23] Ireland, St. Paul, April 8, 1898, to Denis J. O'Connell, O'Connell Correspondence, Box 13.

[24] Ireland, St. Paul, May 2, 1898, to O'Connell, *ibid.*

[25] L. A. Lambert, New York, April 15, 1898, to O'Connell, *ibid.* Father Lambert was editor of the *New York Freeman's Journal.*

[26] *New York Herald,* April 5, 1898, p. 5.

[27] Moynihan, *Life of Ireland,* p. 165.

from our government for settlement of the burning questions confronting us as a nation, based upon propositions emanating from Rome."[28] The following day *The Christian Advocate* echoed this opinion: "Perhaps there is nothing in the oft-repeated statements that the Pope is designated by Spain as a suitable person to mediate between that country and the United States. . . . it may be well to show that such a reference or experiment would not be tolerable to a large part of the people of this country."[29] Popular opinion was such that on April 9 the apostolic delegate to the American clergy, Sebastiano Martinelli, issued a statement to the press that the Pope had not consented to act as an intermediary between the United States and Spain. In reference to Archbishop Ireland he said: "If Archbishop Ireland holds a commission from the Pope to act in any capacity it can only be as a friend of the President."[30]

Although the Protestants had not liked the idea of papal intervention, their attitude toward Catholicism was conciliatory after war was declared. Many of the Protestant journals refused to print items of religious bigotry or make open attacks on Catholics.[31] Most of the religious press united in a strong support of the war effort. *The Churchman's* editorial was typical: "The purpose of the war is altogether good. It is a war undertaken in behalf of a weak neighbor suffering under oppression. It is our response to the cry of the distressed. It is a war upon whose purpose we may properly ask the blessing of Almighty God."[32]

Despite the general conciliatory attitude of the Protestants, enough rumors of Catholic disloyalty circulated to keep most American Catholics on the defensive. Irresponsible, unconfirmed press dispatches caused most of their discomfort. Some of these dispatches reported that the Pope had ordered Catholics in the United States not to fight Spain, that 700,000 armed American Catholics were preparing for an uprising, that an explosion of a powdermill in California was caused by the inmates of a nearby Jesuit monastery.[33] In desperation over what it called bigoted writing the Boston *Pilot*

[28] *New York Herald,* April 6, 1898, p. 1.

[29] *The Christian Advocate,* April 7, 1898, p. 548.

[30] *New York Freeman's Journal,* April 9, 1898, p. 5.

[31] Karracker, "American Churches and the Spanish-American War," p. 79.

[32] *The Churchman,* LXXVII (May 7, 1898), 670.

[33] Boston *Pilot,* May 7, 1898, p. 4, May 14, 1898, p. 4; *New York Freeman's Journal,* March 12, 1898, p. 4.

demanded an explanation from the Associated Press of syndicated reports which contended that the Pope had blessed Spanish armies and that priests and nuns in Manila deliberately had led American marines into a mined cave.[34] As the popular reaction to these rumors intensified, even the hierarchy felt desperate. Archbishop Ireland, still smarting from his failure to maintain peace, recognized the difficulties in this new dilemma. He wrote his friend Monsignor O'Connell in Rome: "The provoking feature of this war is that preachers are making much out of the religion of Spain. It is inopportune to answer them directly, lest we be thought Spanish."[35] The situation became so serious that Cardinal Rampolla, the papal Secretary of State, acting through the Apostolic Delegate in Washington, had to issue a formal statement denying any lack of neutrality on the part of the Vatican.[36]

Catholic clergymen naturally resented these attacks on Catholic patriotism. Indeed, individual bishops spoke out to their flocks, assuring them that their Catholicity did not interfere with their duty to their country.[37] Again the press turned to Archbishop Ireland, seeking his assurances of Catholic loyalty. The newspapers quoted his sermon in the Cathedral at St. Paul in which he stated that the duty of Christians was "to accept manfully the mandate of the supreme power of the nation."[38] Archbishop Patrick J. Ryan, of Philadelphia, was also quoted as saying, "The Catholic Church in America is patriotic. All over the country we are asking God's blessing upon the American cause."[39] But in case there should still be any doubt about Catholic loyalty, the archbishops of the country decided to state officially their position. In a pastoral letter signed by all of them, the archbishops declared:

> Whatever may have been the individual opinions of Americans prior to the declaration of war, there can now be no two opinions as to the duty of every loyal citizen. . . . We, the members of the Catholic Church are true Americans, and as such are loyal to our country and our flag and

[34] Boston *Pilot,* May 21, 1898, p. 8.

[35] Ireland, St. Paul, May 11, 1898, to O'Connell, O'Connell Correspondence, Box 13.

[36] *New York Times,* May 10, 1898, p. 6.

[37] *Ibid.,* May 6, 1898, p. 8.

[38] San Francisco *Monitor,* May 14, 1898, p. 4.

[39] Boston *Pilot,* May 21, 1898, p. 1.

obedient to the highest decrees and the supreme authority of the nation.[40]

There can be little doubt about the genuineness of Catholic support for the war effort. Even before war was declared the nuns at the Convent of Mary Immaculate at Key West placed their buildings at the disposal of the United States government to be used as a hospital.[41] Members of other religious orders did much the same thing, especially through volunteering for nursing duty in the war areas.[42] Several priests volunteered to serve as chaplains, although their number was small in relation to the number of Catholic servicemen. According to the newspapers, members of this religion volunteered for active service in the armed forces in large numbers. The San Francisco *Monitor* claimed that they comprised 75 per cent of the California First Volunteers. The colonel of this regiment, James F. Smith, a Catholic, was destined to play a significant role for Catholicism during his long stay in the Philippines.

Each week the Catholic press enthusiastically acclaimed the heroism of its servicemen. Many papers printed descriptions of the day-by-day activities of regiments known to be composed predominately of Catholics. Editors usually gave full coverage to the labors of priests and nuns actively engaged in supporting the war effort. Almost every one of these papers informed its readers that Father John Chidwick was the only chaplain aboard the *Maine* the night it was sunk. The monthly *Catholic World* published photographs and brief biographical sketches of Catholic Army and Navy officers. And, as the War drew on and casualty lists appeared, the papers printed the "death roll" of these men who had died for their country. The press continuously pointed out that Catholic civilians were praying for their country too; they frequently reported accounts of field Masses and public prayers offered for victory and peace.

This oversensitivity concerning Catholic involvement in the war effort was especially evident in those papers whose editors were Irish-American. The Irish were on the defensive because their loyalty in particular had been questioned. Several American news-

[40] *New York Freeman's Journal,* May 14, 1898, p. 1.

[41] *Ibid.*, April 23, 1898, p. 1.

[42] George Barton, "A Story of Self-Sacrifice. Being a Record of the Labors of the Catholic Sisterhoods in the Spanish-American War," *American Catholic Historical Society Records,* XXXVII (September, 1926), 104–192.

papers, and a few English ones, had tried to portray Irish loyalty to Rome to be too great to support an American war against Spain. These articles offered no explanation as to why the Irish were singled out and such large Catholic ethnic minorities as the Germans and the French were ignored. Nonetheless the Irish editors were vitriolic in their defense of everything Catholic and everything Irish. They found nothing incompatible in being both Catholic and American. While the *New York Freeman's Journal* reminded its fellow Americans that there is "no creed in patriotism," the San Francisco *Monitor* wanted to raise a few regiments of Irish soldiers and say "good-bye to Spain."[43] The Boston *Pilot,* the most Irish and perhaps the most Catholic newspaper in the country, labeled as "bigots" and "A.P.A. Idiots" these detractors of the Irish.[44] Its outraged editorials were frequently reprinted in other Catholic papers. In one succinct sentence published in its first issue after war was declared, its editor summarized the entire Irish-American attitude: "It is war [and] . . . no patriotic American can have any doubt of his duty—to support the government even to the last dollar and the last drop of blood."[45]

America's war on behalf of a free Cuba quickly became a war for a greater prize. On May 1 an American naval squadron under the command of Commodore George Dewey completely destroyed the Spanish Pacific fleet in Manila harbor. The dream of an American overseas empire suddenly seemed near fulfillment. If the United States wanted it the whole vast scattered Spanish colonial empire could be hers. A sudden new interest in Mr. McKinley's war arose. Dewey's victory at Manila opened up new vistas of American opportunities and caused an abrupt change in American war aims. What had been originally a war of liberation in Cuba now became a war of acquisition in the Pacific and the Caribbean.

The possibility of Protestant missionary activity in these areas became apparent almost immediately. By mid-summer the Protestant press had aligned itself squarely on the side of those who would take all of Spain's colonial empire. Most of them took for granted that the United States would retain all that it had conquered, and they then planned accordingly. As early as June the *Missionary Review of the World* looked to the future: "When Cuba and the

[43] *New York Freeman's Journal,* April 16, 1898, p. 4; San Francisco *Monitor,* May 14, 1898, p. 9.

[44] Boston *Pilot,* April 23, 1898, p. 4.

[45] *Ibid.,* April 30, 1898, p. 4.

Philippines are free from the Spanish yoke, two more fields will be open for the free proclamation of the Gospel."[46] *The Churchman* observed that "the war with Spain has an added interest, in that the success of American arms in Cuba and Manila may mean the promulgation of a purer and reformed Christianity."[47] *The Churchman* strongly supported permanent acquisition of the Philippines so that the Islands could be given something better than the "danger, oppression and inadequacy of the Roman Communion."[48] The Methodist *Christian Advocate* repeated this sentiment: "Break the clutch which Rome has put upon these people, and give them a chance for a civilization which is something more than Christianized paganism."[49]

Protestant missionary societies were enthusiastic over the prospect of invading these islands and claiming them from Catholicism. "Divine Providence," it seemed, had thrust the islands into American hands for this purpose. To accomplish such a goal mission leaders began discussing the prospects and problems of opening missions in the Caribbean islands and in the Philippines.[50] The American Tract Society by July had prepared Spanish language editions of Protestant Bibles and texts for mass distribution throughout Cuba.[51] Other groups concentrated their plans on Puerto Rico. The greatest interest, however, was shown in the missionary opportunities in the Philippine Islands. Because so many organizations wanted to work in this particular field the Presbyterian Board suggested that they cooperate and form a union mission of all denominations.[52] As nearly all of the societies had become expansionist-minded before mid-summer of 1898 they were almost as jingoistic as the secular press. One even insisted that "the foreign policy of the United States [must be] foreign missions."[53]

Catholics resented this turn in the direction of the war effort. Not only had their patriotism been challenged but they were now being asked to fight a war to extend Protestantism into territories that had

[46] *Missionary Review of the World,* XXI (June, 1898), 462.
[47] *The Churchman,* LXXVII (June 11, 1898), 833.
[48] *Ibid.,* LXXVII (June 25, 1898), 913.
[49] *The Christian Advocate,* LXXIII (September 1, 1898), 1410.
[50] *Outlook,* LIX, 3 (May 21, 1898), 157.
[51] *The Christian Advocate,* LXXIII (July 21, 1898), 1162.
[52] *The Living Church,* XXI (July 16, 1898), 355.
[53] *Methodist Review,* LXXX (September, 1898), 824.

been Catholic for centuries. The *New York Freeman's Journal* reminded its readers that the Cuban insurrectionists were Catholic and therefore the war in Cuba could not be a religious war.[54] The Boston *Pilot* warned that "powerful influences" had been brought against the President to assure that the Philippines, the Ladrones, and the Carolines would be cleared of Catholic religious orders and opened up to exclusive Protestant missionary activity.[55] It insisted that "the United States is not a Protestant country." While some Catholic papers were worried about Protestant activity others predicted failure of attempts to convert native Catholics to Protestantism. Because the War was of such brief duration, however, most waited to see what the peace would bring in the disposition of Spain's colonies. By the end of the summer the general interest of American Catholics was to create a just peace which would at least assure religious freedom in the colonies. Competition from Protestant missionaries did not seem too important at that particular time.

President McKinley had made no statements of the Administration's plans for Spain's colonies. The future independence of Cuba, of course, had been assured by the Teller Amendment, but the future of Puerto Rico, the Philippines, and the Ladrones was an important question. In all of these islands the interests of the Catholic Church were closely entwined with the Spanish government. When, and if, this relationship was broken and a free state established as a result of the peace settlement, there would be many problems directly concerning the Church. A few Catholics, resenting what they labeled a "religious war on behalf of Protestantism," were perceptive enough to see these difficulties. Shortly after the armistice was signed in August, Archbishop Ireland hurried to Washington in an attempt to minimize such future problems at the outset.[56]

Perhaps the most immediate concern to Catholics was the composition of the Peace Commission. Five Americans were to be sent to Paris to negotiate with the Spaniards, and it was expected that probably one would be a Catholic.[57] Archbishop Ireland was rumored as the one person whom the President considered qualified to represent Catholic interests at Paris. But Ireland's appointment

[54] *New York Freeman's Journal,* April 30, 1898, p. 4.

[55] Boston *Pilot,* June 18, 1898, p. 4.

[56] Ireland, St. Paul, September 13, 1898, to Gibbons, Gibbons Correspondence, Box 96; New York *Evening Post,* August 19, 1898, p. 1.

[57] New York *Evening Post,* August 22, 1898, p. 1.

would perhaps complicate European international relations for the Vatican. The choice of the President was Associate Justice of the United States Supreme Court Edward D. White. Justice White was an ideal choice: he was a Catholic; he had practiced law in Louisiana and knew the Napoleonic Code used in the islands; and he was a Democrat. With this background he could represent some of the minority interests in the United States, besides offering good legal qualifications for the role he would play. The announcement of White's selection was well received by the Catholic hierarchy. Cardinal Gibbons wrote the President that the selection was a happy choice and should give general satisfaction.[58] Thomas Conaty, the rector of Catholic University, thanked McKinley for the appointment and wrote that it indicated "another strong evidence of your desire to safeguard all the interests of the countries which your successful administration has brought under the protection of our glorious republic."[59]

Despite the encouragement given to him in both the Protestant and the Catholic press, Justice White declined the nomination. He made no public statement of his reasons for doing so, but the New York *Evening Post* offered a reasonable explanation: "As a Democrat Judge White had nothing to gain by accepting the post. . . . The Democrats have no party capital to make out of this war, except as Republican mismanagement may give them an opening. They naturally desire to have their hands free."[60] Privately, Justice White expressed his conviction that he could not devote himself adequately to the bench if he took on additional duties in other areas.[61]

For reasons best known to himself, the President made no further effort to select another Catholic for the Commission. This was unfortunate because the Catholic press immediately branded the Peace Commission anti-Catholic, claiming that the large proportion of

[58] Gibbons, Baltimore, August 22, 1898, to William McKinley, McKinley Correspondence, Vol. 17. See also Charles C. Dawes, *A Journal of the McKinley Years,* p. 169. *Christian Register* (LXXVIII [September 1, 1898], 978), *The Independent* (L [September 1, 1898], 644), and *Religious Telescope* (LXIV [September 14, 1898], 1157) quoted in Karraker, "American Churches and the Spanish-American War," *passim.*

[59] Thomas Conaty, Washington, August 29, 1898, to McKinley, McKinley Correspondence, Vol. 17.

[60] New York *Evening Post,* September 7, 1898, p. 4.

[61] Sister Marie Carolyn Klinkhamer, *Edward Douglas White, Chief Justice of the United States,* p. 43.

Catholics in the United States who had done their share in the war effort considered this lack of presidential wisdom a deliberate injustice. As a result, until the end of his life McKinley was under constant attack in the Catholic press. "McKinleyism" became a press slogan for alleged acts of anti-Catholicism committed in the islands.

Before the Peace Commission convened at Paris, the Vatican saw fit to send a representative to act as observer. Archbishop Placide L. Chapelle, of New Orleans, was sent from Rome to Paris with the official title of "Apostolic Delegate to Cuba and Porto Rico." A year later his authority would be extended to include the Philippines as well. His duty as apostolic delegate was to act as the representative of the Vatican to the local clergy, but at Paris he was charged with the additional responsibility of explaining to the Commission the Church's stake in the islands. This task required delicate diplomatic skill in order to reconcile American concepts of separation of church and state with protection of the interests of a church that had been established in the islands for over three centuries.

Chief concern for the Catholic Church was the future of the Philippines. If the Islands were returned to Spain the weakened power of that state would be unable to suppress the strong antifriar agitation among the natives.[62] If the Philippines were allowed to be independent the Church would suffer from the anarchy that would probably result; or worse still, some non-Catholic power, such as Germany or Japan, might seize the Islands and drive the Church out. If acquired by the United States the Islands would probably be governed by American concepts of church and state, and native Catholicism would be exposed to Protestant competition. In Rome the last proposition apparently seemed the safest. As early as May, 1898, Monsignor Denis O'Connell cabled Archbishop Ireland from Rome, "Help hold Philippines."[63] If Catholicism had prospered in the free society of the United States it should prosper in an American-controlled Philippines. The majority of the Catholic press supported this view, most of it looking to the day when the Philippine Church would become Americanized and enjoy American religious privileges, free from interference by the state.[64]

[62] See below, Chapter 5.

[63] Ireland, St. Paul, May 2, 1898, to O'Connell, O'Connell Correspondence, Box 13.

[64] San Francisco *Monitor,* June 14, 1898, p. 4.

With the signing of the Treaty of Peace in Paris on December 10, 1898, one colonial empire ended and another began. Spain granted independence to Cuba and ceded Puerto Rico, Guam, and the Philippine Islands to the United States. The system of close Church-state relations was brought to an abrupt end and the principles of religious freedom embodied in the American Constitution took its place. The Treaty attempted to spell out the Church's position in the new dependencies without defining the myriad specific items. In so doing it created confusion that was to plague the American government for almost six years. Article X of the Treaty stipulated a free exercise of religion, but Article VII provided for "the peaceful possession of property of all kinds, of provinces, municipalities, public or private establishments, ecclesiastical or civil bodies."[65]

Even before the Treaty was signed the Catholic organization in the Philippines was attacked. The New York *Evening Post* called for the immediate expulsion of the Spanish friars from the Philippines.[66] The Methodist *Christian Advocate* asked: "May it not be that Providence has something to do with the fact that this great Protestant nation is about to secure control of the splendid Philippine group? Will it not seem likely to Christian people that we have an obligation resting upon us to plant a pure form of Christianity there?"[67] In October the American Bible Society announced that it was taking steps to distribute Protestant Bibles in Puerto Rico and the Philippines.[68] Even though the War was over and peace assured, and no huge armies of Catholics arose against the government, the *Home Mission Monthly* now questioned the rights of Catholics in the islands: "The herdsman of Tekoa asks in one of the chapters of his book, 'Can two walk together except they be agreed?' The pertinency of this question to the subject of Romanism and citizenship goes without saying, since the one represents the boldest despotism, intolerance, bigotry—and the other tolerance, protection, liberty."[69]

Naturally Catholic editors could not ignore these barbed assaults on the Catholic position in the new territories. The *New York Freeman's Journal* asked of the Protestants: "What fruits can American

[65] *Treaty of Peace between the United States and Spain and Accompanying Papers* (Senate Document No. 62, 55th Cong., 3rd Sess.), p. 8.

[66] New York *Evening Post,* September 3, 1898, p. 5.

[67] *The Christian Advocate,* LXXIII (September 1, 1898), 1410.

[68] *Missionary Review of the World,* XXI (October, 1898), 800.

[69] *Home Mission Monthly,* XIII (November, 1898), 3.

Protestant missionaries produce or point to as a result of the vast sums spent by them in Spain or in Spanish American Republics or in any other Catholic country on the globe."[70] In a later issue the same newspaper reported a petition of the "Free Methodists" to ask the President to guarantee religious freedom in the Philippines. The editor asked, "Do the 'Free Methodists' mean the sort of religious freedom exemplified by the Protestants of Boston, where, of the seventy public school principals, not one is a Catholic, though a majority of the population of the city are Catholics?"[71]

During the entire postwar period the religious press became the arena of a heated debate over the religious future of the islands. The Catholic press attempted to answer point by point each criticism leveled against the Church. The *New York Freeman's Journal,* for example, branded as a "Protestant Slander" the rumor that natives were not accepted for the priesthood in Cuba. It listed the names of forty-three Cuban priests in Havana alone.[72] The same paper reprinted from *The Independent* an article by a Methodist bishop who wrote that "A priest is a costly servant." The *Freeman's Journal* then printed a detailed answer written by the Catholic bishop of Havana and concluded its point by demanding an explanation or a retraction from the Methodist, reminding him that "thou shalt not bear false witness against thy neighbor."[73]

Such diatribes and debates in the religious press were only symptomatic of the general religious uneasiness that had come to focus during the brief Spanish-American War. Catholics in the United States had been on the defensive since the days of the Revolution. They had considered themselves a disparate, unwanted, and, for the most part, defenseless minority. But the recent War, its challenge to their loyalty, and its legacy of colonialism presented them with a situation that required a somewhat changed relationship with the rest of the American community. How they reacted to this new situation can best be understood through a brief review of their past experiences in the United States.

[70] *New York Freeman's Journal,* October 22, 1898, p. 4.
[71] *Ibid.,* October 29, 1898, p. 4.
[72] *Ibid.,* January 7, 1899, p. 4.
[73] *Ibid.,* January 21, 1899, p. 4.

CHAPTER TWO

WHO WERE THE CATHOLICS?

CATHOLICS in the United States during the nineteenth century groped for the means to adapt themselves to the Protestant tradition dominant in Anglo-Saxon America. Drawn primarily from French, Irish, and German ethnic backgrounds, they formed a heterogeneous organization that still sensed religious animosities continuing from the Reformation. As new ethnic groups swelled their numbers toward the end of the century these animosities swelled too. Acceptance and assimilation became increasingly more difficult. Their clergy, for the most part educated, if not born, in Europe, reflected these ethnic differences and thereby made effective leadership impossible. No native clergy or native hierarchy developed to encourage active lay participation in American political affairs. On the contrary, Catholic involvement in the political and civic life of the United States was passive and defensive. Even as the century closed European influences were still so great that Catholics were popularly considered as holding two allegiances. Their Americanism was frequently in doubt. They had difficulty accommodating themselves to life in a pluralistic society. Indeed, their energies were directed chiefly at the problem of preserving their identity as Catholics and still finding the means to become acceptable Americans.

The history of the Catholic Church in the United States was entirely different from the history of the Catholic Church in all other countries. Catholicism, like all of the other major religious practiced in the United States, was not native to the country. It was introduced, as they were, by Europeans and allowed to flourish, as they were, without serious interference from the state. Although several of the non-Catholic denominations had had a brief tradition of establishment in some areas of the country, the Catholic Church in the United States had never known state establishment or even preferential state protection. Its growth, therefore, was entirely different from that of its sister branches in French Canada or in Spanish America. The tradition of the Catholic Church in the United States became a tradition unique in the history of the Roman Catholic religion.

This uniqueness of tradition and independence in growth gave American Catholics a different approach to their Church from that of their coreligionists in other countries. Fiercely loyal to the concept of separation of church and state, Catholics nevertheless were willing to seek state participation on their behalf whenever they felt it necessary. The most classic example of this paradox is the century-old debate on the Catholics' desire for state financial aid to their parochial school system. These situations were defensive, however, in order to protect themselves against Protestant influences. Rare, indeed, were nineteenth-century aggressive attempts to expand American Catholic influence. Most Catholics, including the clergy, preferred to submit to the Protestant ethic of society and to accommodate to it as easily and quietly as possible. Actually there was very little in the way of official governmental policy for Catholics to fear, and when governmental involvement occurred it was over local issues. The national government had put forth no great policies to help or hinder the Church's development. But the Spanish-American War, with its challenges to Catholic loyalties, and the colonial period that followed changed the entire role of the federal government in relation to religion. The government began to formulate policies that directly concerned American Catholics.

To understand the Catholic reaction to these policies it is necessary first to determine who these Catholics were, how many they were, and where they were. No official statistical information, except the annual *Official Catholic Directory*, was taken until the U.S. Census Bureau's *Census of Religious Bodies* was tabulated for 1906.[1] To get some reasonable idea of relative Catholic strength in the United States it is necessary to examine these figures, even though they were compiled two years after the close of the period being discussed. Out of an estimated total population of 84,246,252 for 1906, there were 14,210,000 Roman Catholics in the United States, or approximately one in six, a significantly large proportion.[2] Because Catholic communicants comprised 36.7 per cent of the total religious membership of the entire United States this religious minority could be quite influential.[3] United by a well-organized and highly centralized hierarchical system of religious leaders who were armed with the coercive measures of forgiveness of sins, exclusive ministry of worship, and Papal Infallibility, Catholics, it would seem, could exercise unusual pressure on governmental policies. It is necessary, then, to examine this religious minority before any intelligible discussion of Catholic influence can be made.

An analysis of the statistics in the *Religious Census* and in the *Official Catholic Directory* indicates that over 25 per cent of the Catholics living in the United States were concentrated in the ten major metropolitan centers of the country.[4] Their numbers in these large industrial centers were out of proportion to their ratio in the nation as a whole. Their percentage of the *entire* population of these cities ranged from 18 per cent in Baltimore to 48 per cent in New Orleans.[5] Almost half of them, 5,833,000, lived in the northeastern

[1] *Religious Bodies, 1906* (Publication of the Bureau of the Census), 2 vols.

[2] *Ibid.*, I, 35. For purposes of comparison to other denominations, the Census Bureau uses 85 per cent of this total. The 15 per cent deduction is made for Catholic children under nine years of age who, although baptized, are not considered as communicants by the Census Bureau. All subsequent figures quoted, because they are used in comparisons to Protestant denominations, will be the 85 per cent used exclusively in the Census compilations.

[3] *Ibid.*, p. 47.

[4] *Ibid.*; *Official Catholic Directory, passim.*

[5] The approximate percentages of Catholics to total population of the ten largest cities were as follows: Baltimore 18 per cent, Boston 43 per cent, Chicago 28 per cent, Cincinnati 31 per cent, New Orleans 48 per cent, New York 34 per cent, Philadelphia 22 per cent, Pittsburgh 32 per cent, St. Louis 32 per cent, San Francisco 34 per cent (*Religious Bodies* [Census Bureau Pub.], I, Table 6, 380, 402, 403).

part of the country in the six New England states, New York, New Jersey, and Pennsylvania. In some of these states Catholics outnumbered all other churchgoers as much as two to one. In all but one, Pennsylvania, they were the majority of all church members. In addition to the Eastern states they were exceptionally numerous in Illinois, Michigan, Wisconsin, and California, where they also comprised at least half of the church population.[6] Another factor to note is that more than half of them lived in cities of over 25,000 people.[7] Thus by weight of numbers alone Catholics could exercise a tremendous influence on political affairs in the large cities and especially in sections of the industrial East.

But Catholics could not or would not exercise this tremendous potential so feared by their antagonists. A closer examination of the Catholic minority indicates that the divisive factors within the Catholic group were as great in resultant effect as were the unifying factors. Catholics had been immigrating into the United States in large numbers since 1830: the Irish in the 1830's and 1840's, the Germans in the 1850's. After the American Civil War, Catholics came from Italy, Southeastern Europe, and Poland. In addition to these immigrants, there existed in the United States two older national Catholic groups: French Catholics in the lower Mississippi Valley centered about New Orleans, and Spanish-American Catholics in the Southwestern states. In both of these groups the clerical tradition extended from the mother country rather than from Catholic centers of the United States. The Catholic minority really consisted of several large segments of unrelated immigrants and their unassimilated children, each with broad differences in ethnic traditions.[8] Cut off entirely from their old homes, they clustered in little national ghettos, mostly in the large cities of the Eastern seaboard. But more important to the Catholic Church, they clung to the older national tradition in religious worship, demanding priests who could speak their native tongue and often refusing those who could not, and erecting parochial schools where instruction was in the national language. Thus arose national Catholic churches in the United States, with a strong religious affiliation with the mother country, back to

[6] *Ibid.*, p. 55.

[7] *Ibid.*, Table 6, p. 402.

[8] Thomas T. McAvoy, "The Formation of the Catholic Minority in the United States, 1820–1860," *The Review of Politics*, X (January, 1948), 17–18.

which they sent young men for training in the priesthood.[9] Even the more Americanized sections, such as in Wisconsin and Louisiana, continued this practice. Dozens of German-language churches and schools existed in Wisconsin, and no one but a German had ever occupied the episcopal throne in Milwaukee. A similar situation developed among the French at New Orleans.[10]

Through necessity Rome encouraged, in part, this nationalistic development of its Church in the United States. Rome's great fear during this period of heavy emigration from Europe was a serious loss of Church membership through leakage to some other church, or, worse still, complete indifference of the communicants as a result of minimal efforts by the clergy. It was easier and safer for the Vatican to send priests from Poland to the United States and cluster the Polish-American Catholics about them, than to wait until the Polish-American could learn enough English to understand an American priest in the pulpit and in the confessional. As it was, these foreign-speaking priests were often so few in number and were spread so thin among the immigrant groups that serious weakness in Church membership resulted.[11] The situation was desperate enough to inspire a proposal that a formally organized system of foreign bishops, foreign priests, and foreign-language parochial schools be permanently established to care for the Catholic immigrants, each in his own language and tradition. Taken to the extreme, such a proposal would create dioceses of nationalities regardless of where the individual resided within the United States rather than the conventional diocese in which the bishop was responsible for all Catholics living within a given geographic area. This system would preclude the existence of a unified American hierarchy.[12] Although the idea was not accepted, it indicated the extent of the nationalistic problems confronting the Church throughout the century.

On the whole this particular phase of the evolution of the Catholic Church in America produced additional detrimental situations. It made the Church appear foreign to other Americans, instead of demonstrating Catholicism to be as American as other religions.[13]

[9] "Pope Leo XIII's Plea for the Italian Immigrants in America, 1888," John Tracy Ellis (ed.), *Documents of American Catholic History*, pp. 482–485.

[10] *Religious Bodies* (Census Bureau Pub.), II, 602.

[11] G. M. Shaugnessy gives a thorough analysis of this problem in *Has the Immigrant Kept the Faith?*

[12] James H. Moynihan, *The Life of Archbishop Ireland*, pp. 54–60.

[13] McAvoy, "Formation of the Catholic Minority" *(Review of Politics)*, p. 25.

This was the principal reason for the nativist attacks in the 1840's and '50's and again in the 1880's and '90's. It tended also to encourage rather than eliminate national rivalries carried over from Europe. Unfortunately these rivalries were reflected to a great extent in a conflict of leadership among the hierarchy, some of whom feared that bishops of one nationality might dominate.[14] And finally, a difference of opinion developed among the clergy over the best course of action for future Church policy in the United States. The accumulated result of these particular difficulties forced the Church within itself and heightened the growth of separatism.[15] The hierarchy devoted all of its energies to the perfection of the internal structure and had little time for political or civic matters.[16]

Resolving these difficulties in order to make the Church more acceptable seemed to be an insurmountable task. The nationalistic division among the hierarchy extended itself into a debate over the degree to which the Church should try to adapt itself to American conditions. The training and experiences of the clergy led to a variety of interpretations of just what the Church's role in the United States should be. By the end of the century two groups were clearly discernible. A conservative element, led by Archbishops Michael A. Corrigan, of New York, and Patrick J. Ryan, of Philadelphia, wanted to limit the clergy's concern strictly to ecclesiastical questions. With the opposite view, a more liberal group, headed by James Cardinal Gibbons, of Baltimore, Archbishop John Ireland, of St. Paul, and Bishop John Lancaster Spalding, of Peoria, would make the Church in the United States participate in all levels of American life. The aim of this group was to remove the appearance of foreignism that had shackled Catholic activity for years. They encouraged greater Catholic participation in politics, trade unionism, and education. Gibbons defended the Knights of Labor before the Vatican and obtained permission for Catholics to join it.[17] Ireland endeavored to compromise with existing conditions in education and formulated the Faribault plan, which gave Catholics a voice in the school system but eliminated the cost of supporting a dual system of educa-

[14] John Tracy Ellis, *American Catholicism,* p. 48.

[15] John J. Kane, *Catholic-Protestant Conflicts in America,* Chapter 3.

[16] Thomas T. McAvoy, *The Great Crisis in American Catholic History, 1895–1900,* p. 41.

[17] Henry J. Browne, *The Catholic Church and the Knights of Labor,* p. 265.

tion.[18] Bishop Spalding was primarily responsible for establishing the Catholic University at Washington to provide well-educated Catholic leaders for the American community.[19]

These were only a few of the activities of the "liberals" that alarmed the conservative faction of the hierarchy. The conservatives felt that such direct contact in public affairs would water down Catholicism, weaken it, and even cause a future movement for an independent American Catholic Church. To add further to the fires of dissension, an inadequate French translation of Walter Elliot's *Life of Father Hecker* appeared in 1897. Father Isaac Hecker, a convert to Catholicism, was the founder of the Missionary Society of St. Paul the Apostle. The purpose of Hecker's Paulists, strictly an American order, was to bring the Catholic Church to the grass roots of America. He knew America and felt that he knew its needs. He is frequently considered the forerunner of liberal Catholicism in the United States. His teachings and writings, although orthodox in dogma, did not always appear pleasing to many conservative-minded European clerics of the time.[20] The French translator of Hecker's biography did not understand American concepts of such terms as "democracy," "intellectualism," and "liberalism," and through misinterpretation he read into Hecker's writings ideas that drifted toward heresy. To complicate the matter even further, Archbishop Ireland had written an introduction to the original edition, praising Hecker's work and agreeing entirely with his approach of seeking a more direct involvement of the Church in public affairs within the United States. The implications in the French translation excited considerable protest among Catholic clergymen in Europe. A French priest, Abbé Charles Maignen, wrote a series of articles on Father Hecker, which he later published as a book, *Le Père Hecker —Est-il un Saint?* In these articles he attacked Hecker's ideas and gave impetus to a heated controversy over the so-called Americanism of the American hierarchy. Because the Catholic Church had already suffered much at the hands of liberalism in Europe, further attacks upon its dogmatic fabric from across the Atlantic might tend to destroy it. Discussion in all quarters was out of proportion to the

18 Moynihan, *Life of Ireland,* Chapter 5.

19 See Sister Agnes Claire Schroll, *The Social Thought of John Lancaster Spalding.*

20 The best account of Hecker's influence is in Vincent J. Holden, *The Yankee Paul: Isaac Thomas Hecker.*

true characteristics of interpretation at issue. The conservatives in America were particularly chagrined. In their opinion the liberals had certainly weakened the Church in America. On the other hand, the liberals, especially John Ireland, in speeches, sermons, and letters were defending their activities and trying to explain to Europeans how they had misunderstood the entire issue. The intensity of the controversy is quite evident in the correspondence of these men. To a great degree personal animosities flared to the surface and the cooperative spirit that had existed among some of the American hierarchy was temporarily destroyed.[21]

"Americanism" caused an embarrassment to the clergy of the United States that could not be confined to Catholic circles.[22] Even Theodore Roosevelt, staunch defender of all things liberal and American, was deeply concerned for the future of the Catholic Church in the United States. He wrote a longtime Catholic friend, Maria Longworth Storer, the wife of the American minister at Madrid: "A reactionary or in any way anti-American spirit in ecclesiastical affairs would in America in the long run result in a disaster just as certainly as a similar course in political affairs."[23] As the embarrassment spread to Europe, the Vatican attempted to ascertain what truths were involved in the discussion. In January, 1899, in a papal letter entitled *Testem benevolentiae,* which was addressed to Cardinal Gibbons, Pope Leo XIII summarized the situation in an attempt to stop the argument. Leo had praise for what he designated "characteristic qualities which reflect honor on the people of America."[24] But unfortunately the letter was not intended to praise or condemn. Its purpose was to stop a controversy that was of dubious value anyway. Thus it ended the discussion but solved none of the problems, and encouraged both sides to claim that they had been vindicated.

Reaction in the United States to the papal letter did not strengthen the Catholic position, coming as it did when the Church was undertaking negotiations with the government over affairs in the new island dependencies. Apparently the general tone of the letter left much to be desired, despite the Pope's attempts to distinguish between characteristics of the American people on one hand

[21] McAvoy, *Great Crisis,* Chapter 3.

[22] *The Living Church,* XXI (June 4, 1898), 219.

[23] Theodore Roosevelt, Albany, April 30, 1900, to Maria Longworth Storer, Elting E. Morison (ed.), *The Letters of Theodore Roosevelt,* II, 1272.

[24] "Testem Benevolentiae," reprinted in McAvoy, *Great Crisis,* p. 390.

and inaccuracies of religious interpretation on the other. Frederick Z. Rooker, the American secretary to Martinelli, the apostolic delegate in Washington, was very worried over the opinion of government circles. In a series of letters to Monsignor O'Connell in Rome he maintained that Leo's prestige had fallen appreciably in the United States and that many American officials felt that the Vatican had been actually anti-American during the war with Spain.[25] Later he wrote that the letter "has undoubtedly created a very widespread feeling that if the Vatican can get along without America, as the tone of the letter makes manifest, America can manage very well to get along without the Vatican."[26] Perhaps his opinion was exaggerated, but it was quite apparent that the feelings against Catholics were heightened by what Protestants considered to be papal interference in an American theological discussion. With this issue really not settled and the earlier differences of opinion among the clergy still continuing, the Roman Catholic Church in the United States appeared weak and divided to the American people, to the American government, and even to the American Catholics themselves. Its leadership was confused and embarrassed.

Another factor that deeply disturbed Catholics in the United States was the age-old resentment among Protestants against "Romanism." The history of anti-Catholicism in the United States stretched back to the convent burning and the nativism of the 1830's.[27] But in the last two decades of the century a new wave of this spirit intensified the separatism of Catholics and often made them timid in defense of their own rights. The growing antagonism toward Catholicism was vocalized in a book by the Reverend Josiah Strong, entitled *Our Country,* which first appeared in 1886. In this work Strong outlined basic conflicts between the principles of Roman Catholicism and the concepts embodied in the United States Constitution. He endeavored to show how the two were completely incompatible and that no true Catholic could ever be a good, loyal American. Naturally *Our Country* aroused considerable resentment among Catholics, but Strong continued his charges in a later edition

[25] Frederick Z. Rooker, Washington, February 28, 1899, and March 14, 1899, to Denis J. O'Connell, O'Connell Correspondence, Box 13.

[26] Rooker, Washington, April 21, 1899, to O'Connell, *ibid.*

[27] For a detailed account of anti-Catholicism in the United States in the early part of the nineteenth century see Ray A. Billington, *The Protestant Crusade, 1800–1860.*

which appeared in 1891. Strong's idea was that the three greatest perils to the future of the United States were immigration, Romanism, and religion in the public schools. He thus assailed several important aspects of Catholic life in the country.

Strong's attack against immigration typified much of the sentiment of Anglo-Saxon Protestant Americans in the 1880's and 1890's. The huge waves of Slavic, Italian, and Southeastern European immigrants were frightening to the "native" Americans who saw their social, political, and economic position in jeopardy. The fact that a large proportion of these immigrants were Roman Catholics added more resentment toward their ever-growing numbers.[28] The antagonism toward the illiterate, clumsy immigrants went hand in hand with the resentment toward Romanism and finally broke out in a formally organized group known as the American Protective Association. The A.P.A. was the product of Henry F. Bowers and six associates, who founded the organization in Clinton, Iowa in March, 1887. It developed slowly at first, but by the elections of 1894 it had made significant gains, so much so that it was looking toward the election of 1896, when it would be in a position to influence national legislation. For some reason the group found itself stronger among Republicans than Democrats, and therefore it directed its greatest efforts in trying to control Republican policies. No one really knows how many Republican congressmen were members of the A.P.A. after the election of 1894, but the organization claimed an unusual strength in the halls of Congress.[29] However, both major parties ignored the A.P.A. in 1896, and its effectiveness was immediately diminished. Despite the fact that McKinley and Roosevelt strenuously repudiated the A.P.A., its earlier successes with the G.O.P. made Catholics dubious of the future of Republicanism and strengthened the pre-existing tendency of most Catholics to support the Democrats.

The religious bigotry of A.P.A. activities was apparent from the outset. The organization published all sorts of propaganda directed at the Roman Catholic Church, much of it deliberately falsified and designed to frighten Americans. One of the most fantastic items was

[28] The best account of late nineteenth-century nativism is given in John Higham, *Strangers in the Land: Patterns of American Nativism, 1860–1925,* especially Chapter 6.

[29] W. H. J. Traynor, "Policy and Power of A.P.A.," *North American Review,* CLXII (June, 1896), 658.

the publication of an alleged encyclical of Leo XIII commanding American Catholics to rise on the feast of St. Ignatius Loyola, July 31, 1893, and massacre all the heretics in the country.[30] The ideas embodied in the secret oath of the A.P.A. indicate how far its members would work to eliminate Catholicism in the United States. A member promised

> . . . to the utmost of my ability, to labor, plead and wage a continuous warfare against ignorance and fanaticism; that I will use my utmost power to strike the shackles and chains of blind obedience to the Roman Catholic Church from the hampered and bound consciences of a priest-ridden and church-oppressed people; . . . that I will use my influence to promote the interests of all Protestants everywhere in the world that I may be; that I will not employ a Roman Catholic in any capacity if I can procure the services of a Protestant. . . . I further promise and swear that I will not countenance the nomination, in any caucus or convention, of a Roman Catholic for any office in the gift of the American people.[31]

A.P.A. activity met its greatest success on the local level, where it endeavored to boycott Catholic-owned businesses, refused to hire Catholics, and violently opposed Catholics in politics. On this level, too, Catholics had to concentrate their efforts to meet A.P.A. opposition and defeat its purposes. With the aid of a local Catholic newspaper, Catholic clergy and laymen would organize their forces in an attempt to refute this propaganda and prevent any known A.P.A. member from being elected to public office. Typical of such activities were those of Father Peter C. Yorke, editor of the San Francisco *Monitor.* Week after week his paper reported A.P.A. proceedings and examined the background of nominees for public office suspected of belonging to the A.P.A. Father Yorke fought his battle on every level of California politics and by the end of the decade had met considerable success. When the organization was dead he turned his energies into other areas.[32]

30 The impact of the A.P.A. on American politics and the allegations of un-Americanism are given in Humphrey J. Desmond, *The A.P.A. Movement,* and the more recent Donald L. Kinzer, *An Episode in Anti-Catholicism: The American Protective Association.*

31 "The Secret Oath of the American Protective Association," Ellis (ed.), *Documents of American Catholic History,* p. 500.

32 Under the direction of its fiery editor the San Francisco *Monitor* was one of the most outspoken critics of U.S. colonial policies. For a thorough account

If A.P.A. activity forced Catholics on the defensive, it did not unify them. Because the most urgent battles were fought over local issues Catholics expended their energies in local politics and tended to ignore national affairs. Furthermore, Catholic laymen were for the most part small-business men or laborers and factory workers. Only a very slight representative group of professional men and intellectuals existed. There was no national representative Catholic laity that could speak for the Church; in fact Catholic leadership in the United States was really only the hierarchy.[33] With a broken and divided hierarchy Catholics in America were without direction and inspiration in political and social affairs. They fell back on local questions and seemed afraid to voice their collective opinions on national issues.

Catholic influence in the national politics of the United States was almost negligible as a result of these factors. Only a few Catholics held positions of prominence in the federal government: Justice Edward White of the Supreme Court; Joseph McKenna, Attorney General and later a justice of the Supreme Court under McKinley; Charles Bonaparte, Secretary of the Navy and Attorney General for Theodore Roosevelt; Richard C. Kerens, ambassador to Vienna for Taft; Terence Powderly, commissioner of immigration under McKinley; and Bellamy Storer, American minister at Brussels, Madrid, and Vienna. But these few were hardly representative of one sixth of the country's total population. In addition to Catholics in appointive offices several were members of Congress, but they proved most ineffectual. The San Francisco *Monitor* itself claimed that most Catholic congressmen were "as weak-kneed as jellyfish" and praised instead Senator George C. Vest, of Missouri, a Protestant, as being a better defender of Catholic interests than the Catholic congressmen.[34] Perhaps the only exception was Congressman John F. Fitzgerald, a Democrat from Boston, who became something of a hero to the Catholic press.[35]

Even though this reticence of Catholics in national politics prevailed during the decade of the 1890's, the drastic changes wrought by the Spanish-American War led a few of them to doubt the wis-

---

of the activities of this colorful priest see Bernard C. Cronin, *Father Yorke and the Labor Movement in San Francisco, 1900–1910.*

[33] McAvoy, *Great Crisis,* p. 37.

[34] San Francisco *Monitor,* February 11, 1900, p. 4, *et seq.*

[35] Boston *Pilot,* October 6, 1900, p. 4.

dom of such a policy. The *Sacred Heart Review* complained that Catholics of the United States "do not now wield, and have never yet wielded, the influence which their numbers should give them for furtherance of every good and antagonism to every bad cause."[36] This weakness of the Catholic electorate was graphically illustrated in a resolution passed by the German Catholics in the Diocese of Newark. The resolution pledged their fortunes, sacred honor, and lives, if necessary, to the defense of the United States in the event of a just war with the German Fatherland.[37] The *Monitor* was highly indignant that any body of Catholic Americans should have to make statements professing their loyalty. Such resolutions lent plausibility to "the slurs of Apaistic malice which impugn our patriotism."[38] In spite of comments in the press, many Catholics still accepted a second-class role.

Catholic newspapers and journals were the most vocal representatives of Catholic thought in the country. Within the framework of Catholic dogma they discussed a wide variety of subjects touching on every aspect of life in the United States. Where no specific dogmatic statement limited them, especially in topics dealing with such Church-state problems as the public schools or federal subsidies to Catholic Indian missions, their editorial writers ranged freely in expressing a full range of opinions. Most of them represented the particular nationalistic concerns of the ethnic groups that read them. Some reflected the division of opinion among the hierarchy. The periodicals presented no consistent pattern or organization among themselves. Many were official diocesan organs voicing accurately the opinions of the local bishop. Some were published by religious societies to promote a particular intellectual level or discussion. A few, such as the Boston *Pilot,* were privately owned and published by Catholic laymen and were free from influence and direction by official ecclesiastical authority.[39]

These journals created opinion as much as reflecting it. Confining themselves primarily to local issues, many launched crusades to secure specific advantages for Catholics and, in their enthusiasm, dragged both clergy and laymen along with them. Several Chicago

[36] Quoted in San Francisco *Monitor,* September 9, 1899, p. 4.

[37] *Ibid.,* September 23, 1899, p. 4.

[38] *Ibid.*

[39] See Apollinaris W. Baumgartner, *Catholic Journalism: A Study of its Development in the U.S. 1789–1930.*

and St. Louis newspapers were early and intense supporters of Catholic participation in the labor-union movement years before Cardinal Gibbons became interested in the Knights of Labor.[40] One newspaper, Father Peter C. Yorke's San Francisco *Monitor*, prodded lethargic clergy and laity into a cleanup of San Francisco politics and labor discrimination. Its editor was directly involved in the organization of the San Francisco waterfront strike of 1901.[41] Not all Catholic journals were such crusaders, of course, but most seemed to have an intense interest in getting Catholics involved in controversial local issues. Many editors bemoaned the passive attitude of the vast majority of Catholics, who in their opinion seemed to accept discrimination or bigotry much too readily. Wherever the Catholic viewpoint on particular issues needed defending, the journals were usually the first to speak out. The Catholic press, therefore, was vitally important in the formation of Catholic opinion and influence in political affairs.

As might be expected, the greatest interest in foreign affairs came from those Catholic journals published in seaboard cities. Their editors were close to the day-by-day transactions of international commerce and were familiar with the sentiments of newly arrived immigrants. They could not divorce themselves from their own all too recent immigrant background. As much as they pleaded their own Americanism, they were, nevertheless, not objective Americans seeing the United States in its new struggle for great-power status. Perhaps in this connection the most important consideration was the Irish influence on Catholic editorial opinion. Practically all of the editors of these seaboard journals were Irish-American. Their sensitivity to aspersions cast at Irish loyalty during the War simply encouraged further outspoken opinions on American foreign policies. How well their statements reflected the true consensus of American Catholics can never be determined. The non-Irish writers had so little to say, in relative terms, on foreign affairs that it is difficult to measure their sentiments. The important point is that the Irish writers were doing most of the writing on these issues and were being read by non-Catholics throughout the country. These non-

[40] James E. Roohan, "American Catholics and the Social Question, 1865–1900," *United States Catholic Historical Society Records and Studies*, XLIII (1951), 3–26.

[41] Cronin, *Father Yorke*, pp. 70–77.

Catholic readers accepted the opinions of Irish-American editors as being an accurate interpretation of national Catholic opinion.

Consideration must be given, therefore, to the traditional Irish distrust and dislike of the English. Irish Anglophobia colored much of Catholic journalistic discussion of both American colonial policy and American foreign policy for over a decade. This element of the Catholic press was among the first to support American expansionist programs as a check against overweening British power. Yet at the same time Irish editors could not follow through logically with support of a United States imperialist policy of annexation of large areas of noncontiguous territory. They could not condone a policy of exploitation in the new dependencies that they feared would be similar to that followed by the English in Ireland. As a result the Catholic press was much confused over the momentous issues related to American expansion.

One consistent underlying factor of Catholic press opinion, however, remained the fear that Great Britain might expand its dominion in the Western Hemisphere at the expense of the United States, a fear which brought about frequent demands for quick application of the Monroe Doctrine. As early as 1895, during the Venezuela crisis, the Boston *Pilot* lauded President Cleveland's interference.[42] In an editorial very typical of the rest of the Catholic press the *Pilot* indicated how strong a position the United States should take: "England's reply to the American offer of mediation on the Venezuela question is, briefly: Mind your own business. That is just what we are doing: and the fleet of Admiral Meade is in those waters for the express purpose of seeing that England shall not interfere with us in doing it."[43] A few months later the *Pilot*, referring to the withdrawal of British military interests in the Mosquito Coast of Nicaragua, first mentioned the possibility of an isthmian canal: "It is to be hoped that the Nicaraguans will retain possession of the long-disputed Mosquito Coast and put an end to the British attempts at controlling the Eastern terminus of our future interoceanic canal."[44] The *Catholic World*, another enthusiastic supporter of the canal idea, very strongly stated that "control of the Nicaragua Canal by

[42] Boston *Pilot*, March 30, 1895, p. 4.
[43] *Ibid.*, April 13, 1895, p. 4.
[44] *Ibid.*, August 25, 1895, p. 4.

the United States is a first necessity."[45] For several years the San Francisco *Monitor* had been pointing out the importance of Hawaii to the United States as a defensive base for the Canal.[46] However, the most expansionist-minded of the Catholic press remained the Boston *Pilot.* It agitated for the prompt building of the Canal and the ultimate annexation of Cuba and Hawaii to the United States, and it even went so far as to suggest that the government purchase Madeira as an advance base.[47]

With these sentiments generally prevalent in the Catholic press it is not surprising that Catholics, with little urging, joined their fellow Americans in a war on behalf of Cuban independence. What they or the press or the hierarchy did not expect was the legacy of problems that the War would leave them. The weaknesses of their own internal organization could make it difficult for them to withstand the external pressures rising in the postwar era. The "splendid little war" of 1898 forced the Roman Catholic Church in the United States to come of age. The Church had to throw off its tinge of foreignism and do more than merely accommodate itself to American society. To keep control of its destiny it had to reverse its traditional role of indifference to national affairs and try instead to influence the direction of national policies. How well it enacted this reversal depended on how well its members became conscious of themselves and of their numbers as a potential influence on political matters.

[45] Patrick S. Cassidy, "The Nicaragua Canal Project," *Catholic World,* LXII (January, 1896), 507.

[46] San Francisco *Monitor,* April 3, 1897, p. 4.

[47] Boston *Pilot,* January 11, 1896, p. 4, January 28, 1897, p. 4, October 9, 1897, p. 4.

CHAPTER THREE

CHURCH AND STATE IN CUBA, PUERTO RICO, AND GUAM

QUESTIONS of the separation of church and state in the new American dependencies meant different things to different people. To the officials of the United States government it was a simple matter of applying all of the necessary principles of the American Constitution. Colonial administrators would remove all traces of clerical influence from colonial administration and withdraw from the Church all forms of governmental financial support. Regardless of use, state-owned property would be returned to the state and Church-owned property would be returned to the Church. Thus the Roman Catholic Church would be separated from the state and be allowed to stand or fall on its own resources. But to some officials of the Catholic Church in the islands this was not what separation of church and state meant at all. The state influence in religious affairs would be removed and the Church would be allowed complete control of its destinies and be permitted to enjoy the fruits of its labors, both spiritual and financial. The ancient privileges of patronage which had conferred on the Spanish monarchs the right to direct the Church's policies and name its prelates would be revoked. Property built for ecclesiastical use would be Church property and income-producing property, used for the support of the Church, would also become its property. To the Churchmen separation of church and state simply meant the removal of the state from the Church.

Briefly stated, these were the extreme positions that led to the religious controversies in the islands. Obviously, the solutions to the whole controversy had to lie somewhere in between. In most cases the situation required compromise. And compromise required patience, diplomatic skill, and understanding. From 1898 to the end of 1904 individual problems arose that called the attention of civil and ecclesiastical officials to the need for a better understanding of each others' position. Indeed, during the colonial period the leaders of the Roman Catholic Church at the Vatican learned a profound lesson in the true meaning of twentieth-century republicanism while the representatives of the American people at Washington developed a new respect for this ancient church.

All the controversies centered on the constitutionality of each particular issue. Government officials never displayed any deliberate intention to confiscate arbitrarily Church-owned property or to prevent the Catholic Church from functioning within the confines of American authority. The Catholic Church existed in these possessions, and most of the inhabitants were Catholic. This was the premise accepted by the American government. The issue really involved questions of what the Catholic Church owned, what the state owned, how far the Catholic Church should go in administering certain charities and pious trusts, and what policies the public school systems should follow. All these matters could be, and were, settled eventually by a judicious application of American constitutional principles. The desire of the American government and most of the American Catholic prelates was to make the Catholic Church in each of the dependencies as free and self-sufficient as the Catholic Church in the United States.

Two Church-state problems, however, found no solution in American constitutional tradition. Both received considerable attention in the Catholic press but hardly drew a murmur from the American Catholic hierarchy. The first concerned the possibility of opening up to free missionary activity areas that had been closed preserves for the Catholic Church for centuries. The very nature of an American occupation meant that free access to the territories for other religions would mean competition to the Catholic Church. Catholics, even if they had wanted to, could not press the issue legally because to prevent free access would constitute an infringement of guarantees of religious liberty. So the Catholic press took upon itself the duty of watching the insular governments to be sure that Protestants in official positions did not grant undue advantage to non-Catholic missionary groups. The second problem was far more basic than the first and became the most important single Church-state issue in the entire colonial period: the question of declaring four Catholic religious orders in the Philippines *persona non grata* by the American government. The significance of this matter to public opinion and to the creation of official policy requires that it be given separate and detailed analysis in later chapters.

Of all the many religious controversies that developed during the formation of colonial policies certain ones came to the attention of the American people through prominence in the columns of the American press. These particular issues were significant, for they caused a Catholic reaction in the United States. This reaction, in turn, brought about various forms of pressure on the American government and ultimately influenced colonial policies. Although all of the colonies had similar problems, the solution in one colony set the pattern for the settlement of similar situations in the other colonies. The question of the validity of a religious marriage ceremony, for example, arose first in Cuba in early 1899. Official policy on this issue raised such a furor that it was never allowed to reappear in any of the other dependencies. On the other hand, special circumstances incident to the religious problems of individual dependencies required special solutions. Disputed ownership of Church property in Cuba, for instance, had to be settled before the island's administration was turned over to the government of the new Republic of Cuba; this meant quick, arbitrary action by Governor-General Leonard Wood, whereas in Puerto Rico the same difficulty took several years and legislation by the United States Congress before final settlement was reached.

The Church-state controversy in the islands was never over the issue of the disestablishment of the Roman Catholic Church. No critic of American policies who genuinely voiced the American Catholic viewpoint ever desired a continuation of the ecclesiastical-civil status quo that had existed in these areas. Catholics and non-Catholics alike were practically unanimous in wanting to see a complete separation of Church from state. The controversies that arose during the six-year period were over the methods to be used in bringing about this separation and the extent of separation that was to occur. The debate appearing in press, pulpit, and public speeches, then, was over means to an end rather than the end itself.

Perhaps the reason for the intensity of the debate can be found in the isolation of the United States from the currents of anticlericalism that had swirled in Europe since the French Revolution. In France, Germany, Spain, even in Italy, the Catholic Church had been stripped of much of its influence and wealth by anticlerical forces, many of whom were Catholics. Although Catholicism in these areas had not been seriously hampered, most American Catholics did not understand this. The concept of individual freedom of religious conscience had become so ingrained that many of these Catholics considered an attack on the physical structure of the Church as an attack upon their own religious liberty. They honestly feared that legislation designed to minimize certain aspects of the Church's influence in the dependencies might establish precedents that could be used to interfere with Catholic religious activities in the United States. Their century of defense against nativist anti-Catholicism logically drove them into a rabid, shrill defense of everything connected with the Catholic Church in the new American empire.

Catholic journalism clearly illustrated this point. Rarely was an act of the government called "anticlerical"; instead, policies allegedly detrimental to the Church were called "anti-Catholic" or, more often, "anti-Catholicism in action." The Catholic press, representing an attitude naturally more American than European, was more outspoken than the majority of the hierarchy, simply because the hierarchy was kept closer to Church affairs in Europe. This fact explained the comparatively passive tone of such prelates as Archbishop Ireland and Cardinal Gibbons, both of whom traveled widely in Europe. It also explained the more compliant attitude of the Vatican, for its own tradition had taught it how to survive attack since the time of Nero. Thus the Church itself, through its higher clergy, had to lead its American membership to acknowledge its problem: the lack of recognition of reality in the rest of the world.

But the dilemma was not apparent until the Treaty of Peace was implemented. The simplicity of the peace settlement itself appealed to all, Catholic as well as Protestant.[1] In the months immediately

[1] "Archbishop Ireland on the Religious Question," Boston *Pilot,* August 27, 1898.

following the signing of the armistice in August much of the Catholic press supported the Administration's policies in the new dependencies. As a whole, Catholics looked forward to a bright future for the Church now that Spain's influence had ended.[2] Even Manuel Santander, the bishop of Havana, expressed this sentiment in a pastoral letter to his flock in which he encouraged their cooperation with the American authorities. In his words the change from Spanish rule was for the good because it was "God's will."[3]

Some prophets of doom, however, appeared among the Catholics in the United States. They feared that through Americanization the islands would be open to the unlimited access of Protestant missionaries. Archbishop Ireland, despite his general enthusiasm, had warned of this possibility as early as August.[4] The Protestants themselves would create no problem, but their influence might release a wave of bigotry directed at the Church. The *Catholic World*, normally an ardent supporter of the Administration's policies in the Caribbean, refused to ignore these potential dangers:

> . . . a thousand difficulties present themselves. The horror of it all is that perhaps in our country religious bigotry will be violently tempted to vent its spleen in vandalism worthy of barbarians. The art treasures, the churches, paintings, jewels, mosaics, and sacred vessels must not be polluted by irreverent hands. Let us gently and prudently, if we must, separate state officialism from church government, but let us revere as is becoming a liberal Christian nation every expression and embodiment of religion.[5]

Other writers admonished American Catholics to act as watchdogs over affairs in the new territories and "nail" all lies concerning religion.[6] If Americanization meant the establishment of religious toleration in the new dependencies, it also meant the protection of the religious institution already existing in these islands. The very terms of the Treaty of Peace left no doubt about this protection. The United States had solemnly bound itself to recognize the religion of

[2] *Catholic World*, LXVIII (January, 1899), 571.

[3] Boston *Pilot*, November 19, 1898, p. 4.

[4] *Ibid.*, August 27, 1898, p. 1.

[5] Henry O. O'Keeffe, "A Word on the Church and the New Possessions," *Catholic World*, LXVIII (December, 1898), 319–320.

[6] San Francisco *Monitor*, January 21, 1899, p. 344.

the inhabitants and to protect all religious property.[7] The Catholic watchdog labored incessantly to be sure that the terms of the Treaty were maintained.

American ignorance of the real religious problems became apparent within a few months after the American occupation formally began on January 1, 1899. The United States government was attempting to destroy overnight, as it were, an ecclesiastical-political system that had existed for almost four centuries. From the beginning, the power that the Spanish government exerted over ecclesiastical affairs in its colonial empire was unparalleled in the annals of Catholic history.[8] Nineteen years after Columbus first set foot in the New World the Diocese of Puerto Rico was established at San Juan. From that moment on the Roman Catholic Church became inextricably entwined with the Spanish colonial government in the West Indies. The erection of dioceses was necessary to facilitate the spread of Christianity among the natives, an essential purpose of the colonial venture of Spain's rulers. To this end Isabella had ordered that priests accompany Columbus on his first voyage. She and her successors set aside large portions of the colonial budget for the building of churches and missions. The immediate expansion of Catholicism was to accompany the expansion of Spanish power. The governors were supposed to dedicate themselves to encourage the efforts of missionary priests. Besides wanting to obey Christ's command to "Teach all nations," the Spanish government recognized that a Christianized native society would be a pacified native society. The Spanish crown and its representatives became the protector of the Catholic Church in Spanish America.

Authority for this protection, and compensation for its cost, was granted to the rulers of Spain in a series of papal bulls, issued by Alexander VI in 1493 and 1501 and by Julius II in 1504 and 1508.[9] The Popes made these concessions of their power because a great distance separated Rome from America and because they lacked the means to equip such extensive missionary ventures. In addition, the Holy See was pressured to be certain that the authority granted to the Spanish crown was perpetual and all-inclusive. The papal bulls which made the king the patron of the Church in the Indies gave him

[7] Article VIII, *Treaty of Peace between the United States and Spain* (Senate Document No. 62, 55th Cong., 3rd Sess.), p. 9.

[8] J. Lloyd Mecham, *Church and State in Latin America*, p. 43.

[9] *Ibid.*, p. 17.

the authority to determine the size and location of dioceses and parishes, to nominate the bishops and clergy, to supervise missions and monasteries, and to collect all tithes and first fruits. In return for these rights as patron, the government was to provide out of the public treasury the cost of worship and the salaries of the clergy. In effect, the Papacy exerted almost no direct control of Church activities in America; the king had assumed quasi-pontifical powers.[10]

Spanish sovereigns laid claim personally to all the lands that their military explorers might discover. The islands of the West Indies and the Philippines thus became the personal real property of the crown and could be divided up and disposed of in any way as royal largess. To encourage the spread of Christianity the government made large grants of uncleared land to several monastic orders to provide additional income in support of church operations. The Church was then charged with the responsibility of educating children and caring for the aged and infirm, in addition to its regular functions of conducting divine worship and operating missions. In time great landed estates appeared where jungle had been, and wealth accrued slowly but steadily to these religious orders. In some of the principal cities this wealth was used to erect large and beautiful buildings for public as well as religious use. In such important commercial centers as Havana, Santiago, and Manila the business districts often expanded onto land owned by a religious order or by the Church itself. In large sections of these cities many of the business buildings were owned directly by one of these Catholic orders. Yet in other cities the Church built structures on public land, the use of which was donated by one of the branches of government—the crown, the colony, or the municipality.[11]

To complicate the situation even further, the Church or one of the religious orders often fell heir to a benefaction bequeathed by some ardent Catholic or repentent sinner. The Church shared in a great number of these testamentary estates through the centuries. A few of these might have been outright gifts of money or property designated for some specific ecclesiastical use. But most of this inherited wealth came in the form of *capellanias* or *censos,* liens or mortgages

[10] *Ibid.,* pp. 12–43.

[11] *Government for the Island of Porto Rico. Hearings before the Senate Committee on Pacific Islands and Porto Rico* (Senate Document No. 147, 56th Cong., 1st Sess.), p. 193.

against real property which provided that a set percentage of the income of the property be used for some particular religious function, such as offering Masses for the deceased. Taken individually each of these *censos* did not amount to very much, but through the years the aggregation of them provided a huge source of revenue. As the *censos* were always granted in perpetuity, the property was encumbered regardless of who owned it, and several such encumberances on the same piece of property would stifle the initiative of its owner to make improvements. Large portions of what might have been highly productive land were abandoned or allowed to fall into decrepitude; nevertheless Church officials maintained the claim for the Church's share of the property's income.[12]

This situation of ecclesiastical property in the islands might have remained reasonably ordered, had it not been for the actions of the Spanish home government during its revolutionary and counterrevolutionary periods in the nineteenth century. A movement for the confiscation of Church properties and for the suppression of monastic orders received official sanction in a royal decree dated October 25, 1820, and in a series of decrees in 1835 and 1837.[13] The intention of this action on the part of the new liberal government in Spain was to deprive the Church of its power and much of its income, and put this revenue to work for the civil government. The Church lost almost all of its sources of income and was forced to rely on voluntary support from its members. After a tradition of centuries of state support, Catholics in the islands found this change difficult to accept. The Church's poverty was reflected in the meager amount of collections and the sharp curtailment of many of its activities.[14]

During the years of confiscation much Church property in the islands was sold to private buyers and the proceeds turned over to municipal or colonial governments. But popular sentiment against the entire procedure often delayed or prevented these sales and in many areas the Church continued the use of its property despite the statutes made in Madrid. When the counterrevolutionary government came to power in the 1840's the Spanish crown tried to reverse

[12] *Disposition of Church Lands in Porto Rico* (Senate Report No. 2977, 57th Cong., 2nd Sess.), p. 34.

[13] *Ibid.*, p. 24.

[14] J. I. Rodriguez, "The Church and Church Property in the Island of Cuba," *American Catholic Quarterly Review,* XXV (April, 1900), p. 381.

the policy of confiscation or, if this were impossible, at least to mitigate its worst effects. Finally, a concordat reached between Spain and the Vatican in 1851 attempted a settlement and ascertained an honest appraisal of the status quo. Several royal decrees were issued in 1852 to expedite the terms of the concordat. The lands held by the state and still unsold were to be returned to the Church. The Church no longer was to collect tithes and first fruits; instead it was to receive its financial support directly from the civil treasury in compensation for this loss and for the permanent loss of part of its property. Property legitimately purchased from the state was to remain unmolested in the hands of its private buyers. Meanwhile, by papal decree, the Church's large landholdings were to be eliminated. All property of nonecclesiastical use was to be turned over to the government to be sold. The proceeds of this sale were to be returned in the form of government bonds, bearing 3 per cent interest, to the particular diocese where the property was located.[15]

Unfortunately this settlement was overthrown by a revolution in Spain in 1868, and new confiscations and suppressions were carried on throughout the Spanish islands. But after the restoration of the Bourbon king, Alfonso XII, the crown again tried to right the wrongs done to the Church and new royal decrees issued in 1875 and 1876 implemented this policy. Again the remaining unsold Church property was returned to the Church, and new appropriations were made from the public treasury for the support of the clergy, for the repair and maintenance of Church buildings, and for construction of new churches as they were needed. An additional order regularized and listed all salaries for the various ranks of the clergy and set fees for particular religious services.[16]

This was the complicated situation of property ownership that greeted the American military government as it occupied the Spanish islands in the summer and autumn of 1898. When Spanish sovereignty ceased American responsibility began. But how far should American responsibility go? American authorities, who had known only a tradition of a free church in a free state, could not understand these complex ecclesiastical problems. When they replaced the Spanish administration they stopped all payments to the Church from public funds and refused to make any financial grant to support religious

[15] *Disposition of Church Lands in Porto Rico* (Senate Report), pp. 30–33.
[16] *Ibid.*, p. 26.

worship.[17] To establish a liaison to explain the Church's position to the American government the Vatican appointed Americans to high ecclesiastical offices wherever possible. Archbishop Placide L. Chapelle, of New Orleans, was appointed apostolic delegate to Cuba and Puerto Rico in October, 1898. A few months later another American, James H. Blenk, was named bishop of Puerto Rico. The Vatican hoped that through this means United States policy would at least be sympathetic toward the Church and her financial problems in the islands.

Wisdom, understanding, and patience were required of both the Church and the state before these vexatious problems would be settled. Unfortunately the pressures put upon the American administrators made it difficult for them to be objective. The Protestant press was most vociferous about the land question in Cuba, claiming that the Catholic Church had failed its mission and had no right to anything.[18] Other Protestants demanded that the Catholic Church be forced to shift for itself with no help from anyone to recover its debts.[19] Even Congress was petitioned to pass a resolution against appropriations on behalf of the Catholic Church in Cuba.[20] Of course, Catholic journalistic opinion did not remain silent on the issue either. The *Catholic Quarterly Review* pointed out that in 1896 the Church in Cuba had received $403,149 from the Spanish government for compensation of state use of Church-owned land. In 1899 the American government had refused to pay this sum or to return to the Church its property; as a result the Church in Cuba was poverty-stricken.[21]

When Major General John R. Brooke became military governor of Cuba in January, 1899, the process of Americanization moved forward. Through military directives he established what he termed "the quiet severance of church and state . . . this without violating

[17] R. A. Alger, Washington, August 9, 1898, to General Miles, in Adjutant General of the Army (ed.), *Correspondence Relating to the War with Spain, April 15, 1898 to July 30, 1902* (Publication of the Department of War), II, 371.

[18] D. W. Carter, "Cuba and Its Evangelization," *Missionary Review of the World*, XXV (April, 1902), 253–261.

[19] W. A. Chandler, "The Land Question in Cuba," *The Independent*, LIII (July 25, 1901), 1736–1737.

[20] *Congressional Record*, 55th Cong., 3rd Sess., Vol. XXXII, Pt. 1, p. 829.

[21] Rodriguez, "The Church and Church Property in Cuba" *(Am. Cath. Quar. Rev.)*, p. 380.

the legal rights of the Roman Catholic Church."[22] Apparently General Brooke felt that confiscation of alleged Catholic property was not violating the legal rights of the Roman Catholic Church. Public buildings, schools and convents, and cemeteries were turned over to municipal governments or to the insular government. Brooke justified these confiscations on the theory that possession or use determined ownership. Certain churches and convents occupied by the Spanish colonial government for civic purposes in the early 1870's he considered the property of the Spanish government, even though no actual compensation had been made to Catholic authorities. He concluded that under the terms of the Treaty of Paris these properties had come into the possession of the Cuban government. On the other hand, he reversed this theory when he allowed municipal governments to annex and administer cemeteries that had been used exclusively as Catholic cemeteries for years.[23] When officials of the Church protested he announced that if the Catholic clergy desired to maintain their claims to ownership they would have to go to the courts.[24]

Catholics in Cuba and in the United States naturally protested these property confiscations. Priests and bishops in Cuba appealed to the apostolic delegate, Archbishop Chapelle, who in turn appealed to General Brooke and President McKinley.[25] Other Catholics took their appeals elsewhere, especially to Theodore Roosevelt, who by this time was governor of New York. The Catholic press became indignant toward General Brooke and brought its case before the American public.[26] It asserted that the separation of church and state in Cuba was hardly the quiet affair claimed by Governor-General Brooke. These protests, however, were of little avail because of the confusion resulting from the War and the inadequacy of accurate information. As a consequence not much was done during 1899 to settle the property question. Church authorities, refusing to recognize most of the confiscations, filed their protests and waited. But

[22] *Report of Major General J. R. Brooke on Civil Affairs in Cuba* (House Document No. 2, Vol. 7, 56th Cong., 1st Sess.), p. 15.

[23] Order No. 38, *ibid.*, p. 33.

[24] *New York Freeman's Journal*, April 22, 1899, p. 4.

[25] Archbishop and clergy of Cuba, Havana, February 25, 1899, to General Brooke, Chapelle Correspondence, Box II.

[26] *New York Freeman's Journal*, April 22, 1899, p. 4.

for a time the property issue was forgotten in the furor raised over another of General Brooke's decrees.

In April, 1899, the General promulgated a civil-marriage law which automatically invalidated the customary religious marriage ceremony. It was perhaps the most controversial of his actions in Cuba. Based on what he considered sound reasoning, it nonetheless showed a surprising lack of tact and wisdom. He acceded to the request of a large number of native Catholic members of the Cuban government who wanted Church influence removed from as many areas of Cuban life as possible. But he did not examine the religious ramifications behind their proposal.[27] On the surface, the law was intended to serve a good purpose by trying to eliminate concubinage that resulted from the shortage of priests and from the fees charged for the marriage ceremony, exclusively a religious function, and the civil license. Nevertheless, Catholics, in both Cuba and the United States, considered the law an insult.[28] Three parts of the decree were considered obnoxious: only civil marriage was valid; a religious service by itself was not legally binding; and all previous marriages, regardless of duration, had to be validated within a year of the date of the decree (May 31, 1899) with some sort of documentary or eyewitness proof.[29] The last item was perhaps the most noxious, for after years of war municipal archives might be destroyed or possible witnesses dead or missing. The prospect of having a long marriage invalidated officially and the children of that marriage declared illegitimate infuriated Cubans. Despite protests from the Cuban and American clergy and the Catholic press, nothing could make General Brooke modify or revoke his decree.

Other problems beset General Brooke, too. A career army officer who had seen service in the Civil War, he was honest and methodical but entirely too rigid and conservative for the task of preparing the Cubans for national independence. From the beginning of his administration as governor-general his awkward policies were attacked

[27] Major General Leonard Wood, *Civil Report of Major General Leonard Wood, Military Governor of Cuba, 1900* (Publication of the Department of War), I, 81.

[28] *New York Freeman's Journal*, January 6, 1900, p. 4.

[29] Order No. 66, *Report of Major General J. R. Brooke* (House Document), p. 42. It is difficult to ascertain why Brooke was so adamant on this issue; there is no mention of it in a recent study of the U.S. military occupation, David F. Healy, *The United States in Cuba, 1898–1902*.

in Cuba and the United States. He let the government of the island fall into the hands of Cuban professional politicians who were using his authority to build a political machine of their own.[30]

In fact, the whole matter of colonial administration came under attack during the summer of 1899. It required a thorough review by the McKinley Administration. As long as the dependencies were to remain the particular concern of the War Department, President McKinley recognized the need for imaginative leadership in that department. The result was the appointment of Elihu Root as Secretary of War. Root immediately decided that it was too unsafe to leave General Brooke in command of a situation that he could not grasp.[31] In December, Root appointed Major General Leonard Wood as Brooke's successor. General Wood had earned a brilliant reputation as military governor of the provinces of Santiago and Puerto Principe. He had especially endeared himself to the Catholics in these provinces, who considered him friendly, fair, and honest.[32]

Pressure was quickly brought to bear against General Wood to rescind the Cuban civil-marriage law. Cuban and American Catholics, and some non-Catholics as well, objected to the idea that Cuban marriage laws had to be any different from those in the United States. They pointed out that in every state in the Union the religious ceremony was as valid as a civil one. Catholics in particular objected because they considered marriage a divinely created sacrament that was of no concern to civil authority. In Havana a petition bearing 31,000 signatures protesting the law was presented to the General by the bishop of the city, Donatus Sbaretti.[33] The Bishop claimed that the law violated the religious guarantees of the Treaty of Paris. In the United States the Catholic press took up the Bishop's cause. Almost every Catholic newspaper editorialized against the law; some even claimed that this act was typical of the kind of anti-Catholicism that could be expected from the insular administration.[34] What seemed most unusual during all the hubbub over the marriage law was that little was heard from Archbishop Chapelle or from individual members of the American hierarchy. The San Francisco *Monitor* noted this silence and was especially angered that

[30] Herman Hagedorn, *Leonard Wood: A Biography, I,* 235.
[31] *Ibid.,* p. 258.
[32] *Ibid.,* pp. 245–247.
[33] *Ibid.,* p. 316; San Francisco *Monitor,* June 2, 1900, p. 164.
[34] *New York Freeman's Journal,* January 6, 1900, p. 4.

Archbishop Ireland had not spoken out "in the presence of this outrage."[35] The reason for this reticence can best be explained by official concern over the negotiations for the settlement of disputed claims to Church property. These negotiations were far more important to the Church's position on the island, and no one wanted to upset them for what seemed to be a lesser issue.

Nonetheless, General Wood accepted Bishop Sbaretti's petition; he made no commitments, but promised to investigate.[36] In his own opinion Wood felt that Brooke's marriage law was really desired by a vast majority of the Cuban people and it should remain without modification.[37] During the summer of 1900 more important influences from the United States, however, were to make him change his mind. The most significant came from his close friend Theodore Roosevelt, governor of New York. As governor of a state with a large Catholic population and as the Republican vice-presidential candidate, Roosevelt had become increasingly uneasy over the reaction to the law in the Catholic press. He was convinced that the issue was important enough to affect the outcome of the elections in November. In late July he wrote McKinley that he had had a long talk with Wood concerning the marriage law.[38] On August 1 in a letter to a prominent New Jersey Catholic, William Michael Byrne, he tried to explain Wood's unwillingness to revoke Brooke's law as a fear of instigating a wave of anticlericalism in Cuba that would ruin the Church's negotiations over the property question.[39] Yet two days later he again asked Wood to do something as "speedily as possible" to make the law conform to what it was in the United States. Then he warned that unless something was done before September he would send a Catholic priest and a Catholic layman, both friends of his in New York City, to Cuba to "go over the ground" and endeavor to work out a satisfactory solution with the General.[40] Fortunately for Roosevelt this step was unnecessary. General Wood issued a new

[35] San Francisco *Monitor,* July 7, 1900, p. 264.

[36] Wood, *Civil Report of Major General Wood, 1900* (War Dept. Pub.), I, 80–81.

[37] Wood, Havana, July 19, 1900, to Elihu Root, Wood Unpublished Correspondence, Bureau of Insular Affairs Records.

[38] Theodore Roosevelt, Oyster Bay, July 27, 1900, to William McKinley, Elting E. Morison (ed.), *The Letters of Theodore Roosevelt,* II, 1367.

[39] Roosevelt, Oyster Bay, August 1, 1900, to William Michael Byrne, *ibid.,* p. 1369.

[40] Roosevelt, Oyster Bay, August 3, 1900, to Wood, *ibid.,* p. 1372.

order, effective August 13, 1900, rescinding the Brooke law and making both civil and religious ceremonies equally valid. Roosevelt indicated the importance of this final solution in his letter of congratulations to Wood: "The first credit of course goes to you . . . in the next place, if it can be legitimately shown that Root and Hanna and I joined with you in seeing fair play shown the Catholics in Cuba, I think it would be a good thing."[41] The successful outcome of the election so pleased Roosevelt that he offered some advice to the President for future conduct in bettering relations with the Catholics, reminding McKinley that "excellent results followed the action on the marriage law."[42]

The American Catholics, acting as watchdog, also complained of colonial administrators advancing Protestantism in the dependencies through the new public school system. Catholics objected strongly to the establishment of educational systems that excluded religious teaching in countries that were almost entirely Catholic. As long as Cuba was not to become a part of the United States, they asked, why should the United States dictate its own concepts of education as a policy for Cuba, which Cuba might not want.[43] For the other insular possessions they were concerned that a "Godless" public school system would ultimately weaken centuries of the Church's work among the natives. With this possibility uppermost in their minds, Catholic editors in particular watched over the activities of the personnel administering the island school systems. For example, the newspapers considered the appointment of the Reverend Sam Small, a former Protestant minister, as superintendent of schools for Santa Clara Province as an act of anti-Catholicism by the Cuban government. The *Monitor* insisted that it indicated to Catholics "that there is prevalent in a certain class the unexpressed thought of using the power, influence, prestige and machinery of the United States Government in the interests of Protestant propagandism."[44] The Catholic press consistently maintained this distrust of school administrators during the entire colonial era, especially whenever Catholics were not in charge of the educational system.

One unusual program of the Cuban educational system elicited considerable comment among the Catholic press. A plan to send

[41] Roosevelt, Oyster Bay, August 29, 1900, to Wood, *ibid.*, p. 1395.
[42] Roosevelt, Oyster Bay, November 21, 1900, to McKinley, *ibid.*, p. 1413.
[43] Boston *Pilot,* July 28, 1900, p. 4.
[44] San Francisco *Monitor,* March 18, 1899, p. 506.

approximately one thousand Cuban teachers to Harvard for summer school was accepted and encouraged by General Wood in the spring of 1900.[45] On the surface the idea appeared excellent, but to the Boston *Pilot* it was further indication of the attempt to Protestantize the natives through Cuba's educational system. To the Cubans it would show that the ideal school system was nonreligious, a point never accepted by Catholics. The *Pilot* warned that it was the duty of Catholics in and around Cambridge, Massachusetts, to entertain these Cubans and show them that America's educational system was not godless.[46] The idea caused a chain reaction in Catholic circles and a whole plan of cooperation was prepared as the suggestion of the *Pilot* gained support in other Catholic papers and from the Eastern hierarchy. President Eliot, of Harvard, eagerly accepted the offer. He asked the rector of St. Paul's Catholic Church in Cambridge to provide religious services and social programs for the Cubans. The Sisters of Notre Dame at Cambridge opened part of their buildings to house them, while private Catholic families in the area offered their homes as summertime residences. In addition the archbishop of Boston secured several Spanish-speaking priests to be available for them.[47] The entire summer visit of the Cuban teachers was a success for all concerned, Cuban, Protestant, and Catholic.[48]

Disputed ownership of property in Cuba, however, continued to be General Wood's principal civil-religious problem. Encouraged by Wood's sympathetic attitude as governor of Santiago Province, Bishop Sbaretti presented the General with a list of property claimed and desired by the Church.[49] He was altogether willing to accept the idea of settling these claims through an impartial commission rather than resorting to the courts as General Brooke had

[45] Wood, *Civil Report of Major General Wood, 1900* (War Dept. Pub.), I, 118.

[46] Boston *Pilot,* April 21, 1900, p. 4.

[47] *Ibid.,* May 19, 1900, p. 4, May 26, 1900, p. 4.

[48] Sylvester Baxter, "Cuban Teachers at Harvard University," *Outlook,* LXV (August 4, 1900), p. 775.

[49] Donatus Sbaretti, Washington, January 17, 1900, to Wood, Wood Correspondence, Box 28, Manuscripts Division, Library of Congress. Even though the Vatican had sent an American and a Cuban to the sees of San Juan and Santiago, it appointed temporarily an Italian, Sbaretti, primarily for the purpose of settling these property disputes. At first Wood was dubious of Sbaretti's success because of Cuban resistance to his appointment (Wood, Havana, January 13, 1900, to Root, *ibid.*)

proposed. A commission would eliminate the cost of dozens of lengthy cases of litigation to prove ownership of property that the Church claimed was already guaranteed to it by the Treaty of Paris. The Bishop was also shrewd enough to recognize that the religious body would be more successful if the claims were settled before a native Cuban government was established. He feared that "the Cubans would almost certainly deprive the Church of her properties, to the great detriment to religion."[50] For assistance in this particular undertaking he appealed to the American Catholic archbishops during their annual meeting in October. He begged the archbishops to "take a practical interest in the difficulties of the Church in Cuba, and urge on the Government of the United States to have justice done in regard to the properties of the Church in Cuba."[51] In answer to his plea the archbishops authorized the archbishop of New York, Michael A. Corrigan, to secure "the good services of Governor Roosevelt" and also to see the President.[52]

Theodore Roosevelt was apparently willing to help as much as he could. He wrote McKinley, suggesting that he do "strict justice to the Church as well as to the civil population" and that a money equivalent given to the Church for the property might be the best solution.[53] Roosevelt continued to receive appeals concerning these controversial situations and when he thought the appeals were just he helped the Catholics as best he could.[54] By this time Roosevelt's influence was fairly great. It is quite apparent that often after his attention was called to a situation the problem was quickly settled and was usually quite fair to the Catholics. The Brooke civil-marriage law was a case in point; so too was the eventual property settlements in Cuba and Puerto Rico.

Representatives of both the American government and the Catholic Church wished to settle the property question before the Cuban government was turned over to the native administration of the new

[50] Minutes of the Archbishop's Annual Meeting at Catholic University, October 11, 1900, Gibbons Correspondence, Box 98.

[51] *Ibid.*

[52] *Ibid.*

[53] Roosevelt, Oyster Bay, November 20, 1900, to McKinley, Morison (ed.), *Letters of Roosevelt,* II, 1413.

[54] Roosevelt, Albany, November 23, 1900, to Maria Longworth Storer, *ibid.,* p. 1438.

Cuban Republic.[55] General Wood solved the problem in as fair a manner as possible, considering the complexities involved. He appointed a series of judicial commissions to investigate thoroughly and carefully each of the Church's claims. General Wood himself reported that the investigation

> . . . resulted in ascertaining that the claims of the Church were substantially as stated, and were just and fair; accordingly, steps were taken to reach an agreement concerning the property in question. The state purchased outright all "censos" and "capellanias" (forms of mortgages) and paid for them prior to the withdrawal of the Military Government. The sum paid for these was $951,236.97.
>
> An option, for five years, to buy any or all of the real property was obtained, and the state agreed to pay an annual rental, amounting to 5 per cent of the agreed value of urban and 3 per cent of the agreed value of rural property. This rental amounts to $91,027.50 per annum.
>
> The attitude of Bishop Sbaretti, representing the Holy See, was extremely fair and reasonable, and the settlement reached was approximately one-third of the original claims, which amounted to over $7,000,000, or about the same as the property in dispute in the Philippines. The question is settled, and the Cuban Government has a straight business proposition before it, which it can accept or reject as it deems best.[56]

While these negotiations were being conducted in Cuba the Catholic press in the United States continually badgered both General Wood and President McKinley. It claimed that the General's proposal for a commission was merely a smoke screen to deceive Catholic voters. The *New York Freeman's Journal* insisted that the Republicans were circulating a "Ridiculous Report that Pope Leo has Expressed Himself Satisfied with the Treatment of the Church in Cuba."[57] But the press was wrong; it had lost sight of the significance of the difficulties confronting both the Church and the state. In a series of letters written during his stay in Havana, Bishop Sbaretti continually thanked the General for his cooperation.[58] On the

[55] Root, Washington, May 9, 1901, to Wood, Wood Unpublished Correspondence, BIA Records.

[56] Leonard Wood, "The Military Government of Cuba," *Annals of the American Academy of Political and Social Science*, XXI (March, 1903), 26.

[57] *New York Freeman's Journal*, October 8, 1900, p. 1.

[58] Sbaretti, Havana, August 10, 1900, December 11, 1900, and November 4, 1901, to Wood, Wood Correspondence, Box 28, Manuscripts Division, Library of Congress.

eve of his departure for Rome he summed up his, and the Church's attitude: "I feel the duty before leaving Cuba to express to your Excellency my sentiment of friendship and gratitude not only for the kindness shown to me but for the fair treatment of the questions with the Government of the Island, especially the Marriage and Church property questions."[59]

Despite these solutions to problems in Cuba, Catholics in the United States were more concerned over the future of the Church in Puerto Rico. The fact that the island was to be permanently annexed to the United States meant that approximately one million more Catholics would become a part of the Catholic Church in America. The religious welfare of these people as well as their civil and physical needs brought the government's Puerto Rican policies under closer scrutiny. At first the general reaction of Catholics to these policies was quite favorable.[60] When the office of military governor was filled by Brigadier General George W. Davis in May, 1899, Catholics were pleased. General Davis and his wife were Catholics and their presence in San Juan assured those interested Catholics in the United States that the religious position of the natives would be protected.[61] American authorities, realizing the importance of the Catholic position on the island, where 950,000 of the total population of 953,000 were Catholics, extended every courtesty to the Catholic clergy.[62] President McKinley specifically ordered such cooperation.[63] The apostolic delegate, Archbishop Chapelle, was quite gratified with this spirit manifested by the War Department and especially with Secretary Elihu Root.[64]

Thorniest of all the problems, of course, was the ubiquitous issue of settlement of property claims between Church and civil governments. The Catholic Church was not wealthy in Puerto Rico; its people were very poor and it had acquired little valuable property. For years the clergy had been paid the equivalent of $92,000 out of

[59] Sbaretti, Havana, November 4, 1901, to Wood, *ibid.*

[60] Boston *Pilot,* August 27, 1898, p. 4.

[61] *Ibid.*, March 10, 1900, p. 4.

[62] *First Annual Report of the Governor of Porto Rico* (Senate Document No. 79, 57th Cong., 1st Sess.), p. 17.

[63] Adjutant General, Washington, August 28, 1898, to Commanding General, Porto Rico, in Adjutant General (ed.), *Correspondence Relating to the War with Spain* (War Dept. Pub.), I, 402.

[64] Placide L. Chapelle, Washington, August 11, 1899, to McKinley, McKinley Correspondence, Vol. 36.

the public treasury. As in Cuba, this practice immediately stopped after the American occupation began.[65] Although this property interest was small compared to that in Cuba, it was very important to the Church's financial welfare. No problem occurred over ownership of Church buildings, regardless of who had built them or who owned the land on which they stood, for the American authorities immediately established the policy of recognizing the long use and purposes of property for religious services and residences of clergy as equitable title. The property in dispute was income-producing property that was in the possession of the Spanish government when the United States occupied the island but was claimed by the Roman Catholic Church as the rightful owner. This property consisted of three farms totaling 1,548 acres and valued at $30,860, a convent in San Juan valued at $75,000, and *censos* (ground rents) producing an annual income of $1,500.[66]

Opinions on the legality of the Church's claim varied widely among the officials in San Juan. In the case of the convent the Spanish governor had used it as a school but the teaching was done by religious orders. The American authorities had ejected the religious teachers and had planned to use these buildings as public schools.[67] As in Cuba, ground rents were considered un-American and the American authorities prevented their collection.

No settlement was reached in Puerto Rico by local authorities. Archbishop Chapelle's role in the affair was diminished when James H. Blenk was appointed Catholic bishop of Puerto Rico. Bishop Blenk thereafter carried the burden of the Church's claims for several years.[68] He negotiated with the military governors and the Secretary of War, Elihu Root, with little success.[69] When authority passed to the civil government in 1900 Bishop Blenk continued to press the Catholics' claim. Again Theodore Roosevelt's influence was sought on behalf of the Catholics. Roosevelt felt that the settlement

[65] United States Insular Commission, *Report of the United States Insular Commission to the Secretary of War upon Investigations Made into the Civil Affairs of the Island of Porto Rico* (Publication of the Department of War), p. 33.

[66] *Disposition of Church Lands in Porto Rico* (Senate Report), p. 11.

[67] *New York Freeman's Journal,* January 23, 1899, p. 6.

[68] Chapelle, Washington, August 11, 1899, to McKinley, McKinley Correspondence, Vol. 36.

[69] Root, Washington, June 2, 1902, to John Hay, *Disposition of Church Lands in Porto Rico* (Senate Report), p. 7.

in Cuba had been fair to all concerned and suggested that such a policy of investigation might be followed.[70] However, none of the American authorities wanted to take a firm stand on the question, feeling that because annexation was permanent such problems of basic policy could be solved only by Congress.

These questions over the disputed ownership of Church property became temporarily lost in the political hassle over broader questions of American policy in the newly annexed territory.[71] The entire matter, however, was brought before the respective insular committees of both houses of Congress and discussed in committee hearings. A proposal, passed by the House, was to have the United States relinquish all rights to the disputed property in favor of the Catholic Church. But the Senate did not agree. The senators were afraid that such an outright grant would be difficult to defend before a dissatisfied public. Under Chairman Joseph B. Foraker, of Ohio, the Senate Committee on Puerto Rico and the Pacific Islands reviewed the whole Church-property question. Senator Foraker finally proposed a bill which received the encouragement of the Administration. Its intent was to establish a policy similar to that followed by General Wood in Cuba. A committee would be appointed to investigate the Church's claims and then to make recommendations to the President or Congress. Theodore Roosevelt liked the success of the solution in Cuba and so gave Foraker's idea his personal backing. He wrote the Senator: "All Bishop Blenk asks is an opportunity to lay his case before an impartial tribunal and abide by our decision."[72] The friendliness of the Committee's hearings, the limited debate on the floor of each house, and the cooperative spirit of Roosevelt and other administrative officials indicate how willing the American government was to make a fair settlement. Senator Foraker's version of the bill was passed in both houses in June, 1903. A committee was appointed and eventual awards were made to the Catholic Church.

Another item that particularly irritated the Catholic press in the United States was the colonial administration of the military governor of Guam, naval Captain Richard P. Leary. Captain Leary was

[70] Roosevelt, Washington, June 2, 1902, to Root, *ibid.*, p. 6.

[71] For the debate of the entire Puerto Rican question see the *Congressional Record,* 57th Cong., 2nd Sess.

[72] Roosevelt, Washington, February 19, 1903, to Joseph B. Foraker, Morison (ed.), *Letters of Roosevelt,* III, 430.

appointed governor on January 12, 1899, but because of delays in travel and necessary preparations he did not establish his administration until August 10. The tone of his first official statement immediately caught the eyes of Catholic editors. In this proclamation of his assumption of authority he declared:

> All political rights heretofore exercised by the Clergy in dominating the people of the Island, are hereby abolished, and everyone is guaranteed absolute freedom of worship and full protection in the lawful pursuits of life, so long as that protection is deserved by actual submission to and compliance with the requirements of the Government of the United States.[73]

On August 28 the Governor, finding fault with Spanish priests on the island, ordered them all to leave. Only one priest, Padre José Palomo, was allowed to remain. Three other Spanish priests expressed a willingness to become American citizens and remain, but Leary refused to consider this possibility.[74] A third order, dated August 25, 1899, was equally arbitrary. In this the Governor prohibited public celebration of religious feast days and allowed only those public holidays authorized in the United States.[75]

Governor Leary had definite reasons for the arbitrary action of his orders. However, he based his reasoning on what appeared to American Catholics as preconceived prejudices against Spanish Catholicism. He did not consider the effect of his words on American Catholics. The Catholic press naturally protested. The San Francisco *Monitor* called him highhanded and demanded an explanation from Washington.[76] The Boston *Pilot,* labeling him the "King of Guam," feared that as far as that island was concerned the Constitution of the United States was in jeopardy.[77] Other Catholic papers expressed the same sentiment, asserting that the rights of Spaniards still there and the religious freedom of the natives were protected by the Treaty of Paris. They insisted that Leary's orders were in direct conflict with these terms. Until something was done to modify his actions, the Catholic press demanded an investigation.[78]

[73] Henry P. Beers, *American Naval Occupation and Government of Guam, 1898–1902,* p. 22.
[74] *Ibid.,* p. 62.
[75] *Ibid.,* p. 27.
[76] San Francisco *Monitor,* November 4, 1899, p. 84.
[77] Boston *Pilot,* December 2, 1899, p. 4.
[78] *New York Freeman's Journal,* January 20, 1900, p. 4.

Such demands for investigation did not fall on deaf ears. From Manila, Archbishop Chapelle wrote letters of protest to Governor Leary and to members of the Administration in Washington. Because of these and similar protests in the United States, the President ordered Major General Elwell S. Otis, commanding general of the U.S. Army in the Philippines, to investigate. Major General Joseph Wheeler was sent to the island for this purpose in January, 1900. Although Captain Leary and his naval superiors resented the interference in a naval command by Army personnel, General Wheeler carried out his mission. His report, which approved of most of Leary's policies, was considered final and the issue was dropped.[79] Governor Leary was not satisfied, however. On February 8, 1900, he requested that he be relieved of his command by July. His request was granted and he was replaced by Commander Seaton Schroeder on July 19.

The press in the United States read more into Leary's recall than merely his own desire to return to the United States. The New York *Sun,* claiming that the effect of Catholic demands for action had really been responsible for the replacement, reported: "Captain Richard P. Leary's propensity for issuing decrees or general orders in his capacity as Governor of Guam is believed by several officials to be the real reason for the decision of the Government to recall him."[80] The Catholic press, of course, was pleased at the change of command in Guam, although it seemed to some Catholics that the discussion of Leary was given undue prominence. But the *American Catholic Quarterly Review* pointed out that such actions could not be ignored: "Catholics of America may well ponder on this and ask how long will freedom of conscience be left to themselves if the new theory of establishing free institutions by military despotism is tolerated by the American people."[81]

This observation had in it the best explanation of why so many Catholics in the United States were concerned over the activities of government in these distant lands. Acceptance of certain policies in remote islands might serve as precedent for application of simi-

[79] Beers, *American Naval Occupation of Guam,* pp. 36–37.

[80] New York *Sun,* April 2, 1900, p. 2.

[81] Bryan J. Clinch, "Imperialism in the Philippines," *American Catholic Quarterly Review,* XXV (April, 1900), 225.

lar policies in the United States, where the air still crackled with strong anti-Catholic sentiment. Those American Catholics who were shrewd enough to see beyond an individual isolated act were not going to let this happen. They, therefore, continued to maintain themselves as vigilant watchdogs over the direction of American colonial policies. They were especially alert in observing affairs in the Philippine Islands.

CHAPTER FOUR

CATHOLICS AND THE AMERICAN OCCUPATION OF THE PHILIPPINE ISLANDS

AMERICA'S COLONIAL PROBLEMS began in the far Pacific on May 1, 1898. On that day Commodore George Dewey, commanding the United States Far Eastern Fleet, destroyed a Spanish fleet in Manila Bay. With the loss of but a single life, Dewey practically destroyed in one blow all vestiges of Spanish power in the Pacific. The loss of its fleet made the Spanish military force at Manila helpless, and American capture of the Philippine Islands was only a matter of time and the discretion of the United States government. Suddenly America's attention was diverted from the struggle in Cuba and focused on the remote, mysterious Orient. Such names as Zamboango, Cavite, Corregidor seemed as romantic and fascinating as those in the *Arabian Nights*. America's military machine had bridged the Pacific. Whether the United States liked it or not, it was about to become a colonial power in the Orient.

American public interest was immediately captured by this military success. Where were the Philippines? Who were the Filipinos?

Why was the United States there? How long would it stay? These and other questions began to fill the American press. All sorts of information began to trickle in as answers. Men already on the spot with the Army or Navy sent dispatches to the press. As soon as they could, newspapermen went out to get firsthand information. Soon a welter of material accumulated concerning the Islands and their inhabitants, some of it good, most of it misleading. By the time the War ended in August most Americans were convinced that these island people were allies, for they also had been fighting against Spain and were trying to rid themselves of a Spanish colonial government. To these Americans the Filipinos were the same as the Cubans, deserving of American help, cooperation, and protection. But other Americans, on the contrary, were not so certain. Were the natives barbaric or civilized, Christian or pagan? Did they need or deserve American help? What advantage did the United States have in the Philippines?

To decide what its future was going to be in the Orient the United States needed to know something more concrete about its new wards than what was available in newspaper dispatches. Even President McKinley, after praying for divine guidance, still did not know whether or not he had a pig in a poke when he decided that the United States was to continue its control over the Islands. So at various times executive and congressional committees were created to gather enough information to make an intelligible basis for an American Philippine policy. A summary of their findings indicates the general opinion held by the United States government. The Philippines were a group of about 1,400 islands, ranging in size from small rocks that disappear at high tide to the huge island of Mindanao, as large as all the other islands put together. About half of the population was on Mindanao, and the remainder scattered among the larger islands. Most of the islands were uninhabited. As to the Filipinos themselves, approximately 7,800,000 were of a predominantly Malayan stock. Of these, 6,500,000 were Christians, a few were pagan savages in the hills, and the remainder were Moslems under the vague political and religious authority of the Sultan of Sulu.[1] As far as the United States government was concerned, there was no Philippine people, but a scattering of eighty different

[1] *First Philippine Commission (Schurman) Report* (Senate Document No. 138, 56th Cong., 1st Sess.), p. 107.

tribes speaking more than sixty different languages and knowing no other experience in formal government than that of the arbitrary rule of Spain.[2] The people were ignorant, superstitious, well intentioned but lighthearted, and deeply fond of family and religion.[3] At the same time, a large percentage could read and write in Spanish or a native dialect, and many were highly educated either in local schools or abroad.[4] To mar this rather pleasant picture, the Filipinos were accused of cruelty, especially toward their political oppressors —native, Spanish, or American.[5] The most generally accepted conclusion in these investigations was that all of the 6,500,000 Filipino Christians were sincere, devout, loyal members of the Roman Catholic Church.[6]

As in Cuba and Puerto Rico, so in the Philippines Catholicism had expanded with the power and authority of the Spanish government. Catholic missionaries landed with Magellan when he claimed the Islands for Spain in 1517. Some of these friars remained behind to begin Christianizing the natives even before any semblance of civil authority appeared. From the beginning Spanish priests represented everything of Spain to the natives: religion, government, and culture. In the 381 years of Spanish control of the Islands the Catholic Church grew to claim six sevenths of the entire native population and to organize a church with an archdiocese, 4 suffragan dioceses, and 746 parishes, served by 967 Spanish priests and 675 native priests.[7] Though this is a ratio of only one priest to four thousand natives, the Catholic Church enjoyed a tremendous respect and influence among the natives.[8] Even Protestant missionaries visiting the Islands after the American conquest were impressed at how fer-

[2] Elihu Root, "The United States and the Philippines in 1900," Robert Bacon and James Brown Scott (eds.), *The Military and Colonial Policy of the United States: Addresses and Reports of Elihu Root*, p. 44.

[3] William Howard Taft, Manila, July 14, 1900, to Elihu Root, quoted in Henry Fawles Pringle (ed.), *The Life and Times of William Howard Taft*, I, 173.

[4] *Congressional Record*, 57th Cong., 1st Sess., Vol. XXXV, Pt. 7, p. 7243.

[5] "Testimony of Admiral George Dewey," *Affairs in the Philippine Islands. Hearings before the Senate Committee on the Philippines* (Senate Document No. 331, 57th Cong., 1st Sess.), Pt. 1, p. 2957.

[6] "Testimony of Governor Taft," *ibid.*, p. 50.

[7] "Religion," *First Philippine Commission Report* (Senate Document), pp. 107–108.

[8] *Ibid.*, p. 109.

vent the devotion of the Filipinos, both men and women, was to the ritual and belief of the Roman Catholic Church.[9] After spending four years in the Philippines as civil governor, William Howard Taft was thoroughly convinced of this sincerity of Filipino Catholicism.[10]

However, the depth of Filipino Catholicity did not prevent the Filipinos from agitating against Spanish authority. The same unenlightened Spanish despotism that had incited revolutions in South America, Spain, and Cuba provided enough acts of misgovernment in Manila to call for reforms. During the latter part of the century one Spanish governor after another made promises to improve the situation, but the weight of 250 years of a stifling bureaucracy made changes impossible. Spanish officials, being apprehensive, were edgy, cautious, and often exceedingly cruel.[11] Involved in this Filipino hatred of Spanish authority was an equally strong dislike for the Spanish friar priests. These men were often the only Spaniards in remote sections of the Islands, and willing or not, they became instruments of the Spanish government at the same time that they were representatives of the Catholic Church. Accused of acts of misconduct as clergymen and of cruel and unnecessary exactions as landlords, the friars became the whipping boys for every potential Filipino politician who set out to free his country from Spanish dominion.[12]

With the opening of the Suez Canal the Philippine Islands were drawn closer to Europe and to European commerce and ideas. Prominent young Filipinos, educated in Europe, returned to their homeland filled with new liberal concepts. These young men were lionized as the leaders of a popular movement for Filipino autonomy. Around them developed the nucleus of a revolutionary spirit.[13] Through secret Masonic societies known as the Katipunan a revolution was organized and finally broke out in 1896. The military success of the movement was always in doubt, however, even though

[9] *Ibid.*, p. 110.

[10] William Howard Taft, "The Philippines," *National Geographic Magazine,* XVI (August, 1905), 364.

[11] Oscar F. Williams, U.S. Consul, Manila, March 27, 1898, to Thomas W. Gridler, 3rd Assistant Secretary of State, *Conduct of War Department in the War with Spain* (Senate Document No. 221, 56th Cong., 1st Sess.), p. 1208.

[12] See below, Chapter 5.

[13] Charles B. Elliott, *The Philippines,* I, 182–195.

Spanish armed strength was limited. Not enough popular support from the mass of the Filipinos was manifested for a vast uprising against Spanish authority. Many of the early leaders of the revolutionary movement were either captured or bought off. In time, the entire command of the Filipino forces fell to Emilio Aguinaldo. Holed up in one section of Cavite Province after months of desperate fighting, Aguinaldo tried to get terms from the Spanish governor, Primo de Rivera, in August, 1897.

To some Filipinos Aguinaldo's peace terms looked like a sellout to the Spaniards. He and the other rebel leaders were literally bought off with Spanish dollars. They agreed to lay down their arms and withdraw from the Islands for a specific amount of money and the promise that Governor de Rivera would carry out the reforms that they demanded. The principal terms of the Treaty of Biacnabato, signed November 15, 1897, were as follows: (1) expulsion of the religious orders, (2) representation of the Philippines in the Spanish Cortes, (3) equal justice for all—native as well as Spanish, (4) change of laws governing ownership of property, and (5) proclamation of the individual rights of the Filipino. The first two items, the most important ones, were stricken from the Treaty by the Spanish Governor before either party signed it. In essence Aguinaldo made peace without insisting on the expulsion of the friars and representation in the Cortes. Aguinaldo immediately left the Islands for Hong Kong, where $400,000 had been deposited by the Spanish government to the account of "Aguinaldo & Co."[14]

When Admiral Dewey sailed into Manila Bay the old animosities of the Filipinos toward the Spaniards flared up again. None of the promises of Biacnabato had been kept. So in the intervening months Aguinaldo and his colleagues had organized a new revolutionary junta at Hong Kong, using the Spanish blood money to buy arms for a new insurrection. American intervention on behalf of the Cubans excited hope of a similar intervention on behalf of the Filipinos. With Admiral Dewey's aid and protection the rebel leader and his officers were landed on Mindanao and given encouragement to start anew.[15] On June 18, 1898, Aguinaldo proclaimed his new provisional government. By August 6 he claimed to be in complete control of

[14] *Ibid.*, p. 204.
[15] Margaret Leech, *In the Days of McKinley*, p. 283.

fifteen provinces and to have captured over nine thousand prisoners.[16]

Aguinaldo's military successes and the hesitancy of American policy combined to give hope to the oppressed Filipinos, who then turned on their former masters. Most abused of these Spaniards were the friar priests, who had acted as landlords and government officials as well as missionaries in almost every Philippine province. Many of the friars were driven from their parishes and monastic holdings, some were murdered, some imprisoned by the insurgents, and the remainder fled to Manila hoping to be protected by the remnants of Spanish authority.[17] The old cry for the expulsion of the friars and the confiscation of their estates and buildings went up again. In fact, this became one of the chief aims of Aguinaldo's new government.[18]

But the United States government had different ideas. On May 19 President McKinley instructed Secretary of War R. A. Alger to occupy the Philippines. The President stipulated that "all churches and buildings devoted to religious worship and to the arts and sciences, all schoolhouses, are as far as possible, to be protected, and all destruction or intentional defacement of such places, of historical monuments or archives, of works of science and art, is prohibited, save when required by urgent military necessity."[19] Thus, almost from the very beginning, the American government was in the middle of a whole series of Church and state controversies that were to take years to solve.

American policy in the Philippines, as elsewhere, was intended to be strictly neutral in religious problems. The United States was to act as protector and arbiter, not as participant. The terms of capitulation of the Spanish forces as they surrendered Manila to the U.S. Army guaranteed this American point of view. Item 6 stated this provision: "This city, its inhabitants, its churches and religious worship, its educational establishments and its private property of all descriptions, are placed under the special safeguard of the faith

16 *Treaty of Peace between the United States and Spain and Accompanying Papers* (Senate Document No. 62, 55th Cong., 3rd Sess.), p. 438.

17 *First Philippine Commission Report* (Senate Document), p. 126.

18 *Ibid.*, p. 130.

19 William McKinley, Washington, May 19, 1898, to R. A. Alger, *Conduct of War Department* (Senate Document), p. 1233.

and honor of the American army."[20] The ultimate Peace Treaty, in Articles VIII and X, supported these provisions by protecting religious freedom and the ownership of property. In addition, the United States promised to secure the release of all Spanish prisoners, not only its own but also those held by Cuban and Filipino insurrectionists (Article VI).[21] Having given these assurances, the United States entered upon its colonial experiment in the Philippines and found at once that such promises and commitments were difficult to make good.

Immediately the United States became involved in a local religious issue. Aguinaldo held as prisoners approximately 130 Spanish clergymen and nuns, including the bishop of New Segovia.[22] All these Spaniards were members of the four monastic orders that had been singled out by the insurrectionists as the chief oppressors of the Filipinos. Knowledge of this resentment was quite prevalent in Europe, especially in Rome. There was great apprehension for the physical well-being and even the lives of the men. Stories of all kinds concerning their condition circulated in the European press. Soon pressures were brought upon the Administration in Washington to intervene on their behalf.[23] Cardinal Rampolla, the papal Secretary of State, acting through the Apostolic Delegate in Washington, formally requested William R. Day, the American Secretary of State, for this intervention.[24] The American government was willing to comply with the Vatican's request, but rumors and poor communication had made the situation in the Philippines so unclear that the government was not sure what to do. Nevertheless, General Elwell S. Otis, who was commanding the Army in the Philippines, was cabled: "Secretary Vatican advises bishops and priests New Segovia captured by insurgents and brutally treated. If under control, your

[20] "Terms of Capitulation at Manila," *ibid.*, p. 1313.

[21] *Treaty of Peace between U.S. and Spain* (Senate Document), pp. 8–10.

[22] James Cardinal Gibbons, Baltimore, October 24, 1898, to Alger, Gibbons Correspondence, Box 96.

[23] Henry C. Corbin, Washington, August 1, 1898, to Wesley Merritt, in Adjutant General of the Army (ed.), *Correspondence Relating to the War with Spain. April 15, 1898 to July 30, 1902* (Publication of the Department of War), II, 743.

[24] Mariano Rampolla, Rome, September 13, 1898, to Sebastiano Martinelli, *ibid.*, p. 790.

forces protect from inhuman treatment."[25] No instruction accompanied the message for what to do in behalf of the Spaniards if *not* under the General's control.

Meanwhile James Cardinal Gibbons was kept informed of the situation by the missionary vicar apostolic of Hong Kong. As early as August 22 Gibbons had asked the President for help and had been assured of the government's good intentions toward the priests.[26] Continuous requests from Catholic authorities and "distinguished men high in the councils of nations" to protect the Spaniards generated further activity on the part of the American government.[27] Again Otis was cabled instructions: "Considerable anxiety felt about cruel treatment of religious orders by insurgents. You will use your good offices discreetly for their protection."[28] Otis, endeavoring to secure better treatment for the priests, explained to Aguinaldo in a diplomatic note the reasons for the American position. He made no effort to threaten force.[29] Aguinaldo denied imprisoning any nuns, but refused to release any of the priests, including the bishop. The rebel leader, realizing that he could use them to threaten the Vatican, wrote Otis that "when the Filipino priests, unjustly spurned by the Vatican, have obtained the right to appointment to the duties of bishops and parochial priests, then there will be no danger to the public tranquillity in setting at liberty the ecclesiastics."[30] Otis' only reply was that Aguinaldo's position was "untenable."[31]

Otis' position was even more untenable. The uncertainty of the American future in the Islands and the vagueness of his instructions left him little alternative but polite requests. He feared that efforts

[25] Corbin, Washington, September 20, 1898, to Major General Elwell S. Otis, *ibid.*, p. 793.

[26] Luigi Piazzoli, Hong Kong, October 14, 1898, to Gibbons, Gibbons Correspondence, Box 96.

[27] Otis, Manila, November 2, 1898, to Emilio Aguinaldo, *Report of Major General Otis, Commanding the Army of the Philippines* (House Document No. 2, Vol. 5, 56th Cong., 1st Sess.), p. 22.

[28] Corbin, Washington, October 18, 1898, to Otis, in Adjutant General (ed.), *Correspondence Relating to War with Spain* (War Dept. Pub.), II, 804.

[29] Otis, Manila, October 30, 1898, to Alger, *ibid.*, p. 831; Otis, Manila, November 2, 1898, to Aguinaldo, *Report of Major General Otis* (House Document), p. 22.

[30] Aguinaldo, Malolos, November 3, 1898, to Otis, *ibid.*, p. 23.

[31] Otis, Manila, November 10, 1898, to Aguinaldo, *ibid.*, p. 24.

to free the priests would create a charge that he sympathized with the clerical position, a situation in definite contradiction to the concept of religious neutrality of the American government. The issue over the Spanish clergy was a difficult problem and was too critical for Otis to take any action.[32] These religious prisoners remained in Aguinaldo's hands despite all pressures from the United States. Eventually they were released, however, when an American army captured them and a defeated Filipino army sometime after Aguinaldo had risen against United States occupation forces.

The reason for General Otis' untenable position was the uncertainty in Washington. The McKinley Administration wanted the Philippines, but it did not know what to do with them. To find out what to do and thereby resolve the uncertainty, President McKinley appointed a fact-finding commission to go out to the Islands. This commission was to survey conditions there, interview the inhabitants, and then make recommendations and suggestions to the President for a permanent government. The Philippine Commission was headed by Dr. Jacob Gould Schurman, president of Cornell University. He was to be assisted by Charles Denby, former United States minister to China, and Dean C. Worcester, professor of zoology at the University of Michigan. In addition, the Commission included Admiral Dewey and General Otis, both of whom were already in the Islands. The fact that none of these men were Catholics and that they brought no Catholics with them as advisors immediately made the Schurman Philippine Commission suspect in the eyes of the Catholic press. To many Catholics the most unacceptable member was Dean Worcester, who had spent three years in the Philippines on a scientific expedition and on his return had written a comprehensive book about the Islands.[33] Included in his book was a scathing attack against the organization of the Philippine Catholic Church, especially the Spanish friars. This commission, coming as it did so soon after the Peace Commission, which also had no Catholics among its members, was quickly considered anti-Catholic by most Catholic editors.[34]

The work of the Philippine Commission was aggravated by a new uprising of Aguinaldo and his rebel forces. Early in the morning of

[32] Otis, Manila, January 22, 1899, to Corbin, in Adjutant General (ed.), *Correspondence Relating to War with Spain* (War Dept. Pub.), II, 886.

[33] Dean C. Worcester, *The Philippine Islands and Their People, passim.*

[34] San Francisco *Monitor,* November 18, 1899, p. 122.

February 4, 1899, the Filipinos attempted to drive the Americans out of Manila. The delicate situation that General Otis fostered in his negotiations over the imprisoned Spanish priests blew up in his face. The United States was forced into an unfamiliar type of warfare, a bloody, vicious guerilla war that took over three years to consummate. Reasons for the timing of the outbreak are mere conjecture, but it was intended to embarrass the Republican Administration in the United States. The Senate at this particular time was debating acceptance of the Peace Treaty, with its controversial Philippine annexation clauses. Certainly a native rebellion would seriously hinder the work of an investigating committee. Aguinaldo was apparently trying to build up a strong wave of anti-imperialism in the United States to defeat that part of the Treaty which did not provide immediate independence of the Philippine Islands.

Despite Aguinaldo's interference, the Schurman Commission set out to do its work and analyze the problems that would confront a government established in the Philippines. The Commission investigated a wide variety of situations, including such subjects as the capability of the Filipinos for handling self-government, the extent and quality of their educational system, the potential mineral and agricultural wealth of the Islands, and the structure of local and provincial government. The Commission recognized that the religious difficulties of the Islands were serious and had to be resolved before an Americanized government could function adequately. Many of these difficulties were similar to those in the other dependencies: disputed ownership of Church property, a Church-run but publicly supported school system, and Church claims to *censos* on buildings and land. But other problems were unique to the Philippines. One of the most exasperating to American officials was the inability to protect religious property from the vandalism of Filipinos and Americans during the Insurrection. By far the most difficult and most important of the Church-state issues concerned the presence in the Philippines of about one thousand Spanish friars and their ownership of extensive areas of some of the Islands' best agricultural and commercial property. The Filipino insurrectionists had blamed the friars for all the Islands' civil, commercial, and moral ills. Even the liberal Filipinos, who immediately attached themselves to the American occupation government, advocated a quick expulsion of the friars and an arbitrary confiscation of all their holdings. The relationship of the Spanish friars and the American government is so involved and complex that it will be discussed separately in the following chapter. Regardless of the outcries against the friars, after an examination of religious conditions the Schurman Commission reiterated the findings of earlier investigations. It was convinced that "Catholicism is the religion, not only of the majority, but of all the civilized Filipinos."[35] And the Commission warned that it would be a "lamentable measure" to grant "to all religions equal rights to open schools, erect churches, create parishes, have processions and public ceremonies with the Catholic Church."[36]

After the Schurman Commission completed its work and returned to the United States, it submitted its preliminary report to the President on November 2, 1899. On the basis of its recommendation President McKinley appointed the Second Philippine Commission to go to Manila and work with the new military government of General Arthur MacArthur. After reasonable American military control of the Islands was assured, the Commission was to establish a civil government directed by Americans but with as much Filipino participation as possible.[37] Because this Second Commission was charged with the responsibility of finding legal and constitutional solutions to the Islands' many complex problems, President McKinley selected as chairman William Howard Taft, a federal district judge from Ohio. Taft's fellow members were General Luke E. Wright, Dean Worcester, Professor Bernard Moses, of the University of California, and Henry C. Ide, former chief justice of Samoa.

Notwithstanding outcries in the Catholic press of anti-Catholic discrimination in reference to the First Commission, no Catholics were appointed to the Second. Indeed, some Catholics feared that the President deliberately intended to discriminate against them.[38] The reappointment of Dean Worcester seemed to confirm this suspicion. The San Francisco *Monitor* called his continued presence on the Commissions "an insult to American Catholics."[39] The *Monitor* also reported a rumor that Archbishop Ireland was no longer being consulted by the Administration and it warned that dire conse-

[35] "Religion," *First Philippine Commission Report* (Senate Document), p. 109.

[36] *Ibid.*, p. 110.

[37] *Reports of the Taft Philippine Commission* (Senate Document No. 112, 56th Cong., 2nd Sess.), *passim.*

[38] *New York Freeman's Journal,* July 14, 1900, p. 1.

[39] San Francisco *Monitor,* March 10, 1900, p. 465.

quences would result.[40] The Archbishop himself admitted to Monsignor O'Connell that the rumor was correct.[41] The observations of Father Frederick Z. Rooker, whose position as secretary to the Apostolic Delegate kept him in close contact with opinions of the Catholic hierarchy, show how serious the situation had become. He wrote O'Connell as early as April, 1899:

> . . . Everything shows that the success of the war has turned his [McKinley's] head. . . . He seems to have placed his entire confidence in [Secretary of State John] Hay and [Secretary of the Navy John] Long, and these are the only ones who can talk to him with any weight now. I have every reason in the world to believe that they, neither of them, have any use for the Abp. [John Ireland] nor for any other Catholic. They have determined and have made the President determine to go with the settlement of any difficulties which may arise in the new policy of the government absolutely without reference to the existence of Catholic authority. Everything indicates that the Church is to be left out entirely in the final arrangements. Besides this there is a strong opinion among the men at the head of things that the Church has been working its hardest to frustrate the policy of this government.[42]

This apprehension among Catholics became so strong that most Catholic journals violently opposed McKinley's re-election in 1900. The *New York Freeman's Journal* insisted that "McKinley Must Be Beaten."[43]

Religious problems in the new dependencies did seriously embarrass the McKinley Administration. Perhaps the most embarrassing was its inability to put down the Philippine Insurrection, which some Catholic papers claimed was caused by continued anti-Catholic discrimination. Even the *Catholic World* accepted this theory and in-

[40] *Ibid.*, October 7, 1899, p. 1.

[41] Archbishop John Ireland, New York, October 21, 1899, to Denis J. O'Connell, O'Connell Correspondence, Box 14.

[42] Frederick Z. Rooker, Washington, April 21, 1899, to O'Connell, *ibid.* Father Rooker's comments often tended to be exaggerated. His correspondence reveals that he held a low opinion of Archbishop Ireland and most Republicans. As the bishop of Jaro, in the Philippines, from 1903 to 1907, he became a thorn in the side of the Philippine government by committing himself to a defense of the friar cause. Luke E. Wright, then governor of the Philippines, lost respect for him, although he praised the other American bishops in the Islands (Wright, Baguio Benquet, P.I., June 15, 1904, to Taft, Taft Private and Official Correspondence).

[43] *New York Freeman's Journal,* October 12, 1900, p. 2.

sisted that "we always said that it was a mistake to have appointed on the Philippine Commission men who had no Catholic sympathies.[44] However, rumors of looting and desecration of churches in the Philippines quickly crowded reports of the insurrection off the front pages of the Catholic press. At first, these acts of vandalism were minimized; they were considered the normal result associated with the moral wreckage of warfare.[45] But soon, when regiments returning from the Philippines were seen brandishing holy relics as souvenirs, the entire Catholic press denounced McKinley and his policies. "McKinleyism" took on an additional connotation.[46]

Reports of American violation of religious security were first heard in December, 1898. The Boston *Pilot* printed the story of a Captain Lynn, who was sent to investigate supplies at the College of St. Catherine in Manila, but instead broke into the convent and, despite the pleas of the nuns, intruded into the privacy of the cloister itself. The *Pilot* reported that one of the two American Catholic chaplains, Father Francis B. Doherty, protested the incident to General Otis, who relieved Captain Lynn of his duties and sent him back to Washington.[47] In April of 1899 the San Francisco *Monitor* printed an account of a deliberate burning of a Catholic church in Paco *after* the rebels had been driven out of it. The *Monitor* demanded an investigation.[48] Soon, as more frequent news dispatches from the Islands told of acts of desecration and as irate parents received letters from their sons describing some of these acts, Catholics began to demand action from the government.[49] A few Catholic societies, scattered across the country, sent protests to the President,[50] and some sent petitions to Congress. Yet most Catholics remained silent, considering the press dispatches of church looting as merely unconfirmed rumor.

American Catholics overcame their reluctance to protest when they saw the cover picture of the September 9, 1899, issue of *Collier's Weekly* magazine. This photograph, taken by a *Collier's* correspond-

[44] *Catholic World,* LXIX (August, 1899), 714.
[45] San Francisco *Monitor,* May 27, 1899, p. 161.
[46] *Ibid.,* August 5, 1899, p. 365.
[47] Boston *Pilot,* December 10, 1898, p. 3.
[48] San Francisco *Monitor,* April 15, 1899, p. 44.
[49] *Ibid.,* August 5, 1899, p. 361.
[50] *New York Freeman's Journal,* August 26, 1899, p. 1.

ent, showed two American Army officers and an American military telegrapher with a field telegraph set up on the main altar of the Catholic Church in Caloocan. The telegraph wires were strung across the tabernacle itself. One of the officers was smoking a cigarette. Beneath the picture was the simple caption: "Respectfully Referred to the Secretary of War."[51] This photograph touched off a violent reaction against the Administration by the Catholic press and Catholic lay organizations. The *New York Freeman's Journal* demanded that Catholics protest because they were being asked to pay the cost "of a war which has been converted by Protestant bigots into a war against the Catholic Church."[52] The following week the same newspaper wrote: "American Catholics ought not to remain silent whilst their religion is being insulted by informed A.P.A. bigots in the pay of the United States."[53] The San Francisco *Monitor* called the photograph "An Unimpeachable Witness" and noted that ten thousand members of the Holy Name Society in Brooklyn had sent a protest to the Secretary of War.[54]

The incident of the photograph inspired news reporters to seek further visual proof in the United States. *The Institute Journal* of San Francisco, a non-Catholic publication, sent one of its reporters to the Presidio to see if there were any indications of church looting. As San Francisco was the disembarkation point for most of the American troops returning from the Islands, the reporter wrote that he had seen vestments, ciboria, sanctuary lamps, missals, baptismal records, ivory and silver crucifixes, tabernacle veils, and altar cloths brought back by returning soldiers.[55] The Boston *Pilot* quoted another San Francisco reporter, John L. Sullivan, as discovering twenty-six individuals, whom he named, who were in possession of stolen religious goods.[56] The evidence seemed overwhelming, despite assurances by General Otis that Philippine churches were respected.[57] Archbishop Ireland, interviewed in St. Paul on November 1, defended the War Department and its efforts to prevent church looting.

[51] *Collier's Weekly,* XXIII (September 9, 1899), front cover.
[52] *New York Freeman's Journal,* September 9, 1899, p. 4.
[53] *Ibid.,* September 16, 1899, p. 4.
[54] San Francisco *Monitor,* September 23, 1899, p. 514.
[55] Quoted in *ibid.,* October 28, 1899, p. 20.
[56] Boston *Pilot,* November 4, 1899, p. 4.
[57] San Francisco *Monitor,* September 30, 1899, p. 531.

But even he was later forced to admit that he had received a letter from a Philippine veteran offering to sell him part of the loot.[58]

How much of this church desecration could have been prevented by American officers probably will never be known. Officially the government accepted General Otis' curt denial:

> Referring to your cablegram of September 18, sixteen churches, different localities occupied by United States troops; four only partially occupied, and religious services not interfered with; also three convents occupied; these three and ten of sixteen churches formerly occupied by insurgents; church property respected, protected by our troops.[59]

The Schurman Commission in its preliminary reports, dated November 2, 1899, also dismissed the entire issue: "To those who derive satisfaction from seizing on isolated occurrences—regrettable, indeed, but incident to every war—and making them the basis of sweeping accusations, this commission has nothing to say."[60] In addition, two Catholic chaplains, William D. McKinnon and William H. J. Rooney, came to the defense of the American troops. Recently returned from the scene of military operations, both of them emphatically denied seeing or knowing of any deliberate molestation of Catholic churches.[61] Chaplain McKinnon went on to say that if loot was taken from the churches, it was taken by Chinese "who worked usually between the evacuation of a town by the rebels and the entry of American forces. The American soldiers then bought relics as souvenirs from Chinese or from natives."[62]

Although this explanation seemed plausible, the Catholic press still did not accept it. Almost all Catholics felt that it was the duty of the United States to protect the churches, and, if this was impossible, to compel the return of such relics even though they might have been purchased from natives.[63] Long after the official denials

58 Boston *Pilot,* November 11, 1899, p. 5; *New York Freeman's Journal,* November 4, 1899, p. 1.

59 Otis, Manila, September 20, 1899, to Adjutant General, in Adjutant General (ed.), *Correspondence Relating to War with Spain* (War Dept. Pub.), II, 1072.

60 *First Philippine Commission Report* (Senate Document), p. 183.

61 San Francisco *Monitor,* September 23, 1899, p. 520; *New York Herald,* October 19, 1899, p. 5.

62 Boston *Pilot,* October 28, 1899, p. 1.

63 "Open Letter to the President, to the Secretary of War, and to the General Commanding in the Philippines," *Catholic World,* LXX (October, 1899), 141.

very detailed reports of all types of looting activities still circulated in the press. For months reports came from San Francisco describing various religious relics in detail.[64] Eyewitness accounts were also printed, including one by another Catholic chaplain, Joseph M. Gleason of the 30th Regiment. Chaplain Gleason described the looting of a Catholic church at Guadalupe by the Utah Volunteers who stripped the building of everything and even "rifled the graves of the dead priests for possible treasure."[65]

Apparently more church looting was committed than the Administration cared to admit. Governor Taft himself gave ample testimony for drawing such a conclusion. In October, 1901, he wrote Horace Taft, his brother: "The officers take the good houses in the towns and the soldiers live in the church, the 'convento' (which is the priest's house), the school house or the provincial building. . . . The owners are paid an arbitrarily fixed rent and are very fortunate if they get their rent." Almost five hundred of these military posts were scattered throughout the Islands.[66] In February, 1902, before the Senate Committee on the Philippines, Taft repeated this statement that the troops invariably occupied the convents and the churches.[67] Other witnesses before the Committee corroborated Taft's testimony.[68] The question that concerned Catholics, of course, was what happened to the sacred vessels and relics that were in these buildings before they were occupied by American troops. General Otis apparently could not give a satisfactory answer. Archbishop Chapelle, by this time apostolic delegate in Manila, was so disgusted with Otis' evasiveness that he cabled the President: "Urgent the sending of another governor, civil or military, General MacArthur, Smith or Denby. Otis absolutely incapable to defend the credit of your government."[69] McKinley's only reply was "Tell him I'll think about it."[70]

McKinley's hesitation in giving a definite reply to Chapelle's re-

64 San Francisco *Monitor,* November 18, 1899, *et seq.*

65 *New York Freeman's Journal,* May 12, 1900, p. 1.

66 W. H. Taft, Manila, October 21, 1901, to Horace Taft, quoted in Pringle (ed.), *Life and Times of Taft,* I, 213.

67 "Testimony of Governor Taft," *Affairs in the Philippine Islands* (Senate Document), Pt. 1, p. 63.

68 *Ibid.,* pp. 682–683, Pt. 2, p. 1527.

69 Cable: Placide L. Chapelle, Manila, January 19, 1900, to McKinley, McKinley Correspondence, Vol. 44.

70 *Ibid.*

quest is understandable. Information coming from the Philippines concerning the behavior of American troops was so full of charge and countercharge that governmental leaders were as confused as the public. Actually, American occupation forces were being criticized for harassment and torture of Filipino natives as well as the violation of religious buildings. No doubt both situations did occur, but Army officers in the Islands pleaded that such actions were the unfortunate by-products of guerrilla warfare. After lengthy investigations of both issues Congress itself was unable to reach any other conclusion than that offered by the military. Whether or not the acts of violation were necessary and deliberate was beside the point, however, for Catholics in the United States were almost unanimous in demanding protection for Church property by the United States Army.

Still another issue, the same one that had arisen in the other dependencies, heightened the anti-McKinley sentiment among Catholics—the inability of the government to keep Protestant missionaries from swarming over the Islands. Although most Catholic journals recognized that governmental interference in missionary affairs was unconstitutional, this particular question, nonetheless, was raised in quite a few Catholic newspapers. Their editors were disturbed because Protestants in high governmental positions were interfering on behalf of Protestant missionaries. The Protestants themselves added to this illusion by their announcements of new missionary plans for the Philippines, which were constantly publicized by the Protestant press. Henry C. Potter, the Protestant Episcopal bishop of New York, proposed a "Joint Commission on the Increased Responsibilities of the Church" as a cooperative missionary venture of all Protestant churches to make Protestant efforts in the Islands more effective.[71] The Boston *Pilot* reported that the Reverend Charles C. Pierce, Protestant Episcopal chaplain with the Army in Manila, was attempting to raise $100,000 to establish Protestant missions in the city. This action appeared to the *Pilot* as an obvious use of a government position to Protestantize the natives.[72] In May, 1902, Charles H. Brent was appointed Protestant Episcopal bishop of the Philippines and was sent to Manila with $200,000 to build a cathedral and establish missionary branches.[73] Public statements of other prominent

[71] Boston *Pilot,* April 7, 1900, p. 4.
[72] *Ibid.,* April 28, 1900, p. 4.
[73] *Ibid.,* May 31, 1902, p. 4.

Protestants also indicated the strength of this desire to Protestantize the Islands. Speaking before a conference of Methodists in New York, Bishop Earl Cranston, of Portland, Oregon, explained why he deliberately mispronounced the word "Philippines": "We want to remove every vestige of Rome from those islands, and we might as well change the pronounciation of the name."[74] Another Methodist, James M. Thoburn, bishop of India and Malaysia, told the Senate Committee on the Philippines that America's extraordinary success in driving the Spanish from the Philippines was certainly God's will and thus it was God's will that Protestant missionaries be sent there.[75] Congressman William Harris Douglas, of New York, speaking from the floor of the House of Representatives, said, "There is a great field for work among these people by our missionaries and religious bodies generally, if they take up the matter with energy and intelligence there is no question whatever but that most satisfactory results will be accomplished, and especially among the women and children."[76]

A defense of Catholicism in the Islands immediately arose from all sides, even in the Senate chamber. Senator Thomas M. Patterson, a Democrat of Colorado, reminded his listeners:

> . . . it is further shown by indisputable testimony that, commencing with a period shortly after the sinking of the Spanish fleet and continuing for nearly nine months, there was no power in the Philippine Islands except that of the Filipino priests and the officials in command of the insurrection, and that there was peace and quietude and order throughout the island until the Americans commenced the war which has been raging ever since. Mr. President, the people of the Philippine Islands are a Christian people. It may be said that theirs is a primitive Christianity, but they are taught of the Saviour, of his Sufferings, and his Teachings.[77]

The Catholic press energetically denounced Protestant missionary attempts as wasted energy on "rocky ground."[78] The Catholic Truth Society printed and distributed a pamphlet written by a Catholic chaplain in the Philippines, Joseph P. McQuaide, which refuted all of the accusations against the Spanish priests in the Islands.[79] A well-

[74] *Ibid.*, November 24, 1900, p. 4.
[75] *Affairs in the Philippine Islands* (Senate Document), Pt. 3, p. 2677.
[76] *Congressional Record,* 57th Cong., 1st Sess., Vol. XXXV, Pt. 7, p. 7351.
[77] *Ibid.*, Pt. 6, pp. 5968–5969.
[78] Boston *Pilot,* September 16, 1899, p. 4.
[79] San Francisco *Monitor,* July 8, 1899, p. 285.

known Catholic author, Bryan J. Clinch, circulated to the Catholic press an open letter which attacked a speech given before the Academy of Sciences of San Francisco on January 11, 1899. In this speech Professor George Davidson, of the University of California, accused the Catholic priests in the Philippines of charging such high fees that they denied baptisms, marriages, and funerals to the Filipinos. Clinch demanded that Davidson either prove what he said or disclaim it. He called Davidson a liar and then cited the *Estatistica,* the official Philippine directory, as listing 312,000 baptisms, 48,877 marriages, and 164,877 interments during 1896. These figures indicated a fairly close proportion to those in "civilized countries." Clinch thus maintained that since the priests were the only officials responsible for these services, they were certainly ministering to their people and not charging outrageous fees.[80] The *Monitor,* commenting on another of the Protestant speeches, quoted an Episcopal minister who had said, "In Manila the very insurgent soldier bows humbly in adoration before the cross and forms quite as good a Christian as hundreds of thousands of more pretentious and privileged people in this country."[81]

Several Catholic journals proposed that Protestant missionaries in the Philippines might be a danger to the American occupation. These papers feared that the Filipinos would misinterpret Protestant missions as official American policy to convert them forcibly. An editor of the *Catholic World* summed up this concept:

> Were I in authority I would persuade every Protestant minister to stay away from Manila. I would select the most thorough Americans among the Catholic priests of the country and establish an *entente cordiale* between them and the civil authorities. I would appoint as governor-general a broadminded military man—one who understands the inner workings of the Catholic religion. He need not be a Catholic, but he should have no antipathies against the Church, and should strive to gain the sympathetic adherence of the ecclesiastical authorities.[82]

Many Catholics who accepted this idea turned to Theodore Roosevelt to promote it. However his answer was a rebuke of what ap-

[80] *Ibid.,* January 21, 1899, p. 357.

[81] *Ibid.,* September 24, 1898, p. 509.

[82] A. P. Doyle, "Religious Problem of the Philippines," *Catholic World,* LXVIII (October, 1898), 124.

peared to him and the government as a rather preposterous proposal. He explained to Maria Storer the only position open to him:

> I cannot stop, and I cannot urge the stopping of, missionaries going anywhere they chose. I emphatically feel, as I have always told you, that the chance for bettering the Catholic inhabitants of the tropic islands lies by bringing them up to the highest standard of American Catholicism. The worst thing that could happen both for them and for the Catholic Church would be for the Catholic Church to champion the inequities that have undoubtedly been committed, not only by lay, but by clerical, should-be leaders in the Philippines and elsewhere.[83]

But these matters of church desecration and Protestant missionaries were only on the fringes of the difficulties confronting the Church in the Philippines. For Catholics in the United States the heart of the problem was in the official policies of the American government. To them, these policies appeared to weaken seriously the Church and make difficult, if not impossible, the religious work it was already doing. Besides the proposal pushed energetically by most American officials to expel the Spanish friars, Catholics were also concerned with attempts to deny the Church its property and the recommendation to establish a nonsectarian public school system. Any effort to deprive the Church of its income-producing properties and its facilities of education and charity could quickly destroy the Church's position as guardian of its flock. In addition, the plan to create a public school system in which religion would not be taught and in which Catholics would have no voice in managing would make it impossible to maintain the Church as a teacher of the young. In the long run, then, Catholics objected not to Protestants themselves but to what Protestants in control of the Philippine government could do to the Church.[84] After all, six million Catholics lived in the Philippines and most American officials agreed that they were happy and satisfied in the practice of Catholicism.[85] Why then, American Catholics reasoned, should it be necessary to dislocate the Roman Catholic Church on behalf of six million Roman Catholic Filipinos?

[83] Theodore Roosevelt, Albany, May 18, 1900, to Maria Longworth Storer, Elting E. Morison (ed.), *The Letters of Theodore Roosevelt,* II, 1298–1299.

[84] *New York Freeman's Journal,* July 12, 1900, p. 8.

[85] Taft, Manila, June 22, 1900, to Maria Storer, quoted in Pringle (ed.), *Life and Times of Taft,* II, 222.

Governor Taft realized from the beginning of his administration the complexities of property ownership in the Philippines. As in the other Spanish colonies, the close relationship of the Church and the state created a situation unique to American experience. So close had this relationship been that the Church had not thought it necessary to obtain from the Spanish government for the bishop of the diocese a title to the public land on which churches were built. Thus a majority of the churches were built on land that passed to the ownership of the United States by the terms of the Treaty of Paris. This would mean, of course, that the Church could lose most of its houses of worship. Governor Taft, however, took a liberal stand on behalf of the Catholics. Even against protests from the municipal governments, he insisted that through usage equitable title was in the Catholics of each parish and therefore "releases should be made by the Government of the United States to the bishop of the diocese for the benefit of the Catholics of the parish."[86] Taft steadfastly maintained this policy and recommended that such action be confirmed by Congress.[87] By the subsequent Philippine Civil Government Bill of 1902 the problem concerning actual buildings of worship was easily and quickly disposed of.

But ownership of a considerable amount of public-use property was also in dispute. In addition to cemeteries and schoolhouses scattered throughout the Islands, this property included three hospitals, two leper colonies, three almshouses, three orphanages, a charitable pawnbroker, and a savings bank, all of which had been founded with the permission and aid of the royal government and had been placed in the charge of a particular religious order. Many institutions were established by the government itself, while all of them drew part of their support from the insular treasury. Most, however, received the bulk of their income from pious legacies or from rentals of property owned by the religious order.[88] The school buildings in dispute were claimed by municipal or insular authorities as actually belonging to the American government. The religious orders that had been operating them were frequently ejected, and

[86] William Howard Taft, "Civil Government in the Philippines," *Outlook*, LXXI (May 31, 1902), 318.

[87] "Testimony of Governor Taft," *Affairs in the Philippine Islands* (Senate Document), Pt. 1, pp. 186–187.

[88] "Benevolent Institutions," *First Philippine Commission Report* (Senate Document), pp. 41–47.

lay teachers and administrators were put in charge. Included in this group were all of the normal schools, the only secondary school in the Islands, the University of St. Thomas, the College of San Jose, a school of arts and trades, an agricultural college, and a nautical school.[89]

United States military forces often prevented continued use of this property by the religious orders. In some areas Filipino insurrectionists had already driven the friars from their property, and when American troops ousted the rebels they usually refused to restore it to the original occupants. The policy of the military government of General Otis was to turn most of the property over to the administration of local civil authorities without waiting for legislative or judicial action. As soon as Archbishop Chapelle arrived in Manila he immediately protested this arbitrary decision to General Otis. Through the veneer of politeness in their correspondence it is quite apparent that the two men would not compromise on the issue. Archbishop Chapelle especially protested the evictions of the clergy as an abridgment of long-accepted civil rights. His explanation of the Catholic Church's position really became an indictment of Otis' actions as military governor:

> It is an elementary principle that long undisturbed possession carries with it the presumption that the actual holder has valid title. He can not be ousted unless his title is in the first place clearly proven invalid. To decide otherwise would be either confiscation or criminal usurpation, which, I am sure, the Federal judicial authorities will never countenance. I must avow that I am greatly surprised at the opinions given by your legal advisers. Some of them, no doubt, labor under the delusion that the old relation between church and state practically exists yet in these islands, and that an American governor may act in the quality of vice-royal patron of the church as the Spanish captain-generals did. Some other of your advisers seem to me to be animated with a narrow-minded spirit of hostility to the Catholic Church, whilst they should look at the question presented to them from a disinterested and American point of view.[90]

General Otis recognized that he was in a difficult position and refused to reconsider his actions. He would rather defer to "higher authority" whenever it should appear in the Islands.[91]

[89] *Ibid.*, pp. 16–42.

[90] Chapelle, Manila, April 6, 1900, to Otis, *Education in the Philippine Islands* (Senate Document No. 129, 56th Cong., 2nd Sess.), p. 10.

[91] Otis, Manila, April 12, 1900, to Chapelle, *ibid.*, p. 10.

Governor Taft, of course, was that higher authority. His responsibility was to work out a settlement satisfactory to both civil and ecclesiastical administrators. The problem could not be solved by as simple a solution as that of the ownership of buildings used for religious worship. Unfortunately the situation was further complicated by the fact that partial financial support of most of the benevolent and educational institutions came from income derived from the agricultural estates of the Spanish friars. If these priests were expelled from the Islands and their lands confiscated by the insular government their charitable organizations would wither and die. Thus the Catholic Church had a dual stake in the Islands, both aspects of which Taft recognized.[92] Eventual settlement, therefore, was involved in Governor Taft's direct negotiation with the Vatican.[93] It also involved court litigation with Catholic bishops acting as defendants in some cases and as plaintiffs in others. The whole procedure took years, but much of the property was returned to the Church and it received compensation for its lost part-ownership of the rest. In the meantime, Taft endeavored to mitigate some of the Church's difficulties through executive orders which restored to the Church the use of some of the less important properties, especially the cemeteries.[94]

So much confusion resulted in the Philippines from the religious-property question that the Catholic press in the United States made very little issue of it. Most editors tended to fasten their attention on what seemed to be a simpler and yet a far more significant issue, the establishment of a nonsectarian Philippine public school system. As far as Catholics were concerned, this proposal more than any other, with perhaps the exception of the friars' land controversy, endangered the Church's work. As a result, more attacks were directed against it in the Catholic press and more petitions were sent to Congress and the President concerning it than for any other single issue during the colonial era.

From the beginning of the occupation American officials had strongly recommended that a free, secularized public school system

[92] Taft, Manila, August 6, 1900, to Root, Taft Private and Official Correspondence.

[93] See below, Chapter 7.

[94] Gustave L. Solignac, Manila, October 25, 1901, to Chapelle, Chapelle Correspondence, Box 2. Solignac, Chapelle's nephew, was one of the attorneys representing the Church before the Philippine courts.

be established in the Philippines. General Otis, after a preliminary survey of the chaotic conditions existing there, concluded that if the United States was to keep the Islands such schools were necessary and that they should be divorced from religious control.[95] The Schurman Commission's investigation, upholding this recommendation, found that the existing schools were inadequate in both quality and quantity and that the Church's influence made it impossible to train the Filipinos for participation in a democratic government. One of the persons it interviewed, Oscar F. Williams, the former American consul at Manila, summarized this general opinion: "The Filipinos' education has been very narrow, not so limited as some people think in numbers of people who have been somewhat educated, but the education of the individual person has been very narrow—confined largely to church lines—and [lacking in] sufficient liberality and breadth to enable them to appreciate such a form of government as we have."[96] Because of these circumstances the Schurman Commission recommended to President McKinley that "the government established in the islands should promptly provide for . . . the establishment of an adequate system of secularized and free public schools."[97] Accordingly, President McKinley directed that this action be taken.[98]

At first Catholics in the United States had mixed emotions about the proposed Philippine school system. Many of them recognized the difficulties for the Church in the Islands of supporting a parochial system such as that in the United States; so they agreed that public schools would be the best. Others feared that a public school system, unless it were administered by Catholics, would be used to the disadvantage of the Church. They had already become suspicious of similar proposals in the other dependencies. All of them, however, were delighted when they learned that General Otis had appointed a Catholic army chaplain, William D. McKinnon, as superintendent of schools in Manila.[99] This pleasure soon turned to anger, however, when Chaplain McKinnon resigned his position and was replaced by

[95] Report of Major General Otis (House Document), p. 152.

[96] "Hearings before the Schurman Commission," *First Philippine Commission Report* (Senate Document), p. 256.

[97] *Ibid.*, p. 41.

[98] *Message of the President* (House Document No. 1, 56th Cong., 1st Sess.), p. xlix.

[99] San Francisco *Monitor*, October 15, 1898, p. 44.

Lieutenant George P. Anderson, a non-Catholic, whom after a brief investigation of Anderson's activities the San Francisco *Monitor* concluded was a "bigot."[100] His was the first of a long series of appointments to the school system that appeared to many Catholics as a thinly veiled plot to Protestantize the Filipinos through their own schools. The *Monitor* asked "by what right [does] President McKinley of his own volition undertake to regulate the education of a wholly Catholic people?"[101] The *New York Freeman's Journal* insisted that these appointments were part of an "Anti-Catholic Crusade in the Philippines."[102]

Catholic dissatisfaction for the public school system in the Philippines was based on both a fact and an idea. The fact was the recognized Catholicism of the Filipino people, officially acknowledged by the United States government as the religion of all of the civilized natives. The idea concerned the right of the Filipino people to devise their own educational system and not have one forced on them by the Americans. Most American Catholics assumed that the Filipinos were satisfied with the Church-run schools. The confusion over affairs in the Islands and the attempt by General Otis to exercise press censorship only added to this belief.[103] Any reports that the earlier system was inadequate were merely branded as "falsehoods" and were considered indicative of "shameful discrimination against Catholics."[104]

With this attitude prevalent in the Catholic press, Governor Taft, nevertheless, went ahead with his plans to establish a complete secularized public school system throughout the Islands. Commissioner Bernard Moses, as secretary of public instruction, was given the direct responsibility for education. To assist him Fred W. Atkinson was appointed superintendent of schools for the entire archipelago. It became increasingly apparent to Catholic laymen and clergy in both the United States and the Philippines that opposition

[100] *Ibid.*, August 19, 1899, p. 710. There was apparently some truth in the *Monitor's* accusation, for Taft later acknowledged that Anderson's policies were creating dissatisfaction among Filipino Catholics (Taft, Manila, July 26, 1900, to Root, Taft Private and Official Correspondence, Letterpress Books, Box 1).

[101] San Francisco *Monitor*, June 2, 1900, p. 185.

[102] *New York Freeman's Journal*, July 14, 1900, p. 1.

[103] *New York Herald*, October 1, 1899, p. 9.

[104] *New York Freeman's Journal*, July 14, 1900, p. 1.

to the secularized public schools would be fruitless. So they concentrated their efforts on defending what they thought were their rights in matters of curricula, administration, and faculty. One of the first of these problems to come to their attention was the issue of religious instruction as part of the school program. This question arose when some Filipino Catholic laymen requested that religious instruction be offered to their children.[105] Commissioner Moses at first refused to consider the proposition, but Governor Taft worked out a compromise. Qualified priests or ministers could offer religious instruction in the schools after hours three days a week, but any such instructor who created disloyalty to the system or disorder was to be denied the privilege of teaching. In addition, the compromise also provided for the dismissal of any public school teacher who attempted to influence the religion of his pupils. Taft also agreed to recognize twelve religious feast days as school holidays.[106] The Catholic press grudgingly accepted the compromise, although many editors found it a sinister foreboding of the future. The *New York Freeman's Journal* still claimed that the Administration was "Depriving the Filipinos of their Religion."[107] And the Boston *Pilot*, vilifying Moses for his attitude, asserted that "President McKinley evidently knew what he wanted when he excluded Catholics from the [Taft] Commission."[108]

Catholics also became increasingly concerned over the personnel of the Philippine school system. Already dissatisfied with Moses and Atkinson for their stand on the teaching of religion in the schools, the Catholic press began to assail the Administration because of the teachers it sent to the Islands. The *Catholic World* reprinted some hearsay evidence that Catholic teachers were having difficulty getting positions in the Philippine schools, but that "a recommendation from a Y.M.C.A. secretary, a minister, or a Protestant college is an open sesame to good positions. Inducements are held out to native teachers to apostatize from their church. . . . The school teachers act

[105] *Reports of the Taft Philippine Commission* (Senate Document), p. 33.

[106] "Public Laws Passed by the Philippine Commission," *Second Report of the Philippine Commission, 1901* (House Document No. 2, Vol. 9, 57th Cong., 1st Sess.), p. 126.

[107] *New York Freeman's Journal*, February 2, 1901, p. 1; Boston *Pilot*, January 26, 1901, p. 4.

[108] *Ibid.*

in many instances as the agents of missionary societies in the distribution of Bibles and tracts."[109]

Such sentiments caused anxiety to Theodore Roosevelt, who had succeeded to the Presidency in September, 1901. Roosevelt was more sensitive to this type of press criticism than his predecessor. Concerned that the impact of these accusations might impair his leadership of the Republican Party, especially during a congressional election year, he wrote Secretary of War Root: "Don't you think that some report about this ought to be gotten up? I would like to be able to answer such attacks."[110] On orders from Root, the acting governor of the Philippines, Luke E. Wright, investigated the charges and sent a cablegram, which was published in the *Catholic World*. It was a complete defense of the Administration's hiring policy: "About 2700 native teachers employed in the islands, all of whom are Catholics, . . . 2 American Catholic teachers in the normal school, 5 in the Manila schools, and 140 native Catholic teachers in Manila, alone. Exceptional that any graduate is other than Catholic."[111]

The refutation of charges of anti-Catholic discrimination in the hiring of teachers minimized to some extent the pressure on Roosevelt, but did not stop it. When he succeeded to the Presidency his well-known friendship toward Catholics momentarily eased off the agitation for changes in colonial policies. Yet, as Vice-President, he had committed himself to a wholesale support of McKinley's colonial program. During the winter of 1901–1902 he apparently decided against any major modification. Then Catholic dissatisfaction broke out anew, reaching a peak in the late spring of 1902. Roosevelt was confused by what he considered misunderstanding and unnecessary misapprehension of his policies among Catholics.[112] However, he realized how complex the issues were and that there were no simple answers. But he also recognized that perhaps the key to the solution

[109] "The School Question in the Philippines," *Catholic World*, LXXV (July, 1902), 431.

[110] Roosevelt, Washington, June 28, 1902, to Root, Taft Semi-Official Correspondence, Philippine Commission Papers, R. G. 1534–20.

[111] Cable: General Luke E. Wright, Manila, July 9, 1902, to Root, *ibid.*, R. G. 1534–22; *Catholic World*, LXXV (August, 1902), 703–704.

[112] Roosevelt, Oyster Bay, July 12, 1902, to Eugene A. Philbin, Morison (ed.), *Letters of Roosevelt*, III, 292.

would lie in a just and fair settlement of the friars' land question. Before he could evolve a colonial policy of his own President Roosevelt first had to examine the issues surrounding these Spanish friars and then decide what to do about their extensive holdings in the Philippines.

CHAPTER FIVE

THE SPANISH FRIARS AND THE LAND CONTROVERSY

FANTASTIC STORIES concerning the activities of the Spanish friars in the Philippines circulated in the press of the United States. From the beginning of the Insurrection of 1896 to the Taft Mission of 1902, Americans read about the moral laxness and the cruel exactions of these priests. Every visitor to Manila had some comment to make on the power exerted by these men over Spanish officials as well as over the Filipino natives. In a diary entry of November 20, 1897, a French visitor to the Islands wrote:

> . . . the fact is indisputable that women and priests between them rule Manila. One feels from the first moment that *she* is powerful here, and *he* omnipotent. He has flung aside, as a quite unnecessary constraint, the traditional discretion of manners and humility of bearing. The world and the souls that dwell therein belong to him, and he shunts about his domain. . . . We meet him everywhere, lolling back in his barouche, with a cigar between his teeth, and bestowing all and sundry the self-satisfied gaze of a *parvenu* millionaire.[1]

[1] André Bellessort, "A Week in the Philippines," *The Living Age*, CCXXI (May 20, 1899), 472.

Professor Dean C. Worcester, whose years in the Islands earned him a reputation as an authority on Philippine affairs, published his book *The Philippine Islands and Their People* in 1898. The book gave his impressions of society and politics in the Islands and at the time of its publication was considered the most authoritative work on the Philippines written by an American. His opinions had considerable influence on the general public and he was often asked to write articles for contemporary journals. Worcester wrote of the friars:

> While it is by no means true that all of these friars are incompetent or depraved, it is nevertheless a fact that many of them are ignorant beyond belief; are given over to open and brutish licentiousness; practice inhuman extortion, especially in connection with the solemnizing of marriage and the burial of the dead; interfere with the execution of the laws, and themselves openly violate them when it serves their ends to do so. The inevitable result is the utter demoralization of the communities which they control.[2]

The worst aspect of this demoralization was described by a former Philippine revolutionary, Antonio Regidor:

> One result of the domination of the Friars has been to populate the country with half castes. They must be given negative credit for this, for the half castes are very intelligent and a welcome addition to the population. Taking into consideration the abuses of the Friars, however, it might have been better had they faithfully kept their vows of celibacy. Homes destroyed were too common to excite any notice, the scandals occasionally came to light too serious to be passed over in silence. The most notorious was that of Father Maranow, a Franciscan friar, who it was absolutely proven had 160 wives, and was the father of more than 500 children. This caused such an outcry that the head of the order was compelled to move him from his parochial charge, and he was transferred to the *presidency of the Convent of St. Clara, in Manila.*[3]

With this type of information in the American press American opinion understandably was prejudiced against the friars before the United States entered the Philippines. Most of the articles supported the view that because the friars were such despicable characters the Filipinos were justified in demanding their expulsion from the

[2] Dean C. Worcester, "Knotty Problems of the Philippines," *The Century Magazine,* LVI (October, 1898), 879.

[3] Antonio Regidor, "The Filipino Case Against the Friars," *The Independent,* LII (February 7, 1901), 319–320.

Islands. Perhaps all of this information was true, but other writers questioned the legality of any such act under the American Constitution. The United States could not remove the Church establishment simply because it had superseded the Spanish civil government.[4] Still others felt that all of the available information was too one-sided, and that before any American policy could be determined a fair appraisal of the friars had to be presented to the American public. Such an appraisal was difficult to make because of the heated religious opinions already generated among Americans. Neither the Protestant nor the Catholic press was rational on the subject, and the secular press exploited every drop of bitterness toward the friars in order to raise circulation figures.

Who were these friars who caused such a controversy in the American press? They were Spanish members of four old and venerable religious orders of the Roman Catholic Church: Augustinians, Dominicans, Franciscans, and Recollects. Each order was presided over by a provincial general who resided in Spain, and therefore, each of them had very little Filipino leadership or influence in the direction of its policies. The Spanish leadership, however, was the least detrimental factor concerning the orders. The most serious criticism voiced by the Filipinos was the friars' ownership of huge agricultural estates and a number of valuable commercial buildings. The friars ran these estates as medieval manors and exacted rents from their tenants which they used to finance their religious charitable and educational activities. The Filipino people strenuously objected to paying these agricultural rents. Popular leaders of the Insurrection of 1896, who demanded confiscation of the estates by the Philippine government, reasoned that the land really belonged to the tenants and not to the friars. The estates in question totaled some 403,000 acres of farm land scattered throughout the main islands. Of these, 250,000 acres were considered the best agricultural land in the most populous provinces.[5]

The confusion over the validity of Filipino claims to the friars' land and the disparaging comments on the friars' contribution to Philippine society prompted one American newspaperman to go to

[4] Colonel W. Winthrop, "The Problem of the Philippines," *Outlook,* LIX (June 11, 1898), 382.

[5] "Testimony of Governor Taft," *Affairs in the Philippine Islands. Hearings Before the Senate Committee on the Philippines* (Senate Document No. 331, 57th Cong., 1st Sess.), Pt. 1, p. 100.

the Islands in search of a rational answer. Stephen Bonsal, who had a wide readership in the United States as a result of his shrewd, objective observation of the Cuban insurrection, went to the Philippines and there, after several weeks of investigation, wrote a series of articles which were published in the *North American Review*. According to Bonsal, the friars established themselves in the Philippines as missionaries long before there was a civil authority on the Islands. From the very beginning they exercised great leadership among the natives and over the officials sent out from Spain. The civil and military officers came to serve a tour of duty, but the friars came to spend their lives. Their organizations and personal labors developed a permanency about them that administrations of frequent governors-general never attained. The friars organized the defense against the British in 1762 and built the watchtowers and fortifications to protect the natives from the marauding pirates of Jolo and Borneo. The friars, not the civil officials, organized the building of roads, bridges, and irrigation works. The genesis of the monastic estates was the experimental and model farms established to teach the natives improved agricultural methods and to introduce new or better crops to eliminate recurring famines throughout the Islands. The monastic orders carried on this work with little help from local or royal authorities, and none whatever from Spain.[6]

In regard to education, Bonsal found that the Spanish friars' service to the Philippines was far greater than that of other European colonial powers to "other branches of the Malay family under other circumstances and in another environment."[7] From the founding of Manila until 1863 the only schools in the Islands were those presided over by the friars. The College of St. Thomas was founded in Manila in 1620. Its graduates were accepted everywhere in the Islands and became leaders in their communities. Similar educational institutions, including the Islands' only secondary school and several women's colleges were founded by the friars or their related orders of nuns. Each friar parish priest was recognized as inspector of all schools within his parish until 1893, when the entire responsibility was taken from his hands and vested in those of municipal authorities. Bonsal evaluated this change: "Men as hostile to Spanish dominion as Aguinaldo were installed as teachers, and the schools

[6] Stephen Bonsal, "The Work of the Friars," *North American Review*, CLXXV (October, 1902), 451–453.

[7] *Ibid.*, p. 460.

became the hotbeds of the Separatist movement. There is much evidence to show that from this time the attendance at the schools diminished, and the character of the education received by the children deteriorated."[8]

Bonsal's report on the friars praised their endeavors and pointed out that several recent governors-general in their final reports stated that effective governing of the Islands would have been impossible without the friars. But even more important was Bonsal's denial of some common misconceptions about the friars held by most Americans. For one thing, he claimed, they were not really wealthy, but had to be self-supporting: "Their tithes seem to have been paid largely in chickens and eggs."[9] Their lands were not extensive; on the contrary "the monastic estates amount to less than one-hundredth part of the land under cultivation, and less than one five-thousandth part of the land that might be cultivated."[10] The accusations that the friars led dissolute lives he attributed to the existence of Eurasian children in every community: "This phenomenon was often ascribed to the presence of the friars, but it is difficult to say with what justice. It is certain, however, that though for more than four years the friars have been withdrawn, these miserable Eurasian children continue to come into the world in ever increasing numbers."[11]

If what Bonsal wrote about the friars was true, why then did such a strong antifriar feeling exist among the Filipino people themselves? This could be explained in a variety of reasons. Often the friar was the only Spaniard in a locality; and usually against his will, he was ordered by the provincial civil authority to represent the Spanish government. In this capacity he was chairman of the board of education, tax assessor, recruiting officer for the militia, village registrar and clerk, and, if he had any time left, he was also the local schoolteacher.[12] In most of these communities the friar was forced to be the agent for all of the oppression of the Spanish government. Many of the friars' detractors claimed that they modified laws coming from Spain to benefit themselves, but as often they also

[8] *Ibid.*, p. 456.
[9] *Ibid.*, p. 460.
[10] *Ibid.*, p. 453.
[11] *Ibid.*, p. 459.
[12] *Lands Held for Ecclesiastical or Religious Uses in the Philippines* (Senate Document No. 190, 56th Cong., 2nd Sess.), *passim*.

modified laws bearing down on the native population. If Spain's rule was despotic, the friars were caught up in the web of the despotism and blamed for originating it. Furthermore the friars were avowed Spaniards and they could not recognize the value of any insurgence of Filipino nationalism. It was apparently quite true, according to Bonsal, that they detected and reported several planned revolutions in the latter part of the century.[13] Local nationalism was certainly not unique to Spanish colonialism at the time. The French were having difficulties in Cochin-China, and the British in Egypt and South Africa. Thus, if the friars were really hated, they were hated because they were Spanish and not because they were ecclesiastics. The idea that the friars were universally hated in the Philippines was never fully proved. Regardless of its merits, however, the point was accepted by the American government and became one of the fundamental principles involved in the policies of the Administration in relation to religious affairs in the Islands.[14]

All the American officials in the Philippines testified to this conflict between the friars and the Filipino natives. General Otis stated that the trouble arose between the Spanish friars and the native clergy because the Filipino priests were not allowed to perform certain sacraments. But the friars were allowed to perform them; "whereas in no country of Europe can they perform those sacraments except by special permission."[15] General Otis did not say to which sacraments he was referring. Any ordained Catholic priest can administer five of the seven sacraments; the remaining two, Holy Orders and Confirmation, are administered only by a bishop. When it investigated the problem the Schurman Commission attempted to go a bit deeper by trying to separate the animosity toward the friars from an attack on the Catholic religion itself. The Commission questioned several prominent Filipinos to determine how the natives felt toward the friars independently of their feeling for the Church. Manuel Xerez, a Manila-born physician, stated that the mass of the people were in favor of expelling the friars, but they were deeply devoted to the Catholic Church through their own na-

[13] Bonsal, "Work of the Friars" *(No. Am. Rev.)*, p. 457.

[14] *Fifth Annual Report of the Philippine Commission, 1904* (House Document No. 232, 58th Cong., 3rd Sess.), *passim.*

[15] "Testimony of General E. S. Otis," *Affairs in the Philippine Islands* (Senate Document), Pt. 1, p. 833.

tive priests.[16] Jose Luis de Luzuriaga, of Negros, answered that they attacked only the friars, and did not profess to attack religion.[17] Felipe Calderon, a lawyer and an owner of a large plantation, endeavored to sum up the accepted view of the Filipinos of his class: "The friars is the principal question here, and I say to you, Mr. Schurman, that I am a Catholic and have defended the Catholic faith in the congress at Malolos [the Philippine Constitutional Congress held in the summer of 1898], and I am certain that the friars must be expelled if we are to have peace in the country."[18] Further testimony by a Señor Rosario seemed to clinch the argument:

> If the property is returned to the friars an agrarian war will result; that is, such a war as we have now, a war of the agricultural classes against the property owners. If their property is taken away from them and they still remain here they will cause another war, for they have the protection of Rome. When I speak of Rome I refer to the Vatican, to the Papal power.[19]

Señor Rosario was not asked what he meant by papal power or what protection Rome could give the friars.

Certain members of the religious orders themselves were asked to give testimony on the issue. These men represented the four orders —Augustinians, Dominicans, Franciscans, and Recollects—which were under attack, and also the Jesuits, who had been in the Islands only a few years and had created no ill will among the Filipino people. Representatives of all five denied most of the allegations and stressed the vast extent of good works accomplished by the orders.[20] Yet this positive evidence did not seem to outweigh the negative, especially when the Commission was confronted by reports of the wholesale murder of Spanish priests in outlying districts that resulted from the native hatred. The Commission made no effort to go beyond Manila to see the friars and their works face to face, nor did it attempt any genuine canvas of Filipino opinion. Instead it weighed the evidence given in Manila and drew the following conclusion:

[16] *First Philippine Commission (Schurman) Report* (Senate Document No. 138, 56th Cong., 1st Sess.), p. 404.
[17] *Ibid.*, p. 420.
[18] *Ibid.*, p. 146.
[19] *Ibid.*, p. 100.
[20] *Ibid.*, pp. 246, 278–284.

It is a matter of history that great antagonism has existed in the islands against the class of people called by the Filipinos "friars." This hostility was beyond doubt one of the causes of the rebellion of 1896. Then for the first time in the history of the islands several priests in different parts of Luzon were murdered by the populace; many of them were arrested and held as prisoners by the Filipinos.[21]

The fact that the friars were held prisoners by the Filipinos was confirmed by General Otis when an American army defeated some Filipino insurgents in Lepanto Province and caused the release of 150 Spanish priests.[22] The Schurman Commission's suspicions of native opinion were thus substantiated and its recommendation that confiscation of the property of the religious orders "would have good results" was accepted by the American government in Washington.[23]

When the Taft Commission succeeded General Otis and the Schurman Commission in authority and responsibility in June, 1900, all this information on the friar question was turned over to Taft and his colleagues. Because of the serious consequences of the issue Governor Taft attempted to assimilate the previous testimony and start a fresh investigation of his own. He felt that settlement of this matter was the most delicate of all the problems facing the Commission, so he kept the full responsibility of it for himself.[24] Besides instigating a new series of interrogations, Taft also used the reports of the provincial governors. Before the end of 1901 peace had been restored to large sections of the Philippines, and American authorities felt that they could ascertain local public sentiment about the friars. Almost universally the provincial military governors reported a firm desire of the local inhabitants to prevent the return of the friars to their parishes or estates.[25] In addition to a new mass of testimony

[21] "The Secular Clergy and Religious Order," *ibid.*, p. 130.

[22] Major General Elwell S. Otis, Manila, December 13, 1899, to Adjutant General, in Adjutant General of the Army (ed.), *Correspondence Relating to the War with Spain. April 15, 1898 to July 30, 1902* (Publication of the Department of War), II, 1121.

[23] "The Secular Clergy and Religious Orders" *First Philippine Commission Report* (Senate Document), p. 131.

[24] William Howard Taft, Manila, September 8, 1900, to Horace Taft, quoted in Henry Fawles Pringle (ed.), *The Life and Times of William Howard Taft,* I, 221.

[25] "Exhibits Presented to the Senate Committee on the Philippines," *Affairs in the Philippine Islands* (Senate Document), Pt. 1, p. 494, Pt. 2, p. 1924, Pt. 3, pp. 2191, 2410.

collected from Filipinos, Americans, foreign entrepreneurs, and members of the hierarchy in the Philippines, Taft consulted two American Catholic chaplains, William D. McKinnon and Edward H. Fitzgerald. Taft reported that both of these men agreed without qualification that the friars were exceedingly unpopular with the masses of the people and that it would be a mistake to send them back to their parishes.[26]

Results of all this testimony were quite conclusive to the Taft Commission. Despite the difficulties inherent in their solution, the Commission seconded the Schurman Commission's findings and made its recommendations to the President that the Philippine government should purchase at a fair price the income-producing properties of the friars; in return for the purchase, the friars should be withdrawn from the Philippines by Catholic authorities. The land would then be sold to the present tenants in easy payments. To implement this procedure the Commission also suggested that it be empowered to issue interest-bearing bonds in the name of the insular government so that funds would be available for the purchase.[27] Taft tried to make it plain that the friars issue was not a religious question. In his first report (1900) he wrote, "The Philippine people love the Catholic Church. . . . The feeling against the friars is solely political. The people would gladly receive as ministers of the Roman Catholic religion any but those who are to them the embodiment of all in the Spanish rule that was hateful."[28] Taft underscored this point of view by declaring to Congress, "I think the truth is that they have the best titles in the islands."[29] He hastened to assure the leaders of Catholic opinion in the United States that his proposals meant no arbitrary confiscation of the monastic holdings but rather a "fair and just business-like purchase" of the property.[30]

As a whole, Protestant opinion supported the Taft Commission's position as the only reasonable solution to a most difficult problem. *The Independent* pointed to the performance of the governments

[26] *Lands Held for Ecclesiastical Uses in Philippines* (Senate Document), p. 281.

[27] *Second Report of the Philippine Commission, 1901* (House Document No. 2, Vol. 9, 57th Cong., 1st Sess.), p. 149.

[28] *Reports of the Taft Philippine Commission* (Senate Document No. 112, 56th Cong., 2nd Sess.), p. 30.

[29] *Ibid.*, p. 233.

[30] Taft, Manila, June 21, 1900, to Maria Longworth Storer, Gibbons Correspondence, Box 98.

in South America, France, and Italy, where Church property had been arbitrarily confiscated without compensation. Its editor wrote, ". . . it is a very different way of settling the difficulty from what the Filipinos would employ if left to themselves."[31] Other Protestant journals agreed that the only way to peace in the Philippines was the complete removal of every Spanish priest. To illustrate this point *The Christian Advocate* printed a report of the murder of twenty American soldiers by a "Padre Domasco" who had invited them to a feast and then poisoned their food.[32] Most Protestant comments, however, were typical of the view expressed by *The Churchman* which commended the Report of the Taft Commission for its candor and courage. *The Churchman* also agreed that the friars were the great obstacle to peace, but that "they have a right to their property by every title known to civilized man."[33]

Catholics, on the other hand, disagreed. In answer to some of the earlier information the *Catholic World* warned that official American interference with the friars would be disturbing to the religious peace of the natives and would create a native revolt.[34] A Catholic chaplain, Joseph McQuaide, wrote from Manila that he was unable to find any proof of the charges against the friars. His answer to the charges of immorality among the friars was that "the morality of the Filipinos stands out as a glorious thing in the Orient, and testifies amply indeed for the padre."[35] The San Francisco *Monitor* admitted the probability that some of the friars might be unworthy but pointed out that the allegation of venality and corruption for the entire priesthood of the Islands had not been substantiated.[36] However, if the accusations were true, the same newspaper asked, how could the friars exert over the natives the influence that had been imputed to them by their detractors?[37] The *New York Freeman's Journal* believed that the whole story of Filipino hatred actually had been manufactured by the anti-Catholic societies in Manila. It took the extreme position, not usually expressed in the Catholic papers, that the election of William Jennings Bryan in November, 1900,

31 *The Independent*, LIII (December 12, 1901), 2976.
32 *The Christian Advocate*, LXXVII (April 17, 1902), 605.
33 *The Churchman*, LXXXIII (February 2, 1901), 127.
34 *Catholic World*, LXVIII (February, 1899), 711.
35 San Francisco *Monitor*, July 15, 1899, p. 305.
36 *Ibid.*, May 19, 1900, p. 124.
37 *Ibid.*, June 30, 1900, p. 245.

would assure the protection of Catholic interests in the Islands and the assumption of all the guarantees of the Treaty of Paris.[38]

After Bryan's defeat in November and the publication of the Taft Commission's Report in January the Catholic press attacked Taft's proposals. The *Monitor* claimed that the Report was "Proving Too Much" and was merely indicating that certain native and American elements had promoted the idea of the Filipino hatred of the friars "to profit by the destruction of the Catholic Church in our new possessions."[39] When and where, asked the *New York Freeman's Journal*, had the Filipino people demanded the expulsion of the friars: "Was it at a national convention? If so, when and where was this convention held?"[40] Both the *Catholic World* and the Boston *Pilot* claimed that the accusations against the friars were still vague, regardless of the testimony in the Taft Report. They asserted, "It is absolutely true that 90 per cent of the people in the Philippine Islands do want the friars to remain among them."[41] Obviously Catholic press opinion was as heated and its facts were as highly inaccurate as those circulating in Protestant journals. However, the *American Catholic Quarterly Review*, while not necessarily accepting the findings of the Taft Report, brought up the very important question that much of the press on all sides had missed. If Taft's recommendations concerning the natives were put into effect, what would be the consequences to the native religion? The *Review* answered this question:

> The expulsion of the Spanish friars means that five millions of Filipino Catholics must be left without priests, sacraments or religious instruction for at least a generation. There are less than seven hundred native priests for seven millions of Catholic population and there are no priests, either American or European, familiar with the Filipino language or customs except these friars.[42]

Archbishop Chapelle assumed this defense when he arrived in Manila. He was responsible to the Vatican for the Church's welfare

[38] *New York Freeman's Journal*, October 6, 1900, p. 4.

[39] San Francisco *Monitor*, February 2, 1901, p. 365.

[40] *New York Freeman's Journal*, April 19, 1902, p. 4.

[41] *Catholic World*, LXXII (March, 1901), 832; Boston *Pilot*, June 15, 1901, p. 7.

[42] Bryan J. Clinch, "The Work of the Philippine Commission," *American Catholic Quarterly Review*, XXVI (October, 1901), 639.

in the Philippines. If he condoned the government's expulsion of the friars he would be assisting in the removal of almost two thirds of the active clergy in the Islands. His own position on the question was delicate, for the government really left him no middle ground for compromise. If he cooperated he would seriously weaken the Philippine Church. As a result, he took the opposite view and was already prejudiced in favor of the friars before he left the United States. In a letter to President McKinley in September, 1899, he indicated his opinion: "The winning over of the clergy will, I have no doubt, be more efficacious for the pacification of the archipelago than a very large army. It would therefore be a shortsighted policy to antagonize them."[43] The Archbishop did not change his mind after he personally reviewed conditions in the Philippines. Instead, he took an inflexible stand in favor of the friars and became, to a degree, *persona non grata* to Otis, MacArthur, and Taft.[44] Almost immediately he tried to have the military forcibly reinstate the friars in their own parishes. But General Otis refused to permit this, fearing that eventually most of them would be killed.[45]

Archbishop Chapelle found that Governor Taft was as adamant on the issue as General Otis had been. He and Taft saw entirely different aspects of the situation and could never find an area for agreement. Taft reported to Secretary Root that the Spanish Dominican Archbishop Nazaleda, of Manila, had expressed the desire to return to Spain. Taft wrote, "I am told on every side that if Nazaleda could be induced to leave and an American Archbishop appointed to replace him, that half the religious battle here would be won."[46] But Archbishop Chapelle refused to concede the point; he had definitely taken a profriar stand. The Spanish consul at Manila informed Taft that a good many of the friars felt that their usefulness had ended and wanted to return to Spain but Chapelle had prevented their voluntary withdrawal. The consul recommended that his government use influence at Rome to overcome Chapelle's

[43] Placide L. Chapelle, New Orleans, September 20, 1899, to William McKinley, McKinley Correspondence, Vol. 38.

[44] W. H. Taft, Manila, June 10, 1900, to Mrs. W. H. Taft, quoted in Pringle (ed.), *Life and Times of Taft*, I, 117.

[45] Otis, Manila, February 19, 1900, to Adjutant General, in Adjutant General (ed.), *Correspondence Relating to War with Spain* (War Dept. Pub.), II, 1145.

[46] Taft, Manila, August 11, 1900, to Elihu Root, Taft Private and Official Correspondence, Letterpress Books, Box 1.

authority and have the friars withdrawn.[47] Taft openly admitted his resultant dislike of Chapelle.[48] Although he tried to be fair to the Archbishop, Governor Taft had come to the conclusion that Chapelle could no longer accomplish anything in the Philippines. He wrote Maria Storer:

Archbishop Chapelle has become absolutely identified with the Friars. Nobody here regards him as anything but a Friar. Every Filipino is down on him whether he be an insurgent or an Americanista. I do not think it was necessary for him to get into this position, but that is where he is, and while, of course, his sacerdotal office compels respect, politically he has no force whatever.[49]

Archbishop Chapelle's unwillingness to see the American side of the friar controversy became well-known in the United States. Governor Taft's frequent reports to Elihu Root made action by the government necessary. Archbishop John Ireland was called to Washington for a discussion with Root over Philippine conditions. Ireland was to write Cardinal Rampalla, papal Secretary of State, explaining fully the intentions of the American government in reference to religious and educational matters.[50] To be sure that his report to Rampalla was not misunderstood, Ireland also wrote to his friend, Monsignor O'Connell: "Our government is resolved to be more than fair in its treatment of Catholic matters. But neither McKinley nor Root likes Chapelle."[51] Apparently the Vatican understood the message. Ireland wrote Cardinal Gibbons, "From the general tone of Cardinal Rampalla's letters, I can see that Abp. Chapelle does not count for

47 Taft, Manila, October 31, 1900, to Root, *ibid.*

48 *Ibid.*

49 Taft, Manila, December 4, 1900, to Maria Storer, Gibbons Correspondence, Box 98. Taft's frequent letters to Maria Storer indicate an effort on his part to encourage her to use unofficial pressure on the Church. Both he and Roosevelt wrote her regularly, and often would say, "When you see the Pope . . ." or "Tell the Cardinal . . ." Thus this correspondence is very important in indicating what Taft was trying to accomplish in reference to the Catholic Church, because he knew that its contents indirectly would be made known to high Catholic authority.

50 Archbishop John Ireland, New York, May 2, 1901, to Maria Storer, Maria Longworth Storer (ed.), *In Memoriam Bellamy Storer*, p. 55.

51 Ireland, New York, June 7, 1901, to Denis J. O'Connell, O'Connell Correspondence, Box 16.

much."[52] Chapelle was called to Rome to make his report in the summer of 1901. Obviously the Vatican considered his mission a failure, for he was sent back to New Orleans, and Archbishop Donatus Sbaretti was appointed to replace him as apostolic delegate in Manila.[53] His removal from Manila was the first of a series of actions deliberately taken by the Vatican to accommodate the desires of the government in Washington.

In the United States, Catholic public opinion was finally making itself heard. The Catholic press caused some concern in Washington, but individual Catholics and Catholic groups did more than their newspapers could. All during the earlier controversies in Cuba and Puerto Rico most Catholics were silent and refused to bring pressure against the government. But the Philippine crisis was sufficient impetus for the organization of a nationwide body of Catholic laymen to attempt direct Catholic political action. The growth and development of Catholic public opinion on imperialism and colonialism as an organized force became quite apparent in late 1901 and early 1902. Congress and the President began to receive petitions protesting American policies in the Islands.[54] This Catholic opinion emerged not so much to formulate American colonial policies but to prevent any further drift of these policies into what Catholics felt had been deliberate anti-Catholic tendencies. Even though the Administration had made great efforts to indicate that the friar question was one of Philippine politics and not religion, Catholic fears were hard to overcome. To quiet these fears President Roosevelt invited Archbishop Patrick J. Ryan, of Philadelphia, to call on him at Oyster Bay. After the conference with the President, Archbishop Ryan was convinced of the wisdom of the official policies and issued a statement to the press supporting the government.[55]

The recommendations of the Roosevelt Administration on Philippine policy, made to Congress during a congressional election year, quickly became a campaign issue. With no change whatever, the President accepted the Taft Commission's Report on religious conditions in the Philippines and received Administration backing in

[52] Ireland, St. Paul, August 25, 1901, to James Cardinal Gibbons, Gibbons Correspondence, Box 98.

[53] Sbaretti did not go to Manila (see Chapter 6).

[54] *Congressional Record,* 57th Cong., 1st Sess., Vol. XXXV, Pt. 6, pp. 5717, 5785.

[55] Boston *Pilot,* August 9, 1902, p. 4.

Congress, led by Senator Henry Cabot Lodge and Congressman Henry A. Cooper, to present Taft's solutions as part of the overall Philippine Government Bill. This Bill was to authorize the establishment of a permanent civil government until such time as the United States felt the Filipinos were capable of sustaining self-government. The entire debate in both houses of Congress fell upon party lines rather than on any sort of religious basis—Republicans supporting the bill, Democrats opposing. There were, however, a few notable exceptions. A Republican, Senator George F. Hoar, of Massachusetts, was the most outspoken critic, in either party, of the whole concept of imperialism. He and several of his Republican colleagues defied party discipline to air what they thought were evils inherent in this new system of American expansion. But these Republican die-hards were counterbalanced by a group of Southern Democrats who looked upon the religious aspects of the Bill as further vindication of the Protestant Reformation.[56]

Most Democrats deliberately played up the alleged anti-Catholic aspects of the Bill to curry favor from Catholic members of the electorate in the coming election. Senator Thomas M. Patterson, of Colorado, was quoted in the Boston *Pilot* as saying to the Senate that "if 6,000,000 of Christians in the Philippines were Protestant Christians, the cruelties practiced on them by the American authorities would have to stop, as no Member of Congress would be able to withstand the wrath of the Methodists, Baptists, and Presbyterians of this country."[57] Senator George Wellington, of Maryland, told the Senate, "I can see no greater harm in a religious body holding a great body of land than in another corporation doing the same thing."[58] Congressman Henry D. Green, of Pennsylvania, said:

> . . . the history of the country will disclose that the Roman Catholic religious orders have largely contributed to the conversion of these native people to Christianity and at the same time contributed to their education and enlightenment. And it is not all fair to say that all the troubles and suffering and discontent are traceable to them as a source. This is not true. On the contrary, their influence has, in the main, been beneficial.[59]

Republican congressmen attempted to stave off the effects of the Democratic debate. The burden of this defense fell on Representa-

[56] *Congressional Record,* 57th Cong., 1st Sess., Vol. XXXV, Pt. 6, p. 6087.
[57] Boston *Pilot,* March 1, 1902, p. 4.
[58] *Congressional Record,* 57th Cong., 1st Sess., Vol. XXXV, Pt. 6, p. 5731.
[59] *Ibid.,* Pt. 8, Appendix, p. 320.

tive Henry A. Cooper, of Racine, Wisconsin. Congressman Cooper was chairman of the House Insular Affairs Committee. He was responsible on the floor of the House for the Administration's Bill and therefore had to answer all the criticisms of it thrown out by the Democrats. In his remarks Mr. Cooper carefully tried to prove the need of the requirements in the Bill affecting the friars without offending Catholic voters. In reference to the provision to buy up the friars' land he tried to show that the action did not reflect upon the Church itself:

> . . . if five physicians or 50 physicians break the law or violate the ethics of their calling, we do not therefore denounce the whole medical profession. If five priests or ministers or 50 priests or ministers disregard the tenets of their faith and the laws of their country, we do not therefore denounce the church itself, nor heap maledictions upon the whole system of Christianity.[60]

Another Republican member of the Insular Affairs Committee, Edward L. Hamilton, of Michigan, followed this same reasoning: "Discussion of the friars in the Philippine Islands does not in any way involve reflection upon the church. It is not to be inferred that the church has connived at or in any way upheld the abuses in the Philippine Islands. There is no reason to suppose that it would not have controlled the friars long ago if it could have done so."[61] To indicate how fair the government was trying to be, Representative James B. Perkins, of Rochester, New York, said, ". . . certainly we all desire that if the lands of the friars in the Philippines, or if any other land in the Philippines or out of the Philippines, is to be taken by eminent domain, fair compensation shall be given therefor."[62]

Even though Republican congressmen attempted to minimize these controversial provisions in the Philippine Government Bill and to show how just the proposals really were, Catholics across the nation began to protest. Most of the protest was in the Catholic press. On this particular bill, however, more Catholic opinion was voiced to the Congress than ever before. During the debate Catholic lay organizations presented eleven petitions to members of both houses against "alleged disregard of the Catholic faith and institutions of

[60] *Ibid.*, p. 467.
[61] *Ibid.*, Pt. 7, p. 7103.
[62] *Ibid.*, Pt. 8, p. 7434.

the people" in the Philippines.[63] These petitions were the result of local efforts made to organize a more effective expression of Catholic opinion. Eight of them were sent from Pennsylvania, two from Port Huron, Michigan, and one from Cleveland.[64] But nothing was heard from Boston, New York, or Chicago, where Catholic strength could easily make itself felt. Also, no formal expression came to Congress from the members of the hierarchy; if expression was made privately neither the debate nor the voting indicates it. The vote in the House on the Philippine Government Bill was 140 yeas, 97 nays, and 114 not voting, a clear division on party lines.[65] The Senate had already accepted the Bill, 48 to 30 with 10 not voting; again a vote on party lines.[66]

All along, President Theodore Roosevelt continued to feel that the Reports of both Philippine Commissions were fair to the Catholic Church in the Philippines. Because of this belief he worked toward the ultimate completion of Taft's recommendations through congressional action. A year earlier, in June of 1901, he had already expressed this outlook to Bellamy Storer in Madrid: ". . . I agree with you that the excessive possessions of some of the religious orders will have to be in one shape or another made useable by the Filipino people themselves, and I feel to the last point the need of Americanizing the Filipino priesthood."[67] Answering the agitation in the Catholic press against his policies, the President in July, 1902, wrote Eugene Philbin:

> As regards the friars, I am pained and concerned to find that a large number of Catholics seem to feel that the movement to get rid of the friars is in some way a movement against the Catholic Church by the government at Washington. . . . If only these Spanish friars could be taken away, then their places can be at once taken by friars of other nationalities or by other orders, of priests to whom the people will listen; and there is nothing which I should regard as more fortunate for the Philippines than to see the Catholics . . . get a set of priests who would handle them as our American priests do, and who would get the same control in moral and

[63] *Ibid.*, Pt. 7, p. 7277.

[64] *Ibid.*, Pt. 6, pp. 5717, 5785, 6306, Pt. 7, pp. 7277, 7354, Pt. 8, pp. 7489, 7548, 7730.

[65] *Ibid.*, Pt. 8, p. 7487.

[66] *Ibid.*, Pt. 6, p. 6231.

[67] Roosevelt, Oyster Bay, June 22, 1901, to Bellamy Storer, Roosevelt Correspondence, Letterbook 29 D.

religious matters over their congregations. It would mean a great stride toward the complete settlement of all the difficulties in the islands.[68]

Because he was so convinced of the righteousness of this position, Roosevelt anticipated the strength of his following in Congress. After recommending all Taft's suggestions to the Congress and relying on the strong Republican majorities in each house, he decided to proceed and negotiate with the friar orders in the Philippines for their lands. Unfortunately the Taft government in Manila had come to an impasse with Archbishop Chapelle and could not reach an agreement. It had to wait to see what changes in papal attitude would be manifested through the new apostolic delegate. In the meantime various suggestions were made to Roosevelt, and he finally decided upon a rather startling, but logical solution to the entire friar question: go to Rome and settle directly with the Vatican. This unheard-of break with American tradition might cause trouble with the Protestants, but the Administration considered it the best thing to do. In his usual brusque manner, the President did not wait for consent from Congress but instead dispatched Governor Taft to Rome in June, 1902, before the Philippine Government Bill was passed.

The friar question had perplexed the American government for over four years. For the Administration it stood as the principal stumbling block to a peaceful assimilation of the Philippines. With the removal of the friars and the purchase of their lands other lesser problems might then be settled through negotiation or by firmer administration of government policies. The planned settlement of the friar question seemed to be the beginning of the end of American colonial problems. If the Taft Mission was successful and an arrangement made with the Vatican, certainly substantial strides would be made toward meeting the Filipinos' desires and bringing them closer to an acceptance of American sovereignty.

[68] Roosevelt, Oyster Bay, July 16, 1902, to Eugene A. Philbin, Elting E. Morison (ed.), *The Letters of Theodore Roosevelt,* III, 295.

CHAPTER SIX

THEODORE ROOSEVELT AND THE CRYSTALLIZATION OF CATHOLIC OPINION

CATHOLIC OPINION was slow gathering momentum in the three years immediately following the war with Spain. Although Catholics in general were dissatisfied with the colonial policies of the McKinley Administration, there seemed to be no one major issue about which their dissatisfaction could focus. Nor did they have any particular leader or organization capable of bringing them to a unified action protesting the causes of their dissatisfaction. They indicated individual acts of alleged anti-Catholicism and the protests were either satisfied or ignored, but the Administration made no specific change in its attitude toward Catholic interest. For a time, most Catholics felt either that they were powerless to bring about change so protests were futile or that they could rely on the ultimate good intentions of the Administrations and therefore protests were unnecessary. Regardless of the reason, for the first three years of the colonial period Catholic objections were few, scattered, and directed, for the most part, only at specific issues.

This situation was soon to change, however. Three simultaneous events drew Catholic opinion into focus and brought about a change in the official attitude toward the Church in the overseas dependencies. The first, and perhaps the most important, was the succession of Theodore Roosevelt to the Presidency. The second was the formation of the Federation of American Catholic Societies. And the third was the debate in Congress over the Philippine Government Bill. This final item provided the much-needed forum for official discussion of U.S. policy in the Philippines. The Bill as proposed to Congress was the embodiment of all of the Administration's policies affecting the Philippines and as such was both a summary of America's brief experiences as a colonial power and a projection of future attitudes and policies. In proposing this particular piece of legislation the Roosevelt Administration gave Catholic opinion the opportunity to concentrate its attention. And concurrently, during the winter of 1901–1902, Catholics gained some vocal leadership and something else they had never had before—the ear of a sympathetic President.

President William McKinley had not been deliberately unsympathetic to Catholics; yet his policies reflected an indifference to Catholic opinion. He accepted the generally held Republican view that most Catholics voted Democratic. As a result he did little to woo Catholics into his party, although he openly repudiated the A.P.A. just before his nomination in 1896. He did have a few Catholic friends, most notably Archbishop Ireland and Bellamy Storer.[1] And he endeavored to have at least one Catholic as a member of his Cabinet. But after Justice Edward White declined the appointment to the Peace Commission the President made no serious effort to put Catholics in any of the sensitive areas of his colonial administration. The personnel of both Philippine Commissions is indicative.

Catholics saw more in this indifference than McKinley apparently intended. Most of the Catholic press was suspicious of the President during his entire administration. The San Francisco *Monitor*, for example, distrusted his attitude toward Catholics when it reported that he had listened without protest to a Thanksgiving Day sermon in which the preacher claimed the great dangers to the country were "rum, socialism, and Jesuitism."[2] Subsequent actions during his ad-

[1] For the best discussion of McKinley's relationships to Catholics see Margaret Leech, *In the Days of McKinley*.

[2] San Francisco *Monitor*, December 4, 1897, p. 1.

ministration did little to allay their fears. The net result was that most Catholics considered McKinley uninterested and unsympathetic, if not deliberately hostile.

But when Theodore Roosevelt became President, Catholics quickly expected a perceptible, if gradual, change in the Administration's attitude toward their interests. They knew from previous interventions on their behalf that Roosevelt would be a President whom they could trust and respect. As early as 1895 the Boston *Pilot*, normally an outspoken pro-Democratic newspaper, wrote of him: "If the party which Theodore Roosevelt honors with his support were one-tenth as honorable and honest as he is, it would be the only party in America."[3] Again, in 1897 on the occasion of his appointment as Assistant Secretary of the Navy, the *Pilot* praised him: "By this action the Government gains a valuable official and New York loses the best Police Commissioner it has ever known."[4] When the Republicans nominated him for the governorship of New York the San Francisco Monitor gave him its support:

> Colonel Roosevelt is another "man of destiny." He will likely be the next Governor of New York, and then his way is straight for the Presidency. He certainly deserves well of the nation. As Police Commissioner of New York he made an enviable record. The bigots tried to use him, but he quickly told them that a man's religion was a matter that he was entirely indifferent to. A Catholic was as good as any other man so long as he did his duty, and no one who failed in his duty could remain on the force. As a soldier Roosevelt was superb. . . . In peace and war Colonel Roosevelt has shown his great personal worth. He is a man and a ruler of men.[5]

After he became President the Boston *Pilot* urged Roosevelt to break away from McKinley's policies and create his own: "The *Pilot* has perfect faith in Theodore Roosevelt, either as a private citizen, or President of the Republic when he is following the impulses of his own brave and generous heart, for it believes him to be a high-minded, sincere, honest American gentleman."[6]

Roosevelt had earned this respect from the Catholic press. Disciplined by the complexities of New York politics, he learned early in

[3] Boston *Pilot,* September 21, 1895, p. 4.
[4] *Ibid.*, April 17, 1897, p. 4.
[5] San Francisco *Monitor,* October 8, 1898, p. 24.
[6] Boston *Pilot,* May 3, 1902, p. 4.

his political career the value of understanding and aiding the state's many ethnic and religious minorities. As a member of the Legislature in his twenties, as police commissioner in his thirties, and as governor at forty, Roosevelt had experiences with these groups that had been meaningful, and, for the most part, successful. He deliberately cultivated the friendship of the Catholics in New York City by seeking the advice of prominent Catholics, such as attorney Eugene A. Philbin, building contractor J. D. Crimmins, and the Reverend A. P. Doyle, editor of the *Catholic World*.[7] It was not these personal friendships alone that appealed to Catholics but also his attitude toward them. He publicly claimed to have no religious prejudices, and at every opportunity he spoke against bigots and bigoted groups.[8] In answer to a request to support a local A.P.A. branch he wrote: "When I find that a secret association, or whatever may be its principles, does, as a matter of fact, discriminate against certain Americans, no matter whether good or bad, because of their creed, why I cannot approve of any such organization."[9] His political appointments indicated the same attitude.[10] He once wrote Frank C. Travers, another Catholic friend, "When I came to be Governor I wanted to make the highminded Catholic gentleman feel that socially and politically I was incapable of drawing any line between him and his highminded Protestant fellow citizen."[11]

Throughout his entire political career Theodore Roosevelt carried on a lengthy correspondence with a large number of Catholic Americans. These included such political leaders as William Byrne, of Wilmington, Eugene Philbin, of New York, Richard C. Kerens, of St. Louis, John McDonough, of Albany, and Bellamy Storer, of Cincinnati. This correspondence reveals how susceptible Roosevelt was to suggestions from Catholics. On many controversial religious issues he consulted most, if not all, of these correspondents before he made a decision. This manifestation of friendliness indicated to

[7] Theodore Roosevelt, Oyster Bay, June 29, 1900, to Frank C. Travers, Elting E. Morison (ed.), *The Letters of Theodore Roosevelt*, II, 1346.

[8] Roosevelt, Washington, October 15, 1894, to Bishop J. J. Keane, *ibid.*, I, 404.

[9] Roosevelt, Oyster Bay, November 9, 1898, to Andrew Powell, *ibid.*, II, 887.

[10] Roosevelt, Albany, April 30, 1900, to Maria Longworth Storer, *ibid.*, p. 1272.

[11] Roosevelt, Oyster Bay, July 7, 1900, to Travers, *ibid.*, p. 1348.

Catholics how open-minded Roosevelt's policies were going to be. He was popular among Catholics. He knew it and he intended to encourage this popularity.

At the same time that this new personality entered the White House, Catholics were groping their way into the organization of the American Federation of Catholic Societies. A large segment of the Catholic population of the United States had become identified with the anti-imperialist movement. Many of them saw much more antagonism in imperialism than did the rest of their fellow Americans. The early experiences of the government in establishing the separation of church and state in Cuba and Puerto Rico indicated to them that colonialism was not going to be easy on their Church. Some of the basic religious questions had been disposed of too quickly in Cuba and Puerto Rico, often before Catholics knew what was happening. But they recognized that the future of the Philippines was still a question open to debate. It was on this topic, therefore, that Catholics, as well as other anti-imperialists, concentrated their attention. The stakes were high for the Catholic Church in this faraway archipelago; so the religious issues inherent in the American occupation became a primary interest. As these issues developed, Catholic opinion began to take on a new outlook toward colonial affairs. This change coalesced gradually during the first three years of American colonialism until it culminated in an organized effort toward unity of Catholic political activity. All Americans based their opinions of overseas expansion on the same sources of information—books and the press—and the reactions of Catholics and Protestants were at first similar. Catholics had supported the war with Spain, and much of the Catholic press was enthusiastic over the idea of acquiring coaling stations and naval bases on the American defense periphery.[12] This seemed merely prudent military necessity. But many Americans of all denominations regarded permanent occupation of thousands of square miles of overseas territory as "contrary to the traditions and principles of the United States."[13] Referring to the native populations in these islands, the Boston *Pilot* lectured those who would misconstrue the purposes of the war with Spain:

[12] *Catholic World,* LXVII (June, 1898), 246.
[13] *New York Freeman's Journal,* May 14, 1898, p. 4.

We have an excellent chance for proving our own fitness for self-government by not denying the same right to the people of Cuba, the Philippines, and any other piece of territory that may fall temporarily into our power. Imperialism has no place in a republic of honest men who believe in the Golden Rule and not in the rule of gold.[14]

While championing the cause of the tradition of American free institutions, most of the Catholic press attacked imperialism as endangering the basic concepts of the Republic. The San Francisco *Monitor* warned of a black and dreadful future if the policy was accepted.[15] The *New York Freeman's Journal* printed its "Note of Warning . . . A crisis faces us in which every man who is loyal to the Republic is imperatively called upon to fight imperialism with every means at his command."[16] Asking questions deliberately embarrassing to the Administration, the Boston *Pilot* wondered: "What do 7,000,000 emancipated American Negroes think of the Imperialistic-policy which proposes enslaving ten or fifteen millions of other colored people in the Philippines?"[17] The *Catholic Quarterly Review* also echoed the anti-imperialist point of view:

The possible gain to be looked for, then, in a policy of foreign conquest is simply the creation of more large fortunes among American citizens, and this coupled with an enlarged foreign trade. The latter is at best doubtful; the former is distinctly undesirable . . . a colonial empire would greatly increase the burdens of the citizens at home. . . . Increased taxation at home, increased competition in the labor market, and opportunities for accumulating a certain amount of large fortunes for individuals are the material results to be looked for from a policy of foreign empire by the American people.[18]

How well Catholic distaste for imperialism was separated from Catholic fear of Protestant evangelization in the new dependencies is difficult to ascertain. Catholic concern over Protestant influences in the insular governments and over Protestant missionary activity has already been noted. It can be accepted that the Catholic press

[14] Boston *Pilot,* July 30, 1898, p. 4.

[15] San Francisco *Monitor,* November 5, 1898, p. 105.

[16] *New York Freeman's Journal,* December 10, 1898, p. 4.

[17] Boston *Pilot,* November 12, 1898, p. 4.

[18] Bryan J. Clinch, "Imperialism as a Policy for America," *American Catholic Quarterly Review,* XXIV (January, 1899), 158.

on the whole felt strongly against the concept of imperialism per se as an act of injustice and a crime against the American conscience.[19] Yet at the same time it reminded Catholic readers that many non-Catholics had considered the War "a Protestant Crusade."[20] Thus after the Filipinos started their attempt to drive out the Americans, Catholic papers took up their cause as they had done for the Cubans three years earlier. The San Francisco *Monitor* suggested: "Wouldn't it be just as well, to let up for a while on allusions to Spanish despotism? The 'patriots' from whom our yellow journals originally borrowed the phrase think back regretfully to the happy days before this 'despotism' was ended through the energetic efforts of their 'humane saviors'."[21] The *Monitor* declared that this new despotism had been caused by itinerant preachers and anti-Catholic lecturers who followed the American flag and started religious troubles wherever they went.[22] The Boston *Pilot,* in an article entitled "Let Us Prey," reported that forty ministers of the Evangelical League had asked other ministers in the United States to unite to save the Philippines for Christ.[23] The Catholic press soon equated imperialism with anti-Catholicism. "Behind this attempt to enlist the Protestant sects on the side of a policy which is fraught with the gravest dangers to our institutions," wrote the *Freeman's Journal,* "one can see the old anti-Catholic prejudices, blinding men's judgment and making them an easy prey to imperialism or any other promises to gratify their hatred of the Catholic Church."[24]

Two years later the San Francisco *Monitor* was still claiming that American imperialism meant organized anti-Catholicism in the island dependencies. This newspaper said that it had knowledge of "the circulation of petitions by 'missionaries' asking for the transfer of Catholic Church property to be used for Protestant services. . . . the evangelizers evidently have in mind a little church property confiscation on their own hook."[25] The *Monitor* was referring to a request by some Methodist converts in Manila for the use of a Catholic chapel which they said had been abandoned by the Spanish

[19] San Francisco *Monitor,* February 18, 1899, p. 421.
[20] *New York Freeman's Journal,* July 23, 1898, p. 1.
[21] San Francisco *Monitor,* July 1, 1899, p. 264.
[22] *Ibid.,* January 7, 1899, p. 301.
[23] Boston *Pilot,* February 11, 1899, p. 4.
[24] *New York Freeman's Journal,* February 18, 1899, p. 4.
[25] San Francisco *Monitor,* February 9, 1901, p. 384.

friars.[26] The *New York Freeman's Journal*, too, continued to equate imperialism and Protestantism. Under the heading "Proselytizing and Imperialism" it attacked the ban on religious instruction in the public schools of Cuba, Puerto Rico, and the Philippines as indicative of the anti-Catholicism inherent in American imperialism. It drew this conclusion: "From this time forth, wherever imperialism casts its black shadow there will be a systematized and energetic anti-Catholic campaign, backed by limitless financial resources."[27]

Although these representative examples indicate the general tenor of the American Catholic press, they do not indicate a similar sentiment among the Catholic clergy. As usual, the press did more to stir up Catholic opinion toward a program of action than did the clergy. On the whole, the clergy remained silent on these issues, considered by some editors to be critical to the welfare of the Church. A few clerics defended the Administration's policies and openly expected the good will and justice of McKinley, Roosevelt, Taft, and Root. Only on rare occasions were members of the hierarchy heard publicly criticizing the Administration. Clerical leadership was still badly shaken and divided in its reaction to the Americanism controversy, and personal animosities resulting from this controversy carried over well into the twentieth century and made unity of action among the hierarchy almost impossible to attain. The correspondence of these men indicated either indifference or indecision.

Indifference and indecision also appear in the minutes of the annual meetings of the American archbishops. The fourteen archbishops, representing the full authority of the Catholic Church in the United States, met at Catholic University usually in October or November of each year. Their purpose was to discuss pertinent situations that had arisen or might arise affecting the general interests of the Church. If the minutes of their annual meetings can be accepted as complete and accurate, they should reveal the major concerns of the American hierarchy. The minutes for the years from 1898 to 1904 show only one official discussion of colonial issues.[28] This was Archbishop Sbaretti's request for assistance in solving the

[26] Homer C. Stuntz, "Catholic Church Titles in the Philippines," *The Independent,* LIII (October 17, 1901), 2469–2470.

[27] *New York Freeman's Journal,* March 22, 1902, p. 4.

[28] Minutes of the Annual Meeting of the Most Reverend Archbishops at Catholic University, 1898, 1899, 1900, 1901, 1902, 1903, 1904, Gibbons Correspondence, Boxes 96–102.

Church-property question in Cuba. Such silence can lead to but one conclusion concerning the dependencies: officially the Catholic Church in the United States apparently preferred to watch and wait rather than to antagonize the United States government.

Although the assembled archbishops took no official action on colonial affairs, individual members of the hierarchy were not bound to remain aloof from the issues. As might be expected Archbishop John Ireland, of St. Paul, unequivocally supported the policies of the Administrations of both McKinley and Roosevelt. He deliberately endeavored to create greater harmony and understanding between the Papacy and the United States government. The day after Dewey's victory at Manila, the Archbishop explained his sentiments to his friend Denis O'Connell in Rome: "The result of this war will be to strengthen and enlarge our navy and reach out for new territory. If the Pope in the future is to have any worldwide prestige, he must deal as never before with America. Tell all this in Rome."[29] He repeated this suggestion in a subsequent letter to O'Connell: "if there is wisdom in the Vatican, it will at once seek influence with English speaking countries, especially America. Unless this is to come at once—humanly speaking, the Church is doomed."[30] Ireland was convinced that Spain's rule in the islands "was an open system of peculation" and any defense of Spain in the Catholic press was unjustified.[31]

Shortly after the signing of the armistice Archbishop Ireland called upon President McKinley. After this conference he expressed to reporters his complete confidence in American protection of the Church.[32] He continued during every crisis in the islands to defend the Administration's actions. Referring to the desecration of Philippine churches he once told reporters, "I am satisfied that the War Department, since the matter was brought to its attention, has issued orders which will prevent further looting, and also that the desecration was not allowed with the knowledge of the War Department or the Army officials at Manila."[33] According to his biogra-

[29] Archbishop John Ireland, St. Paul, May 2, 1898, to Denis J. O'Connell, O'Connell Correspondence, Box 13.

[30] Ireland, St. Paul, May 11, 1898, to O'Connell, *ibid.*

[31] Ireland, St. Paul, May 28, 1898, to Archbishop J. J. Keane, and Ireland, St. Paul, June 18, 1898, to O'Connell, *ibid.*

[32] San Francisco *Monitor,* August 27, 1898, p. 427.

[33] *New York Freeman's Journal,* November 4, 1899, p. 1.

pher, Ireland evidently felt that cooperation with the government would accomplish far more than an attitude of criticism and hostility.[34] Because he continued this support of the United States' policies, he apparently weakened his own position in the hierarchy. Yet his encouraging remarks to the Vatican prompted greater cooperation with American authorities, even though other American prelates did not always agree with him.[35] His pro-American stand on the friars question naturally cost him the friendship of the friar orders at the Vatican. He himself claimed that the Friar Cardinals in Rome really blamed him for the American proposal to expel the friars.[36]

Taking an opposite view of the friars was Archbishop Placide L. Chapelle, the only prominent cleric who had official contact with the United States government. As apostolic delegate to Cuba and Puerto Rico he had been instrumental in bringing about successful settlements of most of the Church-state conflicts in those islands. Later, as apostolic delegate to the Philippines, he generally tried to cooperate with the government, although he strongly opposed the specific policy concerning the Spanish friars. He too endeavored through press interviews to minimize Catholic opposition to the Administration. After a conference with President McKinley just before he sailed for Manila the Archbishop told waiting reporters that he was well satisfied with the President's attitude toward the Church's position in the Islands.[37] Again, a year later, after another conference with the President in October, 1899, he warned reporters that he was still satisfied and had not come to protest the recent wave of church desecrations:

I see that it is said that the object of my visit to the White House on Saturday was to protest against the looting and desecrating of the churches in the Philippines. This was not the case. As to the looting and desecrating of these churches I am informed by a person whose word I cannot doubt, that this looting was not done by our American soldiers, but by the insurgents and the Chinese.[38]

[34] James H. Moynihan, *The Life of Archbishop Ireland,* p. 189.

[35] Frederick Z. Rooker, Washington, October 22, 1900, to O'Connell, O'Connell Correspondence, Box 15.

[36] Ireland, St. Paul, November 13, 1900, to Maria Storer, Maria Longworth Storer (ed.), *In Memoriam Bellamy Storer,* p. 86.

[37] San Francisco *Monitor,* December 9, 1898, p. 192.

[38] *Ibid.,* October 28, 1899, p. 72.

He continued to be satisfied with American policies until the friar question eventually caused him to change his mind. Even then, most of his protests were made in private.

Perhaps James Cardinal Gibbons, of Baltimore, could have been a more important factor in Catholic influence than he actually was. But apparently he chose not to interfere. He too felt that cooperation and friendliness toward the Administration would accomplish more than unbridled criticism of government policies. He expressed his concern over the effect of such criticism in a letter to Denis O'Connell: "I regard the attacks of Protestantism as mild compared with the unprincipled course of these so-called Catholics. Our mission is surely a hard one here. While trying to exhibit the church in all her beauty, we are assailed by those who would exhibit her in an odious light."[39] Gibbons never had a close relationship with McKinley, but nevertheless his offers of cooperation were accepted and he occasionally called upon the President to discuss matters with him.

As might be expected, Cardinal Gibbons exercised a somewhat greater influence after Theodore Roosevelt entered the White House. Only a few weeks after his succession Roosevelt wrote asking him to recommend a "good Catholic priest" to fill a vacancy as Army chaplain.[40] Gibbons' opinion was soon well respected by the President. John J. McCook, a lawyer and former chairman of the Army and Navy Christian Commission of the Y.M.C.A., wrote the Cardinal about Roosevelt's deep concern for the Philippine situation.:

> I told him that you, and you only were in a position to open the way to an early and complete adjustment of the matter, the importance of which could not, in my opinion, be overestimated. The President then said that he would invite you to come over and take luncheon with him at an early day, in the hope of putting the matter in train, so that it could be brought to a definite and satisfactory conclusion as soon as possible.[41]

[39] James Cardinal Gibbons, Baltimore, June 16, 1898, to O'Connell, O'Connell Correspondence, Box 13.

[40] Roosevelt, Washington, October 5, 1901, to Gibbons, Roosevelt Correspondence, Letterbooks, Box 142.

[41] John J. McCook, New York, December 10, 1901, to Gibbons, Gibbons Correspondence, Box 99.

These luncheon dates became a habit between the two men and a spirit of friendliness developed between them.[42] Thus Gibbons, more as a neighbor than as a bishop, was often consulted by the President for his opinion. Roosevelt's confidence in him was strong and therefore the Cardinal's ideas were influential. But on the other hand, the Gibbons-Roosevelt correspondence shows that in almost every case it was the President and not the Cardinal who initiated each discussion of a particular issue. As primate of the Catholic Church in the United States, Cardinal Gibbons could very well have tried to exert a tremendous influence over Roosevelt and the government. It is quite obvious, however, that he never used such pressure outwardly, but his opinions did carry the dual weight of his wisdom and his position.

Even though Archbishops Gibbons, Chapelle, and Ireland attempted to lead Catholic opinion to accept the basic justice behind the government's colonial policies, some members of the hierarchy could not agree with them. Chief among the dissenters was James A. McFaul, bishop of Trenton, New Jersey. Writing for the *North American Review* on the role of Catholics as American citizens, Bishop McFaul made observations and asked questions deliberately designed to arouse Catholic opinion. In defense of Spain he wrote: "Spain has many a crime to answer for; but she has allowed the Church to sit down like a mother, amid the children of the forest and the plain, to save the native races, and teach them the doctrines of Christianity and the arts of civilization."[43] As he continued, he attacked the Administration:

Why were not several Catholic members appointed to our new possession? . . . Instead of approaching, in the spirit of a broad and enlightened statesmanship, the problems presented, the prejudices against our government sown by the Spaniards were allowed to be increased by the conduct of our soldiers, and the desecration of the churches wherein the solemn rites so dear to a Catholic people had been daily performed. . . .

[42] Roosevelt, Washington, March 14, 1903, to Gibbons, Roosevelt Correspondence, Letterbooks, Box 145. For an indication of this friendship see John Joseph Gallagher (ed.), "The Theodore Roosevelt Letters to Cardinal Gibbons" (*Catholic Historical Review*, XLIV [January, 1959], 440–456).

[43] James A. McFaul, "Catholics and American Citizenship," *North American Review*, CLXXI (September, 1900), 326.

Our position is simply this. We are American citizens, entitled to certain rights, and these we must possess.[44]

With these sentiments Bishop McFaul did not stand alone. Other bishops had already voiced a strong warning against imperialism. Thomas J. Conaty, rector of Catholic University and later bishop of Los Angeles, stated his concern for America's future even while peace negotiations were being carried on in Paris. Speaking at a school dedication in Brooklyn in November, 1898, the Bishop said, "We have no mission to settle the political differences of the world except by advice and example—never as conquerors."[45] Bishop John Lancaster Spalding, of Peoria, addressed a meeting of Catholics in Chicago on May 1, 1899. He too warned of this dangerous step the United States was taking:

It is not yet too late to turn from the way which leads through war and conquest and imperialism. . . . And now the American soldier, who should never shoulder a gun except in a righteous cause, is sent 10,000 miles across the ocean to shoot men whose real crime is that they wish to be free—wish to govern themselves. To say that they are unfit for freedom is to put forth the plea of the tyrant in all ages and everywhere.[46]

Another Illinois bishop, James Ryan, of Alton, issued a statement to the Catholic press which expressed similar views. The item, entitled "The Republic is in Danger," called for a withdrawal of United States forces in the Philippines and an abandonment of the policy of imperialism.[47]

One of the most extreme criticism of the Republican Administration's policies came from Bishop Bernard J. McQuaid, of Rochester, New York. In an interview with a reporter from the *New York Herald* just before the presidential election of 1900, the Bishop made some rather startling comments. He told the reporter,

According to my views we are drifting into the ways of European nations, with standing armies, and eventual entanglements, with all European complications. . . . I have never felt entirely satisfied that there was any substantial justification for the war with Spain, and I believe any addition to our territory at any great distance from our shores will be very detrimental to the interests of the country. I pray that that party will

[44] *Ibid.*, p. 330.
[45] *New York Freeman's Journal,* November 26, 1898, p. 1.
[46] *Ibid.*, May 6, 1899, p. 5.
[47] *Ibid.*, January 20, 1900, p. 1.

succeed which will best bring us back to our former state of affairs. This country will be amply engaged if it attends strictly to its own interests.[48]

These remarks by the bishops were the kind of encouragement sought by the Catholic press. Having already flayed the Administration for alleged anti-Catholic tendencies in its colonial appointments and the content of its policies, the Catholic newspapers encouraged the idea that Catholics ought to protest to the government and should insist upon their rights as American citizens. The San Francisco *Monitor,* long a critic of the Administration, called the arbitrary actions of the Taft Commission a "Perversion of an American Principle," and insisted that "In the meanwhile, it comes quite within the province of Catholic American citizens to respectfully protest, through the hierarchy, or by some other medium, against the perversion of the accepted American principle of majority rule, as applied to our colonies."[49] Thus the accumulation of acts of apparent anti-Catholicism triggered the fear that if such anti-Catholicism were not combatted in the islands a dangerous precedent might be established for the United States. The reasonably secure toleration of American Catholics might then be endangered.

Other grievances besides the colonial issues bothered Catholics. Among these were the discontinuance of United States subsidies to Catholic Indian mission schools, the proportionately small number of Catholic chaplains in the armed forces, the delay in being allowed to build a Catholic chapel at West Point, and the seeming unwillingness of the McKinley Administration to grant many political appointments to Catholics. Also some anxiety arose because several organizations were already trying to influence government action against Catholic interests. Senator Cushman K. Davis, of Minnesota, once presented to the Senate a petition from a group of Minnesota voters against appropriations made for the benefit of the Roman Catholic Church in Cuba.[50] These were the appropriations for the purchase by the United States government of the Church-owned property in Cuba (Chapter 3). Many other Congressmen presented similar petitions representing opinion in other states.[51]

As a result of all these factors, Catholic sentiment for an organized

[48] *New York Herald,* October 10, 1900, p. 5.
[49] San Francisco *Monitor,* January 16, 1901, p. 345.
[50] *Congressional Record,* 55th Cong., 3rd Sess., Vol. XXXII, Pt. 1, p. 829.
[51] *Ibid.,* p. 1059.

resistance began to grow. The *New York Freeman's Journal* asked, "What are our Catholic citizens doing that they do not rise up in every city in the land to protest against such indignities?"[52] A few Catholic societies made their presence felt by direct appeals to the President. German Catholics meeting in Chicago in August, 1899, sent a protest to McKinley seeking an end to church desecration in the Philippines.[53] In September the Catholic Young Men's Union demanded that McKinley investigate rumors of church desecration and punish those responsible.[54] By 1900, however, it was apparent that these individual societies could accomplish little, but if united they might succeed. Bishop McFaul addressed the Convention of the Ancient Order of Hibernians in Boston in May of 1900 with this idea in mind: "If we are so organized, can it be supposed for a moment that the present Administration would have passed over in silence the outrages against religion perpetrated in the Philippines?"[55] The Bishop made unity his personal crusade. In speech after speech to Catholic societies he urged that Catholics organize in order to make themselves heard: "We are twelve millions in America, yet how small is our influence."[56] In August of the same year he told the Knights of Columbus at Atlantic City that "recent outrages are simply another example of the disregard of Catholic rights against which we should most earnestly protest."[57]

Bishop McFaul's words produced the desired action. A convention of 250 delegates was held on December 10, 1901, in Cincinnati. Under the guidance of Bishop McFaul and Bishops Sebastian G. Messmer, of Green Bay, and Camillus Paul Maes, of Covington, the group organized the American Federation of Catholic Societies. The general purposes of the Federation were to (1) encourage the Christian education of youth, (2) correct error and expose falsehood and bigotry, and (3) infuse Christian principles into public and social life. All the speakers at the convention made it quite clear that the Federation was not a forerunner of a movement to form a Cath-

[52] *New York Freeman's Journal,* July 22, 1899, p. 2.
[53] San Francisco *Monitor,* August 26, 1899, p. 431.
[54] Boston *Pilot,* September 30, 1899, p. 1.
[55] *New York Freeman's Journal,* May 19, 1900, p. 1.
[56] *Ibid.,* June 9, 1900, p. 1.
[57] Boston *Pilot,* August 11, 1900, p. 1.

olic political party in the United States but merely a means of expressing collective Catholic opinion.[58]

Support for the Federation came from all parts of the country. Most of the Catholic newspapers welcomed the organization and worked for its success.[59] Encouraged by local interest and support, Catholics formed state branches of the national Federation and planned a centralized system. To accomplish this an Advisory Council was established at Cleveland. This Council was to act as a permanent agency to continue the Federation's work between annual national conventions.

Catholics disagreed even on this issue for a unified organization of Catholic societies. It was significant, therefore, that the archbishops in their annual meetings made no reference to the Federation. Without their formal support the organization had no official status, although many of the hierarchy endorsed and encouraged its promotion within their own dioceses. The *Catholic World,* in May, 1902, expressing concern over the necessity of such an organization, pointed out the Federation's weaknesses and the lack of support for it from the higher ecclesiastics and the influential laity. It feared that the Federation might do further damage to Catholics by inciting greater anti-Catholic bigotry and advised waiting until the archbishops of the country gave it their full support.[60] The defender of the Administration, Archbishop Ireland, was one of the Federation's most outspoken critics. He claimed that it was composed of soreheads and grumblers and American monks who wanted to stir up trouble for the government on behalf of the friars in the Philippines.[61]

Despite the opposition, the Federation grew until it represented some two million Catholics. Advocates of the organization hoped that its very existence would make politicians take note. Encouraged by its size, the Federation's leadership endeavored to encourage the organization to be more vociferous in its demands. In August, 1902, Bishop Messmer told the Federation's Second Annual Convention,

[58] *New York Freeman's Journal,* December 14, 1901, p. 5.

[59] *Ibid.,* April 12, 1902, p. 4.

[60] Rev. William P. Cantwell, "Is the National Federation of Catholic Societies Desirable?" *Catholic World,* LXXV (May, 1902), 179.

[61] Ireland, St. Paul, July 29, 1903, to Roosevelt, Roosevelt Correspondence, Letters Received, Box 58.

in Chicago, "It is a great mistake to suppose that politics have nothing to do with religion."[62] Bishop McFaul was even more contentious in his address:

> If this organization had been ready for action at the outbreak of hostilities between Spain and America, the religious difficulties incident to the occupation of our new possessions might have received the immediate attention which would have allayed, if not prevented, the unfortunate friction now so deeply deplored. . . . Why should the administration have been led to believe that Catholics are satisfied with what had been done in the Philippines when the very contrary was the fact.[63]

Thus inspired, the Convention formally moved to express its dissatisfaction in colonial affairs by direct appeals to the President. Even though the Taft Mission to Rome had just been completed, the Convention also adopted a resolution extending its "fullest sympathy" to the friars in the Philippines and dispatched a copy of this resolution to Washington.[64] Following this precedent, during the entire controversial period in colonial affairs the Federation continuously kept the government informed about the Catholic side of each issue. Its ultimate success can only be ascertained by observing the changes in American policy after the winter of 1901–1902.

By 1902 Catholics in the United States had moved a considerable distance in overcoming their timidity of 1890. Although still not organized into a homogeneous unit, they were clearly more powerful politically than in the previous decade. Many of the divisive factors influencing Catholic political activity remained powerful forces and prevented the formation of a genuine Catholic political bloc as that which existed in Germany and France. This was perhaps actually to the Catholic advantage. Their organizations voiced Catholic opinions and demanded a cessation of alleged anti-Catholic tendencies in American policies. That was as far as they wanted to go, for they wished to remain Catholic Americans and not become a body of American Catholics trying to exert political pressure antagonistic to the rest of the nation. In fact, if a measure of pressure in relation to potential political strength was taken in reference to American Catholics in this postwar period—during which vital religious questions were especially dominant—the irrevocable conclusion would be that

[62] Boston *Pilot*, August 16, 1902, p. 1.
[63] *Ibid.*, August 16, 1902, p. 5.
[64] *New York Freeman's Journal*, August 14, 1902, p. 2.

Catholic pressure was very slight indeed. The appearance of men like Bishop McFaul, nevertheless, pointed out to political leaders that a tremendous potential did exist and that it might be turned for or against them.

One politician who worried about this potential "Catholic vote" was Theodore Roosevelt. Although he tried to cooperate with Catholic opinion, he constantly feared having his policies labeled either "pro-Catholic" or "anti-Catholic." Part of his difficulty stemmed from his lack of true understanding of the Catholic Church. His comments after he met Cardinal Gibbons for the first time in 1891 are illustrative. He wrote his sister that he was pleased because the Cardinal, whom he called "the cultivated Jesuit," recognized "that his church must become both Republicanized and Americanized to retain its hold here."[65] Yet while trying to achieve a better understanding of Catholics during the 1890's he was often accused of pandering to the Irish and German vote, even though both nationalities opposed one of his favorite projects, an alliance with England.[66] Despite this confusion, he never disregarded potential Catholic influence on the outcome of future elections.

To capture this influence he deliberately set out early in his career to woo some of the Catholic leadership away from the Democrats. He had always encouraged McKinley to retain at least one Catholic in the Cabinet. On several occasions he told Catholic laymen, privately, that he regretted McKinley's failure to appoint a prominent Catholic to the Philippine Commissions.[67] He even suggested that some American order of Catholic priests, such as the Paulists, be given a "free hand" in the Philippines.[68] When he became President he manifested such sentiments more openly and officially.[69] By the end of the first few months of his administration, despite the criticisms of the American Federation of Catholic Societies, he thus suc-

[65] Roosevelt, Washington, February 1, 1891, to Anna Roosevelt, Morison (ed.), *Letters of Roosevelt,* I, 236.

[66] Roosevelt, Albany, November 23, 1900, to Henry White, *ibid.,* II, 1436; Roosevelt, Oyster Bay, August 11, 1899, to Cecil Arthur Spring Rice, *ibid.,* II, 1049.

[67] Roosevelt, Albany, April 24, 1899, to Maria Storer, *ibid.,* p. 995; Roosevelt, Oyster Bay, July 16, 1902, to Eugene A. Philbin, *ibid.,* III, 295.

[68] Roosevelt, Albany, May 18, 1900, to Maria Storer, *ibid.,* II, 1299.

[69] Roosevelt, Washington, October 4, 1901, to Maria Storer, *ibid.,* III, 158; Ireland, New York, November 6, 1901, to O'Connell, O'Connell Correspondence, Box 16.

cessfully had conveyed his sympathetic attitude toward Catholic interests. In May 1902 the Boston *Pilot*, which had been one of the most outspoken critics of McKinley, had expressed "perfect faith in Theodore Roosevelt";[70] he did not want to discourage endorsements of this nature.

Congressional debate on the Philippine Government Bill, however, brought about a deluge of protests and petitions that indicated a somewhat different sentiment. Congress received memorials from parishes, dioceses, and lay organizations protesting the religious provisions of the Bill and the alleged discriminations against Catholics.[71] Many other Catholic societies petitioned individual congressmen to investigate specific acts of anti-Catholic discrimination; most of their requests were turned over to the War Department to be answered.[72] But the greatest number of appeals from the larger or more significant Catholic groups were directed to the President himself.[73] One of these letters eventually became quite important. Written by the Reverend Hiram F. Fairbanks, a Catholic priest in Milwaukee, known to Roosevelt as an active campaigner for the Republican Party, the letter had threatening implications:

Mr. Coe, the Chairman of the Executive Committee of the Republican Party in this state in the first McKinley Campaign when the state gave, as it also did in the last election, more than 100,000 Republican majority, told me that there are in Wisconsin 40,000 Catholics who are Republican voters. Some years ago the party tried to interfere with school matters, and its course gave the State to the Democrats for four years notwithstanding this normal vote. The same German Catholics who now in all or

[70] Boston *Pilot*, May 3, 1902, p. 4.

[71] *Congressional Record*, 57th Cong., 1st Sess., Vol. XXXV, Pt. 6, pp. 5717, 5785, 6306, Pt. 7, pp. 6529, 7277, 7354, Pt. 8, pp. 7487, 7489, 7548, 7730.

[72] Colonel C. R. Edwards, Washington, July 17, 1902, to Philip P. Cosgrove, Secretary of American Federation of Catholic Societies; letters of Edwards, Washington, August 26, 1902, to Senators Lodge, Platt, Hanna, Beveridge, *et al.* and Congressmen Cannon, Grosvenor, Burton, *et al.*, Taft Semi-Official Correspondence, Philippine Commission Papers, R. G. 1534.

[73] M. P. Mooney, Chairman of the Executive Board, American Federation of Catholic Societies, Cleveland, June 11, 1902, to Roosevelt; John P. Dullard, Secretary of New Jersey Branch of Federation, Trenton, June 27, 1902, to Roosevelt; Bishop and Clergy of the Diocese of Leavenworth, Atchison, Kansas, June 27, 1902, to Roosevelt; *The Catholic Citizen*, Milwaukee, July 12, 1902, to Elihu Root; Bishop, Clergy, and Catholics of the Diocese of Columbus, Columbus, July 16, 1902, to Roosevelt; Catholic Clergy of the Archdiocese of Milwaukee, Milwaukee, July 18, 1902, to Roosevelt, *ibid.*

nearly all their conventions are passing resolutions condemning the American Educational policy in the Philippines were the chief cause of Republican reverses in this state.[74]

Despite these petitions and letters, not all Catholics so thoroughly criticized the Administration. Some of the milder critics were placated when the government, through the Bureau of Insular Affairs, published official investigations which explained away many of the Catholic charges. Such formal statements as Acting Philippine Governor Wright's denial of discrimination in the hiring of Catholic teachers gave other Catholics a reasonable basis for defending Roosevelt's policies. For example, Archbishop Ireland on several occasions used his cathedral pulpit for this purpose.[75] The Catholic press published these sermons widely. Quoting the Archbishop, *The New Century,* a Catholic newspaper published in Washington, attacked the Catholic Truth Society for its allegations of discrimination: "The accusation is so monstrous, so entirely unconnected with facts that to enter a categorical denial seems hardly necessary."[76] In July *The Catholic Citizen,* of Milwaukee, ran an editorial which admitted that its own charges of discrimination published in May had been investigated and had been proven false.[77] Even the Boston *Pilot* accepted the validity of a detailed report of the Bureau of Insular Affairs which denied any discrimination against Catholics in the Philippine schools.[78]

These modifications of Catholic criticisms, nevertheless, were not sufficient to assure Roosevelt's peace of mind. He was especially disturbed by the implications of Father Fairbanks' letter, fearing that any serious dissatisfaction among normally Republican voters would impair his leadership of the party in a critical congressional election year. This letter inspired him to order Secretary Root to investigate the charges of anti-Catholic discrimination in the Philippine public schools. Although the results of this investigation, Governor Wright's cablegram, and the Bureau of Insular Affairs Report seemed to settle

[74] Rev. Hiram F. Fairbanks, Milwaukee, June 10, 1902, to Roosevelt, *ibid.*, R. G. 1534–13.

[75] Ireland, St. Paul, August 14, 1902, to Edwards, *ibid.*, R. G. 1534–35; Ireland, St. Paul, August 5, 1902, to Roosevelt, Roosevelt Correspondence, Letters Received, Vol. 71.

[76] *The New Century*, July 19, 1902.

[77] *The Catholic Citizen*, July 12, 1902.

[78] Boston *Pilot*, August 30, 1902, p. 4.

the particular issue, Roosevelt felt it was necessary to go further to satisfy Catholic opinion.

In July, 1902, Roosevelt asked Secretary Root and Governor Taft to make recommendations for changes in the entire structure of the Philippine government.[79] Taft told Root that Bernard Moses was "the least useful member of the Commission."[80] Taft also inadvertently admitted that some of the Catholic accusations in reference to the schools were not entirely unfounded:

> [Superintendent of Schools Fred W.] Atkinson's selections [of teachers] while they might be very good in a state where there was no issue of Catholicism, I am afraid have been unfortunate in bringing to the front as educators in the Philippines some retired ministers, who feel called upon every time there is a missionary or evangelical meeting to appear and make themselves prominent by speeches and otherwise.[81]

His further comment was that Moses and Atkinson did not get along well together and that it might be well "to let both of them go."

Accepting Taft's recommendations, the President asked him: "What steps should I take about getting Moses out? I think it important to put Judge Smith in. I was greatly impressed by him, and I feel that we ought to have an American Catholic on the Commission."[82] Roosevelt was referring to James F. Smith, a justice of the Philippine Supreme Court. An attorney from San Francisco, Smith, a Catholic and a Democrat, had gone to the Philippines as a colonel of the First California Volunteers when that regiment was part of the first American army to land in the Islands. Serving in various capacities in the military governments of Generals Otis and MacArthur he had risen to the rank of brigadier general. When the civil administration was established Taft appointed him to the newly created Supreme Court. During his years in the Philippines Judge Smith had developed a good reputation among the Filipinos and had demonstrated a loyalty for the policies of the Administration. From the standpoint of his experience, his religion, and his previous political affiliation he was ideally suited for Roosevelt's purposes.

[79] Roosevelt, Washington, June 28, 1902, to Elihu Root, Taft Semi-Official Correspondence, Philippine Commission Papers, R. G. 1534–20.

[80] William Howard Taft, Rome, July 5, 1902, to Root, Taft Private and Official Correspondence, Letterpress Books, Box 1.

[81] *Ibid.*

[82] Roosevelt, Oyster Bay, July 31, 1902, to Taft, Morison (ed.), *Letters of Roosevelt,* III, 305.

In October both Moses and Atkinson resigned, effective January 1, 1903. President Roosevelt immediately announced the appointment of Smith to fill the vacancy on the Philippine Commission. He then wrote Governor Taft:

I think your plan is admirable about the schools—first to get some good man in the place of Atkinson, whose usefulness from what you say is entirely gone, and then to have the schools put under Smith in the partition of work among the Commissioners. . . . In other words, besides being just and fair to Catholics it has become painfully evident that we must take every possible step to show them beyond possibility of misconstruction that we are just and fair. Of course, the same thing applies with reference to Protestants.[83]

In selecting a new superintendent of education for the Philippines, Taft disagreed with Archbishop Ireland's earlier suggestion that this position also be given to a Catholic. He explained his reason to Secretary Root: "The truth is there is no such material in the United States."[84] Instead, he worked out another compromise and appointed Elmer B. Bryan as Atkinson's successor. According to Taft, Bryan had been sympathetic to the Catholic position and was well liked by Filipino Catholics. At Bryan's suggestion a Catholic, G. A. O'Reilly, was appointed superintendent of city schools for Manila. This last appointment was not merely a concession to Catholic opinion, however. O'Reilly, another Californian, had been superintendent of schools for the Ilocos Sur division, and Bryan considered him the most competent of the divisional superintendents and well qualified for the Manila post.[85] Satisfied that these administrative changes not only would benefit the Philippine school system but also should placate Catholic opinion in the United States, Taft remarked to Root, "I should think that even the wildest Catholic editor ought to curb his fury against you and me."[86]

Taft was right. The Boston *Pilot* hailed Smith's appointment as "President Roosevelt's Justice to Catholics."[87] The *Catholic World* indicated that it was satisfied that "the President has shown his de-

[83] Roosevelt, Washington, October 21, 1902, to Taft, *ibid.*, p. 358.

[84] Taft, Rome, July 5, 1902, to Root, Taft Private and Official Correspondence, Letterpress Books, Box 1.

[85] Taft, Manila, November 22, 1902, to Root, *ibid.*

[86] *Ibid.*

[87] Boston *Pilot,* October 25, 1902, p. 4.

sire to meet the demands of the Catholic people."[88] Even the San Francisco *Monitor,* normally hostile to the Administration's Philippine policies, insisted that "Mr. Roosevelt recognizes the mistake that was originally made in forming the Commissions, and has taken the first opportunity to rectify it in part."[89] Yet Roosevelt did even more. In October he announced the appointments of Archbishop Patrick J. Ryan, of Philadelphia, to the Indian Commission and of Bishop John Lancaster Spalding, of Peoria, as an arbitrator on the Anthracite Coal Strike Commission. In January he appointed still another Catholic, John T. McDonough, of Albany, as Smith's replacement on the Philippine bench. McDonough had become a good friend of Roosevelt when he served as New York's secretary of state while Roosevelt was governor. Informing Taft of this appointment, Roosevelt wrote of McDonough: "He is not a great lawyer, but he is a very fair-minded man, accustomed to getting along with other men perfectly. . . . I wish to appoint a Catholic, and yet a Catholic who had always gotten on well with Protestants."[90]

One of Roosevelt's most significant concessions to Catholic opinion received the least publicity—the hiring of American Catholics as teachers for the Philippine public schools. The American Catholic press had long complained that discrimination against Catholic teachers existed in the Philippines. When Acting Governor Wright's investigation proved these charges false, the President was satisfied that his Administration's policy had been vindicated. There would be no question of what a teacher's religion should be. As he explained to Eugene A. Philbin, the philosophy on this matter was quite simple: "We have never asked about the religion of any teacher sent over there."[91] However, he quickly changed his mind about the policy.

Most American Catholics had finally, if grudgingly, accepted the idea of a nonsectarian public school system for the Philippines; yet many of them still insisted that the Catholicism of the young Fili-

[88] *Catholic World,* LXXVI (November, 1902), 279.

[89] San Francisco *Monitor,* October 18, 1902, p. 561.

[90] Roosevelt, Washington, February 14, 1903, to Taft, Morison (ed.), *Letters of Roosevelt,* III, 426; Roosevelt, Washington, January 22, 1903, to Ireland, Roosevelt Correspondence, Letterbooks, Box 144.

[91] Roosevelt, Oyster Bay, July 12, 1902, to Philbin, Morison (ed.), *Letters of Roosevelt,* III, 292.

pinos was endangered unless these children had Catholic teachers. The argument in the Catholic press was quite clear: the Philippines did not have a pluralistic society, so if the vast majority of pupils in the Philippine public schools were Catholics then the majority of teachers in those schools should also be Catholics. The importance of this argument had been overlooked by President Roosevelt, but not by Governor Taft. As early as August, 1900, he tried to hire Catholic teachers in the United States. In explaining this idea the Governor wrote Secretary Root that "The effect of bringing Catholic teachers here can not but be good."[92]

At first Taft was unable to find enough qualified American Catholic teachers willing to spend several years in the Philippines. Nevertheless, mounting pressure from petitions received by Congress and the President in early summer of 1902 caused the Administration to take more positive steps to secure additional Catholic teachers. Roosevelt reversed his earlier position and encouraged Taft to seek help directly from the hierarchy. Taft worked out an arrangement with Archbishop Ireland in which the Archbishop would locate Catholic teachers available for service in the Philippines. With the cooperation of the Civil Service Board and the Philippine Superintendent of Education all of the teachers recommended by the Archbishop would be given pass examinations and would be sent directly to assignments in the Islands.[93] Gratified by this manifestation of the Administration's desire for cooperation, Archbishop Ireland turned to other members of the hierarchy for help in fulfilling all of the requests for teachers. By the end of 1902, 200 teachers recommended by the hierarchy were accepted for Philippine service and another 108 were requested by the Archbishop for the following spring.[94] The Archbishop recognized at once, however, that this arrangement could be politically dangerous to Roosevelt. He warned Cardinal Gibbons of this potentiality and reminded him "that all newspaper publicity about what we are doing should be carefully avoided."[95]

[92] Taft, Manila, August 11, 1900, to Root, Taft Private and Official Correspondence, Taft-Root Correspondence.

[93] Taft, Manila, November 22, 1902, to Root, *ibid.*, Letterpress Books, Box 1.

[94] Ireland, St. Paul, May 4, 1903, to Gibbons, Gibbons Correspondence, Box 100.

[95] *Ibid.*

Despite these pitfalls this procedure continued for at least another year.[96]

This spirit of friendliness between the Roosevelt Administration and the Catholic Church was not one-sided. The Vatican also did its part to establish a spirit of cooperation. All during 1901 papal Secretary of State Cardinal Rampolla corresponded regularly with Archbishop Ireland in an attempt to find some form of smooth contact short of a formal diplomatic exchange between the Vatican and the American government.[97] The Vatican particularly desired the opportunity to deal with an individual American who would have the responsibility for reaching a settlement of several major property disputes in the Philippines. The final solution of this request was the decision by Roosevelt to send Governor Taft directly to Rome. But the Vatican made additional arrangements as well. While Taft was in Rome in the summer of 1902 the Pope specifically made known to the Governor that he wanted to have as archbishop of Manila an American whose selection would be "with the accord and understanding of the President of the United States."[98] In fact, as the Vatican began to reorganize the entire Philippine hierarchy, it appointed to all of the sees American priests who had at least the indirect approval of Roosevelt. Naturally the President was flattered by the Vatican's attitude. But he did not deliberately attempt to nominate any candidates, although Thomas A. Hendrick, appointed bishop of Cebu, had been a close acquaintance while Roosevelt was governor of New York.[99]

The Vatican also tried to please the Administration with its selection of an apostolic delegate. This was the crucial appointment, for the delegate was the direct representative of the Papacy in the negotiations over the sale of the friars' lands and the settlement of the ownership of the other properties. When the Vatican realized that as

[96] Ireland, Washington, October 16, 1903, to Roosevelt, Roosevelt Correspondence, Letters Received, Box 62.

[97] Ireland, St. Paul, August 25, 1901, to Gibbons, Gibbons Correspondence, Box 98.

[98] Taft, Naples, July 22, 1902, to Root, Taft Private and Official Correspondence, Letterpress Books, Box 1.

[99] Roosevelt, Oyster Bay, July 30, 1903, to James F. Smith, Morison (ed.), *Letters of Roosevelt,* III, 534; Bishop B. J. McQuaid, Rochester, April 23, 1903, to Gibbons, Gibbons Correspondence, Box 100.

far as Governor Taft was concerned Archbishop Placide L. Chapelle had overstayed his usefulness in Manila it withdrew him.[100] Cardinal Rampolla preferred to send an Italian for these negotiations; so his next appointee was Donatus Sbaretti, who as archbishop of Havana had participated in the settlement of the Cuban property questions. Rampolla learned through Archbishop Ireland, however, that Secretary Root disliked Sbaretti.[101] Rampolla then recalled Sbaretti, who had gone as far as New York on his way to Manila, and selected another Italian, Giovanni Baptiste Guidi. Before Guidi was to arrive in Manila the Cardinal sought confirmation by asking Bishop Thomas O'Gorman, of Sioux Falls, to inquire of the President if Guidi would be acceptable to him and Taft.[102] There was no objection to this appointment. In fact, it proved eminently satisfactory, for Taft and Guidi worked out a series of successful arrangements and in the process developed a great respect for each other.[103]

These attempts by Roosevelt to settle differences with Catholics and their Church and to meet some of their demands eventually changed the Catholic attitude toward him and his Administration. But until the effects of these attempts became widely known the Catholic press still castigated the Administration. Despite the pleasant relations Taft had established with the Vatican during the summer of 1902, some members of the hierarchy still found fault with Roosevelt's policies. Bishop James McFaul, unaware of the Taft-Ireland arrangement to send Catholic teachers to the Philippines, continued to insist that anti-Catholic discrimination existed in the hiring of teachers. In a speech at the Federation's annual meeting in August he claimed that of 967 American teachers in the Philippines only 19 were Catholics.[104] Later on, in the summer of 1903, he complained personally to Roosevelt about the activities of Philippine

[100] Ireland, New York, June 7, 1901, to O'Connell, O'Connell Correspondence, Box 16; Taft, Manila, June 23, 1901, to Root, quoted in Henry Fawles Pringle (ed.), *The Life and Times of William Howard Taft,* I, 224; Ireland, St. Paul, August 25, 1901, to Gibbons, Gibbons Correspondence, Box 98.

[101] Ireland, St. Paul, March 29, 1902, to Maria Storer, Maria Storer (ed.), *In Memoriam,* p. 66.

[102] Thomas O'Gorman, Sioux Falls, October 17, 1902, to Roosevelt, Roosevelt Correspondence, Letters Received, Vol. 75.

[103] Taft, Baguio Benquet, P.I., June 15, 1903, to Root, Taft Private and Official Correspondence, Letterpress Books, Box 1.

[104] Boston *Pilot,* August 16, 1902, p. 5.

Commissioner James F. Smith.[105] Exasperated by this accusation against his principal Catholic appointee, Roosevelt replied in a warning letter to the Bishop:

Let me urge you, not merely in the interest of the country but in the interest of the Catholic Church, to be cautious about committing yourself on this Philippine matter until you are absolutely sure of your ground. It seems to me that when a Catholic layman like Smith, and a Catholic priest like Vattman, stand so absolutely for the present policy; and when I am simply carrying out the policy which they and scores of other Catholics . . . out of full knowledge advocate, it at least warrants caution in condemning what has been done.[106]

Disappointed that some segments of the Catholic community still misread his intentions in the Philippines, Roosevelt appealed to other Catholics to come to his aid. Acknowledging Archbishop Ireland's past assistance, the President again wrote him, giving additional information concerning his policies.[107] He specifically requested Commissioner Smith to "get at certain Catholics here and lay the facts as they actually are before the Catholics of the United States."[108] Ireland continued his public defense of the Administration and Smith published a thirteen-page report which described and defended all of the religious policies of the Philippine civil government. When he submitted this report to the President, Smith pointed out that

. . . the Philippine Government has endeavored, by every means in its power, to secure to the ministry of the Catholic Church the rights, powers and liberties enjoyed by other citizens. The statement that the Friars have been refused permission to return to their parishes is as false as the statement that they have been denied the protection of the law.[109]

While he was defending his Philippine policies as not being anti-Catholic, President Roosevelt was assailed by some Protestant or-

[105] James A. McFaul, Trenton, July 28, 1903, to Roosevelt, Roosevelt Correspondence, Letters Received, Box 58.

[106] Roosevelt, Oyster Bay, July 29, 1903, to McFaul, *ibid.*, Letterbooks, Box 145.

[107] Roosevelt, Oyster Bay, July 31, 1903, to Ireland, *ibid.*

[108] Roosevelt, Oyster Bay, July 30, 1903, to Smith, Morison (ed.), *Letters of Roosevelt,* III, 534.

[109] Smith, Manila, October 24, 1903, to Roosevelt, Roosevelt Correspondence, Letters Received, Box 62.

ganizations and journals as being too pro-Catholic. Among these was an interesting group known as the Order of United American Mechanics. During the congressional debate on the Philippine Government Bill several state chapters of this organization petitioned the President and individual congressmen to prevent any official aid to the Catholic Church or cooperation with it. A typical resolution called upon the President and Congress

> . . . to maintain none but patriotic Protestant Americans in the control of our Public School system in the Philippines which, like our Public Schools in the United States, are daily being assailed by the Jesuits and Roman Catholic Church.[110]

Some Protestant papers echoed these sentiments. When the *Religious Telescope* reported the appointment of James F. Smith to the Philippine Commission it warned its readers that the Philippine schools were about to become "Romanized."[111]

These criticisms, coming from both the extreme Catholic and the extreme Protestant positions, confused and frustrated Smith and Taft as well as Roosevelt. Taft took them personally. He recognized that in the United States he was accused of being at the same time too anti-Catholic and too pro-Catholic. Fearing that a person so "doubly damned" would be an embarrassment to Roosevelt, Taft offered to resign as civil governor.[112] Smith, too, felt the sting of unexpected criticism and offered his resignation. Roosevelt refused, however, to be so pressured and rejected both resignations.[113] His subsequent loyalty to Taft, offering him a United States Supreme Court vacancy, appointing him Secretary of War, and selecting him as his successor in the Presidency, is well known. But Roosevelt was equally loyal to Smith. He sent strong letters to several Catholic bishops in which he upheld Smith's activities in the Philippines, and when the opportunity occurred he insisted that Smith become civil governor of the Philippines even though another member of the

110 "Resolution of the Order United American Mechanics to President Theodore Roosevelt," St. Louis, June 18, 1902, Taft Semi-Official Correspondence, Philippine Commission Papers, R. G. 1534–16.

111 *Religious Telescope,* n.d., *ibid.,* R. G. 1534–46.

112 Taft, Manila, March 4, 1903, to Roosevelt, quoted in Pringle (ed.), *Life and Times of Taft,* I, 244.

113 Roosevelt, Oyster Bay, July 11, 1904, to Smith, Morison (ed.), *Letters of Roosevelt,* IV, 854.

Commission, Henry C. Ide, wanted the position and Smith did not.[114]

Eventually Roosevelt's determination to be fair on Philippine matters won him general Catholic approval. Cardinal Gibbons wrote him: "I am happy to say that the suspicions and criticisms manifested towards the government by some religious journals in this country are gradually diminishing in proportion as new light is thrown on the situation in the Philippines."[115] Archbishop Ireland also informed him that many Catholic bishops were "unanimous in praising" him and that "among Catholics you have far more supporters than you could well believe."[116] Archbishop J. J. Harty, the new American archbishop of Manila, told him: "Your words and deeds have been an inspiration to the people of the Islands. The Government at Washington has made a wholesome impression on all classes."[117] The Federation of the Catholic Societies of Kansas directed a resolution to Smith, Taft, and Roosevelt, which expressed its appreciation "of their efforts on behalf of the welfare of Filipino Catholics."[118]

Gradually the Catholic press, too, indicated the change in its temperament. The *Catholic World* expressed complete satisfaction with the solution of Philippine religious questions.[119] A *New Century* editorial declared, "So it strikes *The New Century* that it is about time to stop the clamour about discrimination against Catholics; about time to cease attacking a policy which so it seems to us, accentuates that splendid American characteristic—the love of justice and fair play."[120] The San Francisco *Monitor*, so hostile in the past, gave Roosevelt an indirect compliment in an editorial dated August 6, 1904: "The apparent indifference of Mr. Roosevelt to the religious complexion of his appointees, has had no little to do with the beat-

[114] Taft, Washington, January 15, 1906, to Henry C. Ide, Taft Semi-Official Correspondence, Philippine Commission Papers, Miscellaneous.

[115] Gibbons, Baltimore, December 2, 1903, to Roosevelt, Gibbons Correspondence, Box 100.

[116] Ireland, St. Paul, July 29, 1903, to Roosevelt, Roosevelt Correspondence, Letters Received, Box 58.

[117] J. J. Harty, Manila, April 29, 1904, to Roosevelt, *ibid.*, Box 72.

[118] "Resolution of the Federation of the Catholic Societies of Kansas" to Roosevelt, Smith, and Taft, Leavenworth, May 16, 1907, Taft Semi-Official Correspondence, Philippine Commission Papers, R. G. 1534–78.

[119] *Catholic World*, LXXVIII (October, 1903), 136.

[120] *The New Century*, September 12, 1903.

ing down of the barrier of national and religious bigotry in politics, noticeably in the past two or three years."[121] A surprising article appeared in the *Monitor* during the 1904 election campaign:

It becomes more evident every day as this campaign progresses, that it is essential that a Republican House of Representatives should be elected this Fall. . . . we may mention that the Boston *Pilot*, the *Irish World*, and other representative Catholic papers, have heartily endorsed Mr. Roosevelt's nomination and are earnestly advocating his election.[122]

How well these changes in Catholic opinion contributed to Theodore Roosevelt's political success in 1904 is impossible to determine. Roosevelt did win the presidential election with a sizable plurality, but he also won areas of large concentrations of Catholic voters, areas that had supported Bryan in 1896 and 1900. Regardless of the existence or validity of election statistics, Roosevelt believed that his attitude on colonial affairs was partially responsible for his victory. He was especially pleased with his own ability to allay Catholic fears of his intentions. As he wrote Finley Peter Dunne, the Irish-American humorist,

One of the things I am most pleased with in the recent election is that while I got, I think, a greater proportion of the Americans of Irish birth or parentage and of the Catholic religion than any previous republican candidate, I got this proportion purely because they know I felt in sympathy with them and in touch with them.[123]

Roosevelt was not the only one to benefit from the change in Catholic opinion. In particular, Governor Taft shared in the new Catholic acceptance of the Administration's colonial policies. The Catholic press was full of praise for him when it learned of his retirement as civil governor and appointment as Secretary of War. The San Francisco *Monitor* warmly congratulated him and extolled the qualifications of his successor, Luke E. Wright.[124] In all of this praise perhaps the *Ave Maria* summarized more clearly than any other Catholic journal the new attitude toward Taft:

[121] San Francisco *Monitor*, August 6, 1904, p. 6.

[122] *Ibid.*, October 22, 1904, p. 14. This item may have been a political advertisement, although it was not labeled as such; regardless, its presence in the pages of the *Monitor* is noteworthy.

[123] Roosevelt, Washington, November 23, 1904, to Finley Peter Dunne, Morison (ed.), *Letters of Roosevelt*, IV, 1042.

[124] San Francisco *Monitor*, January 9, 1904, p. 281.

Judge Taft's mission to the Philippines was one of extraordinary difficulty, and it is only fair to say that he seems to have fulfilled it as satisfactorily as any other citizen could have done, in view of the conglomerate condition of our people . . . all this stamps the statesmanship of the retiring governor as large-minded, straightforward, and in harmony with the best traditions of our country.[125]

Roosevelt's elation over his success in allaying Catholic fears was well justified. He had consistently tried to maintain honesty and intelligence in handling the highly controversial Church-state issues in the dependencies. Yet he had done more than this. His attitude helped foster a better relationship between American Catholics and their non-Catholic fellow citizens. By officially recognizing the validity of Catholic interests Roosevelt helped the Catholic Church in the United States come of age within American society. His policies reduced mutual distrust and misunderstanding. The climax of these policies, sending Governor Taft to Rome, was Roosevelt's attempt to deal directly on the major issues. He did more in this personal diplomacy with the Vatican to satisfy Catholic opinion than in all of his other efforts. Although it did not fulfil all of his expectations, the Taft Mission to Rome, nonetheless, was Roosevelt's principal solution to the religious problems in the Philippines.

[125] *Ave Maria,* LVIII (February 13, 1904), 214.

CHAPTER SEVEN

THE TAFT MISSION TO ROME

IT IS NOT CERTAIN who originally conceived the idea of sending an official representative from the United States to negotiate directly with the Vatican for the purchase of the friars' lands. Both the Schurman and the Taft Commissions had recommended buying these properties, but neither suggested a method of procedure. The relationship between Archbishop Chapelle and Governor Taft was so strained that negotiations in Manila between these two officials could not be undertaken. Yet these were the two most logical men to reach any sort of settlement. To the Roosevelt Administration the friars' own representatives appeared too anti-American and were expected to demand a high price for their property. If Taft could not negotiate with Chapelle, then some other arrangement would have to be made unless a satisfactory settlement of the entire issue were to be postponed indefinitely.

No one recognized the importance of the situation more clearly than Cardinal Rampolla, the Secretary of State for the Vatican. In the summer of 1901, in a series of letters to Archbishop Ireland, he suggested that only direct negotiation between Washington and Rome seemed possible. At Rampolla's request, Archbishop Ireland proposed to Secretary Root that it would be quite acceptable to the Vatican for some representative of the United States government to go to Rome to reach a settlement. It was to be understood from the very beginning that this would be a special and temporary mission and would imply no future diplomatic relationship between the two governments.[1] The whole idea was acceptable to Root, who after some further correspondence with Taft in Manila, proposed it to the President and the Cabinet.

By November, President Roosevelt with his customary enthusiasm had committed himself to the proposal. Closeted with the Archbishop, Secretary Root, and Secretary of State John Hay, the President discussed all ramifications of the project and subjected it to criticism in order to ascertain public reaction when an official announcement was made.[2] During this initial planning Archbishop Ireland played a significant role on behalf of his church. He saw the President often and made suggestions that apparently were followed.[3] Cardinal Gibbons gave enthusiastic support and assured Roosevelt that he anticipated no serious objection from any quarter.[4]

The question then turned on who was to lead the mission. Judge James F. Smith, of the Philippine Supreme Court, was proposed because he had been in the Islands for several years and was familiar with the situation. And, of course, he was a Catholic.[5] But Protestant opinion was equally important to the Administration. Senator Henry Cabot Lodge, of Massachusetts, feared a Protestant reaction to the whole project, and caused Secretary Root to have some misgivings.[6] But the President was adamant on the basic idea. He was willing to compromise, however, on the leadership of the mission. He, too, was

[1] Archbishop John Ireland, St. Paul, August 25, 1901, to James Cardinal Gibbons, Gibbons Correspondence, Box 98.

[2] Ireland, St. Paul, November 3, 1901, to Bellamy Storer, Maria Longworth Storer (ed.), *In Memoriam Bellamy Storer*, p. 57; Theodore Roosevelt, Washington, November 7, 1901, to Elihu Root, Elting E. Morison (ed.), *The Letters of Theodore Roosevelt*, III, 189.

[3] Ireland, Washington, November 7, 1901, to Gibbons, Gibbons Correspondence, Box 99.

[4] Gibbons, Baltimore, December 10, 1901, to Roosevelt, Roosevelt Correspondence, Vol. 56.

[5] Ireland, Washington, December 3, 1901, to Bellamy Storer, Maria Storer (ed.), *In Memoriam*, p. 58.

[6] Ireland, Washington, December 8, 1901, to Bellamy Storer, *ibid.*, p. 61.

concerned over the effect on Protestants and asked Archbishop Ireland to discuss the plan with Lyman Abbott, of *Outlook*, and William H. Ward, of *The Independent*.[7] Both of these editors and their journals were considered high-level spokesmen of Protestant religious opinion in the United States. Their influence behind the Administration would be absolutely essential for success. Compromise on the membership of any mission to Rome would probably be more successful.

Abbott and Ward agreed to back the Administration and work up popular Protestant support.[8] Immediately after Archbishop Ireland's visit to them in New York they fulfilled their promises. The editorial columns of both *The Independent* and *Outlook* made the suggestions that the best solution to much of the Philippine question *might* be more easily reached in Rome than in Manila.[9] By leading Protestant opinion along in subsequent articles, these two editors materially assisted in bringing about an understanding of the government's aims. With this support and the strong backing of Ireland and Gibbons, Theodore Roosevelt and his advisors announced their proposal.

On the whole the Catholic press greeted the official announcement of the mission to Rome with reserved support. The Boston *Pilot* saw in it the handiwork of Archbishop Ireland and, therefore, approved.[10] The *Catholic World* called it "another evidence of the saner methods now being adopted towards the Church."[11] Nevertheless, some Catholic papers considered the mission further evidence of anti-Catholicism, especially when the President announced that Governor William Howard Taft would head the three-man commission. The other members were to be Justice James F. Smith and Major John Biddle Porter. Perhaps as much in bigotry as in ignorance the *New York Freeman's Journal* attacked the composition of the mission because "Judge Smith and Major John Biddle Porter, both of whom, with Taft himself, are Protestants, an arrangement

[7] *Ibid.*

[8] Ireland, Washington, December 21, 1901, to Roosevelt, Roosevelt Correspondence, Vol. 56.

[9] *The Independent,* LIII (December 19, 1901), 3029; *Outlook,* LXIX (December 28, 1901), 1051.

[10] Boston *Pilot,* March 29, 1902, p. 4.

[11] *Catholic World,* LXXV (April, 1902), 132.

[which is] fully in accord with the 'no papist need apply' principle so far rigidly observed in American high official appointments in connection with Government in the Catholic Philippine Islands."[12]

Governor Taft was the most logical person for this assignment. He had returned to the United States in the late fall of 1901 for a serious operation. During his convalescence his presence in the United States was important to the Administration for supplying much needed firsthand information. Everyone in government circles trusted and respected him. And he could easily carry on the negotiation with the Vatican on his return to Manila, going by way of New York, Rome, and Suez rather than by San Francisco and Tokyo. Fortunately the Governor's recovery was rapid; by February 1 he was able to go before the Senate Committee on the Philippines for several days of interrogation concerning the proposed Philippine Government Bill. The decision that Taft go to Rome was finally made in February.[13]

The *New York Freeman's Journal* attack upon this new Taft Commission was entirely unjustified. Not only was it in error about the religion of Justice Smith, but it entirely ignored the late addition to the Commission of Thomas O'Gorman, bishop of Sioux Falls. Bishop O'Gorman, an intimate of Archbishop Ireland, was another defender of the Administration. Judge Taft felt that such a man would be invaluable as part of the Mission and suggested that the Bishop precede him to Rome to prepare the way.[14] Thus the Taft Mission as finally constituted was officially made up of four men, two of whom were Catholic. Despite this organization, strong sentiment in the Catholic press still argued against it. One of the chief opponents was St. Clair McKelway, editor of the *Brooklyn Eagle*. Roosevelt wrote him on April 1, trying to explain why he wanted to send Taft to Rome.[15] But apparently he had little success, for he had to ask Arch-

[12] *New York Freeman's Journal,* May 17, 1902, p. 4.

[13] William Howard Taft, Washington, February 24, 1902, to Mrs. W. H. Taft, quoted in Henry Fawles Pringle (ed.), *The Life and Times of William Howard Taft,* I, 226.

[14] Taft, Cincinnati, April 8, 1902, to Thomas O'Gorman, Taft Private and Official Correspondence, Letterpress Books, Box 1.

[15] Roosevelt, Washington, April 1, 1902, to St. Clair McKelway, Morison (ed.), *Letters of Roosevelt,* III, 251.

bishop Ireland to call personally on McKelway and get him to ease the pressure on the Administration.[16]

Besides placating the Catholic press, the Roosevelt Administration continued to seek support from the hierarchy. Before he left for Rome, Governor Taft visited Cardinal Gibbons in Baltimore.[17] A few weeks later the President invited the Cardinal to the White House to discuss the prospects of Taft's success.[18] Roosevelt certainly knew that his favorable words about the Church and his cooperative spirit over the negotiations in Rome would be made known to the Vatican, as well as to American Catholics, through Gibbons. At any rate, Ireland wrote O'Gorman in Rome that "Public opinion in America is quiet—in a waiting mood."[19] Even the Boston *Pilot,* usually critical of the Administration, stated: "The appointment of this commission has been an act of political wisdom, and its good results will astonish those unhappy bigots who live in fear that justice to Catholics means the transference of the seat of civil government to the Vatican."[20] Americans, Protestant and Catholic alike, were waiting to see how well Governor Taft would be received in Rome and how far the Vatican would go to cooperate with him.

Governor Taft and his official party were treated cordially at the Vatican.[21] They arrived in Rome on June 1 and presented their credentials to Cardinal Rampolla on the second. At 12:30 on June 5 they were received in a private audience with the Pope. Leo XIII, at this time in the twenty-fourth year of his pontificate, was a frail man over ninety years old. But he was quite a surprise to Taft. The Governor wrote his wife, "The old boy is quite bubbling with humor. He was as lively as a cricket."[22] The Pope presented gifts to each member of the Taft party and also a beautiful mosaic of himself which was to be given to Roosevelt. Taft in turn presented the

[16] Ireland, Washington, April 16, 1902, to Bellamy Storer, Maria Storer (ed.), *In Memoriam,* p. 69.

[17] Gibbons, Baltimore, May 7, 1902, to Denis J. O'Connell, O'Connell Correspondence, Box 17.

[18] Gibbons, Baltimore, June 12, 1902, to O'Connell, *ibid.*

[19] Ireland, St. Paul, May 26, 1902, to O'Gorman, O'Gorman Correspondence.

[20] Boston *Pilot,* June 14, 1902, p. 4.

[21] Ireland, St. Paul, June 14, 1902, to O'Gorman, O'Gorman Correspondence.

[22] Taft, Rome, June 7, 1902, to Mrs. W. H. Taft, quoted in Pringle (ed.), *Life and Times of Taft,* I, 228.

Pontiff with a white leather-bound edition of the President's literary works. Then Governor Taft read a prepared statement to the Pope concerning the intentions of the American government. In this he briefly outlined the history of antifriar agitation in the Philippines and pointed out the desire of the United States to effect a fair settlement that would return peace to the Islands. He called the Pontiff's attention to the bold facts of the case and the necessity of a quick solution. "The justice or injustice of this hostility is, as I conceive, aside from the issue," he said. "An attempt by them [the religious orders] to assume the right of landlords or to become parish priests again, will, it is confidently believed, seriously disturb the peace and order of the islands."[23] The Governor's tone and the Pope's attitude were both warm and friendly. Leo did not discuss the American's instructions point by point, but instead said that he had turned the matter over to a committee of cardinals to negotiate with Taft and to make recommendations to himself.

Secretary Root's instructions to Taft appeared to the Americans as open, fair, and just. There seemed to be no reason why Taft could not get quick agreement from the Pope and settle the matter immediately without further negotiation while he was in Rome. The opening paragraph of these rather lengthy instructions indicated, however, that the Administration was uncertain of the reaction in Congress to the Taft Mission. Although committees of both houses had reported favorably on the Philippine Government Bill, Congress had not acted on it when Taft departed for Rome. As a result Root hoped that Taft would reach an immediate agreement with the Vatican and thereby present Congress with a solution that it would have to accept.[24] The Secretary obviously was more concerned over a possible negative vote in Congress than the loss of cooperation from the Vatican, for the tone of his instructions in reference to the friars was quite definite and uncompromising:

3) By reason of the separation the religious orders . . . are no longer capable of serving any useful purpose for the church. . . . They will not be voluntarily accepted again by the people, and can not be restored to their positions except by forcible intervention on the part

[23] "Text of Address by Governor Taft to Leo XIII," *Papers Relating to the Friars' Land Negotiations* (House Document No. 2, Vol. 1, 57th Cong., 2nd Sess.), p. 237.

[24] Root, Washington, May 9, 1902, to Taft, *ibid.*, p. 233.

of the civil government, which the principles of our Government forbid.

4) It is the wish of our Government . . . that the titles of the religious orders to the large tracts of agricultural lands which they now hold shall be extinguished, but that full and fair compensation shall be made therefor.
6) The titles to the great amount of church lands and buildings in the islands, other than those of the religious orders and now apparently owned by the states, should be settled fairly.
7) Provision should be made for ascertaining what rentals, if any, ought to be paid for conventos and other church buildings which have been occupied by United States troops during the insurrection. . . .
8) The rights and obligations remaining under the various specific trusts for education and charity which are now in doubt and controversy ought to be settled by agreement if possible, rather than by the slow and frequently disastrous processes of litigation, so that the beneficent purposes of these foundations may not fail.[25]

Quite clearly the success of the entire negotiation would turn on the question of the withdrawal of the friars. Taft realized this and waited over two weeks for Vatican officials to prepare an answer to his original instructions and the requests of his government. On June 22 Cardinal Rampolla sent a reply to the Governor. He expressed the Vatican's willingness to cooperate with the American government and its gratitude for the American desire to settle quickly and generously all property claims made by the Church. To accomplish this the new apostolic delegate would be instructed to work for an equitable understanding with the Philippine government. In addition, the Holy See would try to promote better ecclesiastical education and training in pastoral functions for the native clergy in order to have them gradually replace the friar orders. But, the Cardinal continued,

As to the Spanish religious in particular belonging to the orders mentioned in the instructions, not even they should be denied to return to those parishes where the people is disposed to receive them without disturbance of public order; and, if in some parishes where it is evident that they are desired, or are favorably regarded by the whole or the great majority of the people, obstacles and difficulties should be interposed on the part of some disturber of peace, the Holy See trusts that the American

[25] *Ibid.*, pp. 234–235.

authorities by the ordinary means of civil justice will know how to protect the right of religious themselves and the wish of the people.[26]

The Vatican was willing to do everything but withdraw the friars from the Philippines. Because these Spanish priests comprised two thirds of all the clergy in the Islands and since there were as yet no replacements, Filipino or American, Rampolla had no alternative but to remain adamant on this particular point.

Governor Taft was dissatisfied with the Cardinal's reply; nonetheless he considered it a firm basis for further negotiation. In the meantime his position had been strengthened by the passage of the Philippine Government Bill, which gave his mission official status and provided with the necessary means to raise funds to purchase the friars' property. After communicating with the Secretary of War he formulated a *modus vivendi* in the form of a contract that, if signed while he was still in Rome, would go a long way to providing an immediate end to the difficulties. He objected to the sending of another apostolic delegate, for he felt that a delegate would impair the personal relationship he had just established between himself and the Vatican. Instead, he proposed a contract which would be both a statement of mutual agreement on fundamental principles and an acceptance of a board of arbitrators. The five arbitrators, two selected by the Vatican, two by the Philippine government, and one by a disinterested third government, would evaluate claims and counterclaims to property, establish the sale price of each piece of property, and settle the validity of claims to rents and pious trusts. In summary, the contract would commit the Philippine government to (1) buy all agricultural lands owned by the orders, (2) release by legislative act "all lands or enclosures upon which Roman Catholic Churches and conventos now stand," and (3) compromise with the Holy See where possible on charitable and other trusts. In addition the United States government would pay reasonable rentals or damages for property used by United States troops. In return the Roman Catholic Church was expected to provide adequate titles for all property purchased and to withdraw all of the Spanish members of the four orders by the end of two years after the Philippine government made the first payment toward the purchase of the property. An exception to this provision would be granted to those friars

[26] "Memorandum of Cardinal Rampolla to Governor Taft," *ibid.*, p. 241.

who were peaceably active in parishes outside of the city of Manila.[27]

On July 9, Cardinal Rampolla replied to the Governor's propositions with a new set of counterpropositions of his own. In essence, the Vatican and the Philippine government were in agreement except on the basic issue of the friars. Rampolla's statement of the Church's position is clear:

If we now pass to an examination of the difficulty itself, it is very easy to prove that the Holy See can not accept the proposition of the Philippine Government to recall from the archipelago in a fixed time all the religious of Spanish nationality—Dominicans, Franciscans, Augustinians, Recoletos, and to prevent their return in the future. In effect such a measure, not justified by reason of force majeure, would be contrary to the positive rights guaranteed by the Treaty of Paris, and would put, consequently, the Holy See in conflict with Spain, who would have every reason to protest. Much more, such a measure would be, in the eyes of the Filipinos and of the entire Catholic world, the explicit confirmation of all the accusations brought against the said religious by their enemies, accusations of which the falsity, or at least the evident exaggeration, can not be disputed.[28]

It was apparent that neither government was willing to give in on this very vital issue.

The United States government, despite its offer to settle all of the religious-property questions with a minimum of litigation, found itself still caught in the perplexities of the presence of the Spanish friars. The government certainly could not force the Vatican to withdraw the friars; so it had to recognize that a different approach to a solution was necessary. Taft forwarded to Cardinal Rampolla a new statement from the Secretary of War. In this document Root acknowledged the willingness of the Vatican to negotiate as "a sure basis of mutual consideration and just treatment in the future relations between church and state in the Philippines."[29] Again he defended the American insistence on the withdrawal of the friars not as a religious or racial question and not as involving "any confirma-

[27] "Response of Governor Taft to Cardinal Rampolla," *ibid.*, pp. 243–252.
[28] Rampolla, Rome, July 9, 1902, to Taft, *ibid.*, p. 253.
[29] Root, Washington, July 14, 1902, to Taft, *ibid.*, p. 256.

tion of any accusations against the persons withdrawing or the orders to which they belong." On the contrary, he continued,

It is to be observed that we have made no such accusations. It would simply recognize the existence of the conditions which for several years past have been and are now preventing these particular agents from serving the church in the stations to which they were assigned and which would make their re-employment injurious to the community. In this matter the United States representatives in the Philippines are merely endeavoring to meet the wishes, as well as the needs, of the Philippine people.[30]

However, since the Vatican refused to concede this point, the Secretary instructed Governor Taft to change the entire tactic of the American negotiation. No matter how well-couched in the language of diplomacy these new instructions were, they nevertheless meant an abrupt withdrawal of the American offer to purchase outright all disputed properties after a value had been set on them by an impartial tribunal. Taft was instructed to accept the appointment of a new apostolic delegate and plan on negotiating each and every claim with him in Manila. This meant that the process would be slow and laborious, with each side setting a valuation on the property and then trying to reach a compromise settlement without the assistance of outside arbitration.

On the surface Taft's mission to Rome appears to have been a failure. Certainly he had not accomplished his purpose of buying the friars' property outright and having the friars withdrawn from the Philippines. Naturally he was disappointed and could not ascertain why such a generous offer would have been declined by the Vatican. In his report to Secretary Root he tried to offer a few conclusions. His observations were very interesting, even if based only on conjecture. He wrote:

The answer of the Vatican was a great disappointment and surprise to me. . . . Bishop O'Gorman is of opinion that some communication was received from Spain protesting against the reflection upon Spain implied in our agreement. It is possible that some of the religious orders stirred Spain up to this, though I doubt it. . . . Cardinal Satolli and other Cardinals have not hesitated to express themselves as of [the] opinion that the Committee of Cardinals committed a stupid mistake in not accepting our original proposition, and that they have allowed a great opportunity to

[30] *Ibid.*

slip through their fingers. My impression is that the Pope feels the same way, but the grip of the monastic orders is too strong to permit him to overrule a commission constituted as this was.[31]

Actually the Mission to Rome was not a failure. If Taft's observations on conditions in the Holy See were correct, ample pressure was exerted within the Vatican to increase cooperation with American authorities. Certainly Taft and his colleagues laid the basis for further understanding between Church and state, and upon this smoother plane ultimate solution of all problems seemed far more feasible than it had appeared before. The final exchange of communications between Taft and Rampolla indicates how close to an understanding both men were.[32]

In the Philippines Taft found that his stopover in Rome had not been a failure. The fact that he had endeavored to negotiate with the Vatican for the removal of the friars enhanced his popularity. The welcome provided for him upon his return to Manila in August was tumultuous.[33] Reviewing affairs in the Islands several weeks later, he wrote Roosevelt, ". . . I do not state it too strongly when I say that the visit to Rome has done us a great deal of good in this country."[34] Taft had made many friends while he was in Rome, and learned something of how to get along with Catholic prelates. He also understood Vatican politics and realized that the advanced age of Leo XIII meant that aspirants were jockeying for position in preparation for the next conclave. His growing friendliness toward Churchmen was indicated in the reception he gave the new apostolic delegate, Archbishop Giovanni Baptiste Guidi, upon his arrival in Manila in November.[35] He continued his friendliness the following March when he sent personal congratulations to Pope Leo on the twenty-fifth anniversary of his pontificate.[36]

[31] Taft, Naples, July 22, 1902, to Root, Taft Private and Official Correspondence, Letterpress Books, Box 1.

[32] *Papers Relating to the Friars' Land Negotiations* (House Document), pp. 259–260.

[33] Pringle (ed.), *Life and Times of Taft*, I, 232.

[34] Taft, Manila, September 13, 1902, to Roosevelt, Roosevelt Correspondence, Vol. 73.

[35] Taft, Manila, November 23, 1902, to O'Connell, O'Connell Correspondence, Box 17.

[36] Taft, Manila, March 3, 1903, to Root, Taft Private and Official Correspondence, Letterpress Books, Box 1.

But the friendliness toward the Catholic Church that Taft demonstrated in Rome and Manila was not enough for the Roosevelt Administration. The President was still worried about the attitude of Catholics in the United States. If Pope Leo had agreed to all of the terms of the American offer and had ordered the removal of the Spanish friars from the Philippines, the Pope would have tacitly admitted that all of the charges against the friars were true. By refusing to do so he put President Roosevelt in a perplexing situation. The entire basis for the negotiations was the idea that if the government purchased all of the friars' property the priests would no longer have an interest in the Islands and thus they would return to Spain. The failure to conclude this aspect of the expected solution forced the Administration to back down from its position on the entire friar controversy and left it open to severe criticism. Much of the Catholic press found the Pope's refusal a clear indication that all of the charges against the friars were pure calumnies. Some still considered Governor Taft and his commission quite bigoted. Catholic societies again began to send protests to the President while congressmen filed more petitions indicating a new wave of Catholic sentiment.[37]

A mass meeting of Catholics was held on June 7 in Leavenworth, Kansas, where a resolution was adopted in the name of the clergy and the bishop of the Diocese of Leavenworth protesting the policies of the Administration in the Philippines. A copy of the resolution was sent to the President.[38] In July a similar meeting was held in Grand Rapids, Michigan. The group of over four thousand resolved that "we, the Bishop, clergy and Catholics of the City of Grand Rapids, Michigan, as citizens of the United States . . . protest against all the wrongs and unjust acts perpetrated on our fellow-Catholics in the Philippines."[39] Similarly, other Catholic organizations called the President's attention to their particular opinions on affairs in the Philippines or on the Taft Mission.[40]

President Roosevelt called all these protests "an entire misunder-

[37] *Congressional Record,* 57th Cong., 1st Sess., Vol. XXXV, Pt. 7, p. 7354.

[38] *New York Freeman's Journal,* July 12, 1902, p. 4.

[39] Boston *Pilot,* July 19, 1902, p. 5.

[40] Roosevelt, Oyster Bay, July 31, 1902, to Taft, Morison (ed.), *Letters of Roosevelt,* III, 303–304.

standing of the facts."[41] He had already provided an investigation of the charges of anti-Catholic discrimination in the hiring of teachers for the Philippine public schools, but he still intended to answer all of the protests and attempt to minimize the agitation. To further the defense of his policies he again relied on Archbishop Ireland. The Archbishop spoke for the Administration before the Second Annual Convention of the American Federation of Catholic Societies, held in Chicago in July. After the Convention adjourned he wrote the President: "It is my duty to do all I can to guard Catholics against false opinions which ignorance and malice seek to foster. Of course, at the bottom of the agitation there are various motives at work. But one motive is surely politics. Democrats are glad to conceal their warfare beneath the mantle of religion."[42]

As spokesman for the Republican Administration, the Archbishop had too many Republican sins to live down. Commenting on his speech to the Federation, the Boston *Pilot* wrote, "The *Pilot* cannot agree with Archbishop Ireland. . . . The fact that at the very outset of our occupation of those islands a commission was formed on which Catholics were not represented, was a sufficient reason for fear that the interests of the Church would suffer.[43] Bishop McFaul, the spiritual advisor of the Federation, replied vigorously to Ireland and continued to maintain his position that Roosevelt's policies were aimed at doing damage to the Church.[44] According to most of the Catholic press, the Administration still had not satisfied Catholic opinion.

Catholic societies and newspapers continued to protest after the Taft party returned to Manila with no clear-cut record of achievement. The press widely published a current letter from the Philippine Catholic Center in Manila. This group, reported to be the strongest and most representative body of Catholic laymen in the Islands, addressed its thanks to the American Catholics who had protested on their behalf and requested that it be made known in Washington that they wanted the Spanish friars to remain in the

[41] Roosevelt, Oyster Bay, July 21, 1902, to James D. Fox, Secretary of St. Catherine of Sienna Holy Name Society, Roosevelt Correspondence, Letterbooks, Box 143.

[42] Ireland, St. Paul, August 5, 1902, to Roosevelt, *ibid.*, Vol. 71.

[43] Boston *Pilot*, August 2, 1902, p. 4.

[44] *New York Freeman's Journal*, August 9, 1902, p. 5.

Philippines.[45] This was the first expression of popular Filipino sentiment in favor of the friars to appear in the Catholic press. It brought a few more profriar protests to Congress from irate Catholic groups.[46]

President Roosevelt received the brunt of this Catholic antagonism. Because he felt that he had tried to follow a just path, he was amazed by the opposition to the Taft Mission that came from Catholics. He wrote Senator Henry Cabot Lodge, "There has been a ferocious *Catholic*—instead of A.P.A.—attack against Taft! It is on behalf of the friars."[47] He also wrote Taft about his anxiety over the situation:

> I was prepared to be attacked by the extreme anti-Catholic people for your going there [to Rome], but I was completely taken aback by the violent attack made upon us by the Catholics. . . . A curious feature of the situation is that the anti-Ireland Catholics—those who have called themselves antiliberals—are now strenuously insisting that it was an outrage for the United States to depart from its traditional policy and try to open negotiations with the Vatican.[48]

Roosevelt was most concerned over the effect of the Taft Mission on the coming congressional elections. His observations to Taft could not conceal his bitterness and disappointment:

> Taken together, the matters have rather complicated the political situation here. I am afraid we may be hurt thereby this fall in the congressional elections. . . . We have tried to persuade the church to enter into an arrangement which would be for its own financial interest and for the interest of its Catholic parishioners—an arrangement by which the Catholic laymen of the Philippine Islands would receive Catholic priests to whom they would listen. The church has refused, and our position has been so misunderstood as to cause great bitterness among the Catholics here. . . . I feel that, unless you with your superior knowledge of the situation see controlling reasons to the contrary, we should sit still and let the friars get along as best they can.[49]

[45] San Francisco *Monitor,* October 18, 1902, pp. 562, 577.

[46] *Congressional Record,* 57th Cong., 2nd Sess., Vol. XXXV, Pt. 1, p. 23, and Pt. 2, p. 1164.

[47] Roosevelt, Oyster Bay, July 30, 1902, to Henry Cabot Lodge, Henry Cabot Lodge (ed.), *Selections from the Correspondence of Theodore Roosevelt and Henry Cabot Lodge,* I, 521.

[48] Roosevelt, Oyster Bay, July 31, 1902, to Taft, Morison (ed.), *Letters of Roosevelt,* III, 303–304.

[49] *Ibid.*

Nevertheless, Roosevelt could not ignore the American Catholics. Almost immediately after it became apparent that Taft had not met success in Rome the President endeavored to recover his prestige before the Catholics in this country. He asked Taft to get for him further information concerning the real opinion of leading Catholic laymen in the Philippines as additional testimony to prove the government's position.[50] He also recognized that the settlement of other Philippine questions on a pro-Catholic basis might overcome the detrimental effects of the Mission to Rome. At this particular time he decided to put a Catholic on the Philippine Commission. He again asked prominent Catholics to defend himself and his Administration. To Eugene A. Philbin, of New York, he wrote, "As regards the friars, I am pained and concerned to find that a large number of Catholics seem to feel that the movement to get rid of the friars is in some way a movement against the Catholic Church by the government at Washington."[51] He wrote to Archbishop John Ireland, "I have been very indignant at the attacks that have been made, and indeed at many of the petitions that have come to me."[52] And to John Crane, of Baltimore, he pointed out, "In the first place, remember that in what we advocated doing at Rome we not only acted upon the request of Archbishop Ireland but with the cordial support of Cardinal Gibbons."[53] In answer to a specific Catholic protest he severely lectured James D. Fox, the secretary of a parish Holy Name Society in New York: "The United States authorities, as far as they are concerned, have not the slightest feeling against the friars. But it is simply foolish to ignore what is practically the unanimous will of the Catholics of the parishes in which the friars once were."[54] In addition to these letters the President encouraged two American Augustinian friars to pioneer a movement to send American priests out to the Philippines to replace the Spaniards.[55]

Fortunately for the Roosevelt Administration, many Catholics de-

[50] *Ibid.*

[51] Roosevelt, Oyster Bay, July 16, 1902, to Eugene A. Philbin, *ibid.*, p. 296.

[52] Roosevelt, Oyster Bay, July 23, 1902, to Ireland, Roosevelt Correspondence, Letterbooks, Box 143.

[53] Roosevelt, Oyster Bay, July 31, 1902, to John Crane, Morison (ed.), *Letters of Roosevelt,* III, 306.

[54] Roosevelt, Oyster Bay, July 21, 1902, to Fox, Roosevelt Correspondence, Letterbooks, Box 143.

[55] Boston *Pilot,* September 27, 1902, p. 5.

fended the President. Archbishop Ireland already had addressed the Chicago Convention of the Federation of American Catholic Societies. In late July he held a press conference in St. Paul in which he enthusiastically praised Roosevelt: "Never . . . [has there been] in the White House a man more fair-minded and impartial in religious matters than Theodore Roosevelt." He insisted that the Taft Mission was genuine proof of this fair-mindedness.[56] Throughout the late summer and early autumn of 1902 he made further speeches and interviews on behalf of the President and his policies.[57] Another influential Catholic, a Republican from Wilmington, Delaware, William M. Byrne, was quoted at great length in the *Catholic World:* "The most cordial relations now exist between the two great parties to this question, and if a rupture comes I hope it cannot be traced to the intemperate utterances of Catholic Americans."[58]

A large segment of the Catholic press began to accept the Roosevelt position. The *Catholic World* heaped praise and confidence on the Administration, complimenting it on the sincerity of purpose behind the Taft Mission.[59] The Boston *Pilot* eagerly followed developments in Rome and came to the conclusion that "the Pope and President Roosevelt equally recognize the inevitable."[60] In August the *Pilot* printed the story of the Pope's statements concerning the Taft Mission and then commented, "When the Pope and the President are satisfied, the Catholics in America have no cause to complain."[61] The non-Catholic press, too, went all out in defense of Taft and Roosevelt. *The Independent* claimed that too much of the Catholic press was unfair to the government and was "more Papal than the Pope" on the friar question.[62]

Opinion of Taft and Roosevelt was also high at the Vatican. Taft's friendly negotiations over the friar lands manifested the American spirit of cooperation. And, the willingness of Roosevelt to practically bend over backwards in favor of Catholics in the Philippines prompted the Papacy to meet the Americans halfway. In January,

[56] *Ibid.,* August 2, 1902, p. 5.

[57] Ireland, St. Paul, September 6, 1902, to Maria Storer, Maria Storer (ed.), *In Memoriam,* p. 71.

[58] *Catholic World,* LXXV (September, 1902), 847–850.

[59] *Ibid.* (August, 1902), p. 701.

[60] Boston *Pilot,* July 12, 1902, p. 4.

[61] *Ibid.,* August 23, 1902, p. 4.

[62] *The Independent,* LIV (August 7, 1902), 1913.

1903, Leo XIII issued an encyclical directed to the Church in the Philippines. In this letter he set up a whole new Philippine hierarchy, divorced entirely from Spanish clerical authority. He created four new dioceses to add to the existing three dioceses and archdiocese, and placed them all under the authority of the archbishop of Manila, who was to be known as a "Metropolitan" and was to be directly responsible to Rome. Leo also directed that each diocese establish a seminary to encourage the training of natives for the priesthood, and that a pontifical university be made from the Catholic University at Manila. "Above all things," he warned, "the clergy should hold to the rule that they are not to allow themselves to be mixed up in party strifes. . . . We deem it necessary that men in holy orders in the present condition of affairs in the Philippine Islands should avoid this in a special manner."[63] To encourage further cooperation, Leo allowed the remaining Spanish bishops to resign, and filled all of the vacancies, including the new ones, with American clergymen. When he found that the appointment of Donatus Sbaretti as apostolic delegate to Manila was not satisfactory to Taft and Root he offered the name of Giovanni Guidi instead.[64] By such actions the Pope indicated that he was satisfied with affairs in the Philippines. Bishop O'Gorman assured Roosevelt that there should be no reason for any further attack on him and Taft, or their policies, in the Catholic press.[65]

Adverse Catholic opinion soon abated after the November, 1902, election. With the promulgation of Pope Leo's encyclical on the Philippine Church in January, the air cleared for serious negotiations between the Apostolic Delegate and Governor Taft. Negotiations started immediately after the first of the year. But by April, Governor Taft was discouraged over the slow progress. Apparently the friars were not cooperating in supplying Archbishop Guidi with the necessary information as to surveys, titles, and deeds. According to Taft, "[The friars fear] that the Pope will take all the money, as he will, for the Philippine Church and they are anxious to defeat him in this. . . . Guidi is very vigorously hated by the friars and this

[63] Leo XIII, "The Church in the Philippines," *American Catholic Quarterly Review,* XXVIII (April, 1903), 373–377.

[64] Ireland, St. Paul, March 29, 1902, to Maria Storer, Maria Storer (ed.), *In Memoriam,* p. 66.

[65] O'Gorman, Sioux Falls, October 17, 1902, to Roosevelt, Roosevelt Correspondence, Vol. 75.

attitude of the friars towards him makes him correspondingly popular with the better class of Filipinos."[66] As late as June, Taft reported to Secretary Root that the friars were still hampering the Delegate.

Not until the summer of 1903 was there any revival of Catholic agitation on colonial questions. This was brought on by another letter from the Philippines. Published widely in the Catholic press, it told how some American Catholics residing in the Philippines had petitioned Archbishop Guidi to allow the friars to remain in the Islands.[67] This new letter aroused Catholic opinion again and momentarily revived the friar issue in the press. The additional fact that negotiations over the Church property were going slowly added further force to the argument that the government was deliberately pursuing a negative attitude toward the Church in the Islands. The *Monitor,* failing to revive strong popular agitation, was quite disgusted with the apparent indifference of American Catholics who, it claimed, continued "mute under every provocation."[68] As usual the agitation worried Roosevelt, for he tried again to explain to Catholics why his government was following its particular policies. He could not understand why, after all his efforts on their behalf, they still would not accept what had been done and was being done.[69] Despite these isolated criticisms, Roosevelt found encouragement and satisfaction in a letter from Cardinal Gibbons:

> I have every hope that the religious conflict will be appeased. . . . The sources of my confidence lie in the judicial temper of Commissioner Smith, the arrival of the Bishops at their respective posts and the calm conciliatory temper of Mgr. Guidi, the Apostolic Delegate; and above all the earnest desire of yourself and your administration to be guided by a lofty sense of justice and impartiality.[70]

While Roosevelt was meeting renewed criticisms in the United States, Taft was developing a great respect for Guidi. In order to

[66] Taft, Bangino, Benguet, P. I., April 14, 1903, to Root, Taft Private and Official Correspondence, Letterpress Books, Box 1.

[67] San Francisco *Monitor,* June 27, 1903, p. 242.

[68] *Ibid.,* May 2, 1903, p. 84.

[69] Roosevelt, Oyster Bay, July 31, 1903, to Ireland, Roosevelt Correspondence, Letterbooks, Box 145, Vol. 11.

[70] Gibbons, Baltimore, December 2, 1903, to Roosevelt, Gibbons Correspondence, Box 100.

speed up the negotiations he decided to help the Archbishop work out a compromise.[71] The chief difficulty was the inability to determine the actual monetary evaluation of the friars' holdings. Taft felt that the demands of the friars were exorbitant; and although he might raise his original offer of $5,000,000, he could not possibly meet the friars' price.[72] Unfortunately negotiations were delayed further by the death of Leo XIII in the early summer of 1903, and they were not resumed again until after the election of the new Pope, Pius X, and issuance of his instructions to continue on the basis accepted by his predecessor. Surprisingly, Pius' Administration seemed to speed up affairs, even though his Secretary of State, Cardinal Merry del Val, was a Spaniard. In September, Archbishop Guidi informed the Governor that $10,700,000 was the lowest possible figure that he could get from the friars.[73] Taft, although willing to go beyond his original figure, still felt the Philippine government could not go to the extremes requested by the friars. Nevertheless, through Archbishop Guidi's efforts they finally reached a compromise and Taft agreed to pay $7,239,000 for 410,000 acres of land.[74] Preliminary contracts were signed December 22, 1903, and final purchase was to be made subject to new accurate surveys.[75]

The most difficult of all the Philippine Church-state problems had finally been settled. The way was now clear to take up the remaining ones. Even though the land purchase had been intended originally as a means to eliminate the Spanish friars, the negotiations, of course, as finally decided upon, ignored these priests. The question of their presence gradually disappeared. At the beginning of the controversy over the friars in 1898, according to an official census, 1,013 friars were in the Islands. By the end of 1903, when the land question was settled, this number had fallen to 246.[76] This reduction resulted from a combination of factors: the normal loss of men through death or retirement, death caused by native hostilities, and the voluntary return to Spain of individual friars. Of those who did

[71] Taft, Bagino, Benguet, P. I., June 15, 1903, to Root, Taft Private and Official Correspondence, Letterpress Books, Box 1.

[72] Pringle (ed.), *Life and Times of Taft,* I, 227.

[73] *Ibid.,* p. 230.

[74] *Fourth Report of the Philippine Commission, 1903* (House Document No. 2, Vol. 6, 58th Cong., 2nd Sess.), p. 43.

[75] *Ibid.,* p. 28.

[76] *Ibid.,* p. 45.

remain in the Islands most stayed in Manila, where they ministered to the rapidly increasing nonnative colony. A few did return to their native parishes, where they were received with a minimum of friction.

The settlement of the friars' lands was hailed in the United States as an indication of the patience and skill of William Howard Taft. Archbishop Ireland congratulated President Roosevelt because the Governor had removed "all further room for agitation in the States or in the Islands."[77] The Boston *Pilot* called the termination of the Philippine difficulties the result of "President Roosevelt's Wise Policy."[78] *The Independent* also praised the Administration as well as Governor Taft.[79] Taft's success as an administrator and diplomat in the Philippines was part of the reason why President Roosevelt decided to recall him to Washington to replace retiring Elihu Root as Secretary of War. In January, 1904, William Howard Taft took up his new duties and turned over the governorship of the Philippines to Luke E. Wright, who had been vice-governor since 1900. Even the San Francisco *Monitor* now joined with the ranks in praise of Governor Wright. Its editor wrote:

> From all accounts no better selection of a successor to Judge Taft as Governor of the Philippines, could have been suggested than that made by President Roosevelt. General Luke Wright appears to possess the necessary experience, temperament and qualifications to discharge the important duties of the office intelligently and with a conscientious regard for the best interests of the natives as well as the American proprietary.[80]

Certainly Roosevelt, his Administration, and his policies had come a long way in the favor of American Catholic press opinion. The ultimate success of the Taft Mission in Rome and Manila ended any serious reasons for Catholic antagonism on colonial questions. Although never entirely silent, the Catholic press never again took up the cudgel against officials in Washington and Manila as it had done in the years between 1898 and 1903.

This does not mean, of course, that all the religious difficulties were solved before Governor Taft left the Islands, but he had laid

[77] Ireland, St. Paul, December 23, 1903, to Roosevelt, Roosevelt Correspondence, Box 65.

[78] Boston *Pilot,* January 2, 1904, p. 1.

[79] *The Independent,* LVI (February 18, 1904), 390–392.

[80] San Francisco *Monitor,* January 9, 1904, p. 281.

the groundwork for smoother negotiations on the other issues. Next important on the agenda was the settlement of rentals of Church-owned buildings occupied by United States troops. Governor Wright and Archbishop Guidi continued negotiations on a friendly basis and were reaching a compromise agreement. The untimely death of the Archbishop in June, 1904, however, prevented a final settlement until a new delegate could be sent out. Taft, as Secretary of War still responsible for affairs in the Philippines and still interested in them, considered the death of Archbishop Guidi a personal loss.[81] While in Washington he continued to cultivate the friendships he had made among the clergy in Rome. Reminding papal Secretary of State Cardinal Merry del Val that a new apostolic delegate should be quickly sent to Manila to solve the remaining difficulties, he wrote:

> Your Eminence will understand that while the Philippine Government may not contribute to the support of the Roman Catholic Church of the islands, it is deeply interested in a restoration of the church to a condition of prosperity and increased usefulness, because the happiness and welfare of a large majority of the Philippine people are closely connected with the Roman Catholic Church.[82]

Before the end of 1904 the major problems in the Philippines were in the process of being settled or were already settled. Catholic opinion on the issue, such as it was, appeared satisfied, and little more was heard, even though the American government stuck to its original policies. Why had Catholic opinion apparently changed so quickly? Several factors may indicate an answer. For one thing, Catholics in general were actually not very much interested in the issues. The tongue-lashings in the Catholic press over Catholic indifference attested to this fact. Without popular Catholic support on each issue the Catholic press had to back down. The hierarchy was split over the role the Church should play in colonial questions. The open debate between Bishop McFaul and Archbishop Ireland since the summer and fall of 1902 was certainly not conducive to organizing any effective unity among Catholics or their clergy. The political potential of the Roman Catholic Church in the United States therefore was never fully utilized, either through its hierarchy or through

[81] Cable: Taft, Washington, June 25, 1904, to Merry del Val, Private and Official Correspondence, Letterpress Books, Box 16.

[82] Taft, Washington, August 3, 1904, to Merry del Val, *ibid.*, Box 2.

its millions of members. On specific issues, such as the Brooke marriage law or the hiring of teachers in the Philippines, certainly enough Catholic strength appeared at the right time to demand and get some pro-Catholic action. How much of this acquiescence to Catholic opinion was caused by fear of a Catholic vote is open to conjecture. The facts that the settlement of the Brooke marriage law was rushed before the elections of 1900, and that the announcement of the appointment of James F. Smith as a member of the Philippine Commission was made in late October, 1902, lend plausibility to this conclusion.

Perhaps the greatest factor that contributed to the changing attitude of the Catholics was the performance of the Roosevelt Administration itself. As an experienced politician the President knew what issues were critical and how to win votes. As a man attempting to be fair Theodore Roosevelt apparently inspired confidence among Catholics. Certainly by the election of 1904 Catholic agitation had all but disappeared. This respect for Roosevelt came from his direct handling of the most controversial religious questions. By sending Governor Taft to Rome to negotiate with the Pope over the land issue in the Philippines, the President used a just procedure. If the Pope was satisfied then Catholics would also be satisfied. The Taft Mission to Rome thus became the climax of Roosevelt's colonial policies as far as Catholics in the United States were concerned.

Though the Catholic Church had a new problem in the Philippines—arising from the schism in the native or Philippine Catholic Church, known as the Aglipayan movement—the relationship between the United States government and the Roman Catholic Church vastly improved as a result of the Taft Mission.[83] The attitude of Governor Taft was maintained by his successor in a spirit of cooperativeness. As Secretary of War, Taft continued his friendliness toward the hierarchy and in June, 1904, he was able to return the hospitality that Cardinal Francis Satolli had shown him during his stay in Rome. Satolli had come to the United States as the new apostolic delegate to the American clergy. Both Taft and Roosevelt felt that in some manner official recognition of the Apostolic Delegate should be made. To do this, Taft invited members of the Eastern hierarchy and well-known Catholic laymen to a dinner party in

[83] See James A. Robertson, "The Aglipay Schism in the Philippine Islands," *Catholic Historical Review*, IV (October, 1918), 315–344.

the Delegate's honor.[84] The Cardinal could indicate how warm the relations actually were between the United States government and the Vatican. Speaking as the official representative of Pius X, he thanked Taft for the hospitality and then carefully pointed out what the Vatican thought about the final settlements in the Philippines:

Again, may it be pleasing to His Excellency Mr. Taft to accept the tribute of a grateful heart for all the great good he has done in the government of the Philippines, with admirable equity and prudence, and for his respect and deference, as far as it was in his power, for the interests of Catholicity in those islands which, under the wings of the American eagle, already feel the warmth of a new life, and which give promise of the most happy future, both political and civil, intellectual and Christian.[85]

[84] Taft, Washington, June 14, 1904, to Patrick J. Ryan, to Gibbons, to James Farley, *et al.*, Taft Private and Official Correspondence, Letterpress Books, Box 2.

[85] "Speech of Cardinal Satolli," June 20, 1904, *ibid.*, Box 87.

BIBLIOGRAPHICAL ESSAY

Research concerning the history of the Catholic Church in the United States at the turn of the century has been limited not so much by a scarcity of material as by a scattering of it. Ascertaining the opinion and the activities of the hierarchy becomes almost a monumental task because the higher clergy were inconsistent in the practices of preserving their personal records. Diocesan records—baptismal, death, ordination, etc.—are carefully preserved, but not so the kind of information that reflects the Church as a force for political action. Only a few of the bishops preserved the correspondence that they received and fewer still made copies of that which they sent; that correspondence which has been preserved is scattered across the country in the archives of a hundred and more American dioceses. For the correspondence of those members of the clergy who were direct participants in affairs pertaining to the Spanish-American War it was necessary to turn to the collections of their letters deposited in the archives of the last diocese over which each had jurisdiction. From these papers emerges a rather sketchy knowledge of the opinions of the clergy.

James Cardinal Gibbons as primate of the Church in the United States was both moderator between Catholic conservatives and progressives and also official spokesman for the American Church to the Papacy and to the government of the United States. His papers, deposited in the Chancery of the Archdiocese of Baltimore, are a rich source of correspondence representing personal opinions, requests for aid, suggestions of policy, and reports of action already taken. These archives also contain the minutes of the Annual Meetings of the Catholic Bishops of the United States, in themselves important as indicators of official Church policies. The other prominent cleric with a role of official spokesman for the Church was Placide L. Chapelle, appointed apostolic delegate to Cuba, Puerto Rico, and the Philippines while still remaining Archbishop of New Orleans.

Unfortunately the collection of his papers in the Chancery at New Orleans is brief and limited by long gaps, especially for the crucial years between 1902 and 1904. However, the best record of his views and activities pertinent to this study is given in his correspondence with General Elwell S. Otis, published as part of the congressional document, *Report of Major General Otis, Commanding the Army of the Philippines.* Although he acted in no official capacity, Archbishop John Ireland, of St. Paul, was the most vocal member of the hierarchy. He scribbled off notes to almost everyone who was concerned with colonial matters. The result is that his views are more widely scattered among the manuscript collections of his contemporaries than in the vast number of his papers which are in the archdiocesan archives of St. Paul. Ireland's protégé Bishop Thomas O'Gorman, of Sioux Falls, played a brief but significant role when he accompanied the Taft Mission to Rome in 1902. A few of his letters pertinent to the Mission are in the archives of Catholic University in Washington, D.C. But the most valuable of the collections is the correspondence received by Bishop Denis J. O'Connell which are in the archives of the Diocese of Richmond (Virginia). During the colonial period O'Connell was vicar of Gibbons' titular church in Trastevere, Italy. In this capacity he was expected to keep the American hierarchy informed of events in Rome and at the same time to be informed by them of events in the United States. He became the recipient of a steady flow of correspondence from prominent clerics in the United States, especially from Archbishop John Ireland.

Fortunately, the attitudes and opinions of the policy-makers in the United States government are easier to ascertain. The Manuscripts Division of the Library of Congress provides the personal papers of Presidents William McKinley and Theodore Roosevelt as well as the private and official papers of Governor William Howard Taft. During the period of April, 1900, to October, 1903, Taft wrote biweekly informal reports to Secretary of War Elihu Root; letterbook copies of these are in his semi-official correspondence, deposited with the Philippine Commission Papers among the Bureau of Insular Affairs Records kept in the National Archives in Washington. This is also the location of the papers of General Leonard Wood, military governor of Cuba. Much of the official correspondence involving representatives of the United States has been published by the government either as separate items or as congressional documents. Several of these are extremely important, for they include letters and cablegrams sent and received by the military governors of the dependencies. Most valuable are *Correspondence Relating to the War with Spain, April 15, 1898 to July 30, 1902,* edited by the Adjutant General of the Army, and *Conduct of War Department in the War with Spain,* published as a Senate document. Of particular importance for the initial statement of U.S. religious policy vis-à-vis the dependencies are *Correspondence Relating to the Treaty with Spain* and *Treaty of Peace between the United States and Spain and Accompanying Papers.*

Best sources of information concerning policy making and day-to-day problems in each of the dependencies are separate series of reports published by the government. Among the items listed in the Bibliography the most valuable for Cuba are General Leonard Wood's twelve-volume *Civil Report of Major-General Leonard Wood, Military Governor of Cuba, 1900* and General J. R. Brooke's *Civil Affairs in Cuba;* for Puerto Rico, *Report of the United States Insular Commission to the Secretary of War upon Investigations Made into Civil Affairs of the Island of Porto Rico,* and, of particular interest, *Disposition of Church Lands in Porto Rico.*

Because of the political interest within the United States over the controversy concerning permanent annexation of the Philippine Islands, Congress was quite prolific in calling for and publishing a wide variety of reports and collections of documents pertaining to almost every aspect of life in the Islands. In addition to the first six issues of the *Annual Report of the Philippine Commission,* for the years 1899–1904, published as Senate or House documents, the most informative of these specialized reports are *Communications Between the Executive Departments of Government and Aguinaldo, etc.* and *Charges of Cruelty, etc. to the Natives of the Philippines,* because they indicate the source for the Administration's view that the Filipinos insisted on the removal of the Spanish friars. On the highly complex subject of Church-held property the most complete sets of documents are published in: *Education in the Philippine Islands, Papers Relating to Friars' Land Negotiations,* and *Lands Held for Ecclesiastical or Religious Uses in the Philippine Islands.*

Of secondary importance, but perhaps only slightly less valuable as sources concerning the thinking of the leading participants discussed in this study, are the published editions of their letters and autobiographical materials. The most numerous of these pertain to

Theodore Roosevelt: Elting E. Morison's edition of *The Letters of Theodore Roosevelt;* Joseph Bucklin Bishop's *Theodore Roosevelt and His Time Shown in His Own Letters;* Henry Cabot Lodge's *Selections from the Correspondence of Theodore Roosevelt and Henry Cabot Lodge;* and John Joseph Gallagher's "The Theodore Roosevelt Letters to Cardinal Gibbons," *Catholic Historical Review.* There are no published collections of Taft papers for this period, but Henry F. Pringle's *The Life and Times of William Howard Taft* contains some of Taft's letters to members of his family that are not available elsewhere. Mrs. William Howard Taft's reminiscences of her stay in Manila are described in her *Recollections of Full Years.* These give fairly important descriptions of Taft's contact with the Filipinos and their problems. The best available indications of what Governor Taft felt that he was doing are given in several articles which he wrote for American periodicals. The most significant of these are "Civil Government in the Philippines," *Outlook,* LXXI (May 31, 1902) and "The Philippines," *National Geographic Magazine,* XVI (August, 1905).

Published collections of the works of others supplemented the sources for the period. By far the most valuable is the collection of the letters of the Bellamy Storers, *In Memoriam Bellamy Storer,* edited and privately published by Maria Longworth Storer after her husband's death. Although Bellamy Storer had nothing to do with the forming of colonial policy, both he and his wife were in the middle of an interesting stream of communication. Zealous Catholic converts and active Republicans, they corresponded with almost everyone of importance during the period, including Roosevelt, Taft, Root, Gibbons, and Ireland. Some of the letters presumably not expected to be preserved, especially Roosevelt's, are most informative because they are quite candid. In addition to these collections, the published addresses of Elihu Root indicate the overall sentiments of the Roosevelt Administration; these appear as *The Military and Colonial Policy of the United States: Addresses and Reports of Elihu Root,* edited by Robert Bacon and James Brown Scott. William Roscoe Thayer's *Life and Letters of John Hay* indicates some of the general concern for the colonies in relation to foreign policy. H. Wayne Morgan's recent edition of Whitelaw Reid's running memoir of the peace conference, *Making Peace With Spain: The Diary of Whitelaw Reid,* is interesting but not vital, for it indicates among the peacemakers no thought of future religious problems. It has but two references to Archbishop Chapelle, although he was a continuous observer of the negotiations. Perhaps somewhat prejudiced but nonetheless valuable is Dean C. Worcester's *The Philippines: Past and Present.* Written mainly as a memoir of his years in the Philippine government, it remained as hostile to the Catholic Church as his previous study (1890) of the Islands. Of an opposite, but no less prejudiced, view is Archbishop John Ireland's *The Church and Modern Society.* In this, Ireland, who was considered one of the most liberal members of the Catholic hierarchy, presents his opinions of the Church's role, but gives little indication of his personal activities on its behalf. Ireland also wrote frequently in the non-Catholic press such articles as "The Religious Conditions in Our New Island Territory," *Outlook,* LXII (August 26, 1899).

Contemporary periodicals represented a reasonable cross section of public opinion. In this context the religious newspapers are more valuable than the secular press. Most of the Catholic newspapers, however, were independent of diocesan control and therefore usually reflected only the opinion of the editor and not that of the bishop or an influential lay society. Many Catholic papers were published in this period, but the current journalistic practice of reprinting editorials from other newspapers somewhat simplified the measuring of Catholic press attitudes. The three newspapers selected as principal sources for this study—Boston *Pilot, New York Freeman's Journal,* and San Francisco *Monitor*—were the most outspoken critics of the Administration among the Catholic press and consequently are significant not necessarily for reflecting a genuine nationwide Catholic opinion but rather because the Administration thought they reflected such opinion. Several other Catholic journals, however, indicate a wider range of Catholic thinking; among these the most important are *American Catholic Quarterly Review,* which was generally anti-Administration, and *Catholic World,* which remained fairly loyal to Roosevelt and his policies. Non-Catholic religious periodicals, too, represent a wide range of opinion. The most dispassionate are *The Independent, Outlook, The Christian Advocate,* and *The Living Church.* The more outspoken, and the more anti-Catholic, are *Home Mission Monthly* and *Methodist Review.* For representation of the secular press the best sources and reporting on colonial religious questions are in *North American Review, The Century Magazine,* and *Forum.* Of the daily newspapers the *New York Times* and the New York *Evening Post* have fairer and more thorough coverage of controversial events, particularly concerning the desecration of churches in the Philippines.

Monographic and biographical studies pertaining to the era of the Spanish-American War are numerous, although unfortunately spotty in the treatment of religious issues. For this reason the two best biographies are Margaret Leech's *In the Days of McKinley* and John Tracy Ellis' *The Life of James Cardinal Gibbons, Archbishop of Baltimore, 1838–1921.* James H. Moynihan's *The Life of Archbishop Ireland* and Sister Agnes Claire Schroll's *The Social Thought of John Lancaster Spalding* are scholarly, but give perhaps a too Catholic account of the ideas and activities of these two prominent clerics. Because of its obvious overly Catholic sentiment, one of the most disappointing works is Frederick Zwierlein's *Theodore Roosevelt and Catholics.* Important to the background of the activities of Catholics in this period are three fairly thorough biographies: Sister Marie Carolyn Klinkhamer's *Edward Douglas White, Chief Justice of the United States;* Patrick H. Ahern's *The Life of John J. Keane, Educator and Archbishop, 1839–1918;* and Frederick Zwierlein's *The Life and Letters of Bishop McQuaid.*

Several good studies consider the relationships of the Catholic Church in the United States to the rest of the community. These are essential for a thorough understanding of the internal dissension within the Church structure and the extensive pressure exerted on the Church from external sources. Among the most helpful, in a chronological sequence, are: Vincent J. Holden's study of the founder of the Paulists, *The Yankee Paul: Isaac Thomas Hecker;* Henry J. Browne's *The Catholic Church and the Knights of Labor;* Colman J. Barry's *The Catholic Church and German Americans;* and Thomas J. McAvoy's *The Great Crisis in American Catholic History, 1895–1900,* an extremely thorough treatment of the Americanism controversy, which so divided the hierarchy. The impact of organized anti-Catholicism is best described in three fairly recent objective works: Ray A. Billington's *The Protestant Crusade, 1800–1860;* John Higham's *Strangers in the Land: Patterns of American Nativism, 1860–1925;* and Donald L. Kinzer's *An Episode in Anti-Catholicism: The American Protective Association.* An older study, *The A.P.A. Movement,* although perhaps not as objective, is valuable because its author, Humphrey J. Desmond, was a contemporary Catholic journalist and an active combatant of the A.P.A. A modern overall discussion of church-state matters is presented by Anson

Phelps Stokes in *Church and State in the United States,* although he barely touches on colonial questions. The same is true of John Tracy Ellis' *American Catholicism,* which is the best survey history of the Church in the United States, but it entirely ignores the religious issues incident to the Spanish-American War.

Of the many investigations regarding the War itself, only a few concern the deeper issues involved in it. Julius W. Pratt in his *Expansionists of 1898* discusses the general attitude of American churches toward Spanish Catholicism, but does not break down the study by religious groups. William A. Karraker's unpublished dissertation, "The American Churches and the Spanish-American War," analyzes the subject much more thoroughly, examining all the major denominations. M. M. Wilkerson's *Public Opinion and the Spanish-American War* is important for a view of general opinion; unfortunately it has little reference to the opinions of the churches. A very colorful and somewhat cynical account of the attitude of Americans toward Spain, Cuba, and war was given in Walter Millis' *The Martial Spirit.* Quite different is Orestes Ferrara's *The Last Spanish War,* which presents the Cuban viewpoint. Recent studies of the period add new interpretations to the age of imperialism and are therefore useful, but all of them seem to ignore any concern for Catholic opinion among Republican party leadership. Ernest R. May's *Imperial Democracy: The Emergence of America as a Great Power* treats the background and build-up of American expansionism, while H. Wayne Morgan's *William McKinley and His America* concentrates more on McKinley's role and attempts to be more sympathetic than Margaret Leech's biography.

Most of the literature referring to American involvement in the several dependencies mentions only briefly the religious aspects. Several works, however, are valuable discussions of the details of the American occupation. Of these the most thorough is Henry P. Beers' *American Naval Occupation and Government of Guam, 1898–1902.* For the Philippines the best-balanced treatment is in James A. LeRoy's *The Americans in the Philippines: A History of the Conquest and First Years of Occupation.* Other authors on the Philippines, stimulated by the controversy that developed over the idea of permanent annexation of the Islands, produce an interesting variety of partisan writing. The most important criticism of American policy is Moorfield Storey's and M. P. Lichanco's *The Conquest of the Philippine Islands by the United States, 1898–1925.* The Filipino point of view is well analyzed in Maximo M. Kalaw's *Self-Government in the Philippines.* Defenders of occupation policies were most often Americans who had served in the Philippine civil government. The first of these and, therefore, the most important to this study is Jacob Gould Schurman's *Philippine Affairs: A Retrospect and Outlook.* Fred W. Atkinson, somewhat disappointed in his experiences as an educator in the Islands, discusses the problems confronting the Americans in *The Philippine Islands.* Two other participants offer later and fairer defenses of U.S. policy. James Henderson Blount, a district judge in the Islands during the early years, expresses his views in *The American Occupation of the Philippines, 1898–1912* and William Cameron Forbes, a former civil governor, took advantage of the perspective of the time in *The Philippine Islands,* written in 1928.

Too little research on specific situations of Catholic relationships to the War has been published in scholarly journals. The few such articles available are therefore noteworthy because of their appearance. An all-too-brief survey of Catholic attitudes toward the War is Benjamin J. Blied's "Catholic Aspects of the Spanish-American War," *Social Justice Review,* XVIII (August, 1933). But a very informative long article is George Barton's "A Story of Self-Sacrifice. Being a Record of the Labors of the Catholic Sisterhoods in the Spanish-American War," *American Catholic Historical Society Records,* XXXVII (September, 1926). The only survey of the activities of the Taft Mission to Rome is given in Edward F. Goss' "The Taft Commission to the Vatican, 1902," *American Catholic Historical Society Records,* XLVI (September, 1935). A recent article derived from the research of the present study is Frank T. Reuter's "American Catholics and the Establishment of the Philippine Public School System," *Catholic Historical Review,* XLIX (October, 1963).

BIBLIOGRAPHY

PRIMARY SOURCES

Unpublished Correspondence

Chapelle, Placide L., Archbishop of New Orleans. Correspondence. Archives of Archdiocese of New Orleans, Chancery, New Orleans, Louisiana.

Gibbons, James Cardinal, Archbishop of Baltimore. Correspondence. Archives of Archdiocese of Baltimore, Chancery, Baltimore, Maryland.

McKinley, William. Correspondence. Manuscripts Division, Library of Congress, Washington, D.C.

O'Connell, Denis J., Bishop of Richmond. Correspondence. Archives of Diocese of Richmond, Chancery, Richmond, Virginia.

O'Gorman, Thomas, Bishop of Sioux Falls. Correspondence. Archives of Catholic University, Washington, D.C.

Roosevelt, Theodore. Correspondence. Manuscripts Division, Library of Congress, Washington, D.C.

Taft, William Howard. Private and Official Correspondence. Manuscripts Division, Library of Congress, Washington, D.C.

———. Semi-Official Correspondence. Philippine Commission Papers, Bureau of Insular Affairs Records, National Archives, Washington, D.C.

Wood, General Leonard. Unpublished Correspondence. Bureau of Insular Affairs Records, National Archives, Washington, D.C.

———. Correspondence. Manuscripts Division, Library of Congress, Washington, D.C.

Published Personal Documents, Memoirs, Diaries, Correspondence, Directories

Atkinson, Fred W. *The Philippine Islands*. New York: Ginn and Company, 1905.

Bacon, Robert, and James Brown Scott, eds. *The Military and Colonial Policy of the United States: Addresses and Reports of Elihu Root*. Cambridge, Massachusetts: Harvard University Press, 1916.

Bishop, Joseph Bucklin, ed. *Theodore Roosevelt and His Time Shown in His Own Letters*. 2 vols. New York: Scribner's, 1920.

Dawes, Charles C. *A Journal of the McKinley Years* (Bascom N. Timmons, ed.). Chicago: Lakeside Press, 1950.

Ellis, John Tracy, ed. *Documents of American Catholic History*. Milwaukee: Bruce Publishing Company, 1956.

Gallagher, John Joseph, ed. "The Theodore Roosevelt Letters to Cardinal Gibbons," *Catholic Historical Review*, XLIV (January, 1959), 440–456.

Ireland, John. *The Church and Modern Society*. St. Paul, Minnesota: Pioneer Press, 1905.

Lodge, Henry Cabot, ed. *Selections from the Correspondence of Theodore Roosevelt and Henry Cabot Lodge*. 2 vols. New York: Scribner's, 1925.

Morgan, H. Wayne, ed. *Making Peace with Spain: The Diary of Whitelaw Reid*. Austin: University of Texas Press, 1965.

Morison, Elting E., ed. *The Letters of Theodore Roosevelt*. 8 vols. Cambridge, Massachusetts: Harvard University Press, 1951–1954.

Official Catholic Directory. New York: P. J. Kenedy, 1898–1905.

Pringle, Henry Fawles, ed. *The Life and Times of William Howard Taft*. 2 vols. New York: Farrar and Rinehart, 1939.

Roosevelt, Theodore. *Theodore Roosevelt: An Autobiography*. New York: Scribner's, 1929.

———. *The Works of Theodore Roosevelt: Presidential Addresses and State Papers*. 24 vols. New York: P. F. Collier and Son, 1917.

Schurman, Jacob Gould. *Philippine Affairs: A Retrospect and Outlook*. New York: Scribner's, 1902.

Storer, Maria Longworth, ed. *In Memoriam Bellamy Storer*. Boston: privately published, 1923.

Taft, Mrs. William Howard. *Recollections of Full Years*. New York: Dodd, Mead and Company, 1914.

Thayer, William Roscoe, ed. *Life and Letters of John Hay*. Boston: Houghton Mifflin, 1915.

Worcester, Dean C. *The Philippine Islands and Their People*. New York: Macmillan Company, 1898.

———. *The Philippines Past and Present*. New York: Macmillan Company, 1914.

Publications of the United States Government

The Bureau of the Census

Abstract of the Twelfth Census. Washington, D.C.: Government Printing Office, 1904.

Religious Bodies, 1906. 2 vols. Washington, D.C.: Government Printing Office, 1909.

The Congress

Congressional Record. 55th–58th Congresses. Washington, D.C.: Government Printing Office, 1898–1904.

HOUSE DOCUMENTS

Commission to Revise and Compile Laws of Porto Rico (House Document No. 52, 57th Congress, 1st Session, Serials 4372). Washington, D.C.: Government Printing Office, 1901.

Fifth Annual Report of the Philippine Commission, 1904 (House Document No. 232, 58th Congress, 3rd Session, Serials 4853). Washington, D.C.: Government Printing Office, 1904.

Fourth Report of the Philippine Commission, 1903 (House Document No. 2, Vol. 6, 58th Congress, 2nd Session, Serials 4632). Washington, D.C.: Government Printing Office, 1903.

Message of the President, December 5, 1899 (House Document No. 1, 56th Congress, 1st Session, Serials 3898). Washington, D.C.: Government Printing Office, 1899.

Papers Relating to Friars' Land Negotiations (House Document No. 2, Vol. 1, 57th Congress, 2nd Session, Serials 4443). Washington, D.C.: Government Printing Office, 1903.

Report of Major General J. R. Brooke on Civil Affairs in Cuba (House Document No. 2, Vol. 7, 56th Congress, 1st Session, Serials 3904). Washington, D.C.: Government Printing Office, 1900.

Report of Major General Otis, Commanding the Army of the Philippines (House Document No. 2, Vol. 5, 56th Congress, 1st Session, Serials 3902). Washington, D.C.: Government Printing Office, 1899.

Second Report of the Philippine Commission, 1901 (House Document No. 2, Vol. 9, 57th Congress, 1st Session, Serials 4276). Washington, D.C.: Government Printing Office, 1901.

Third Report of the Philippine Commission, 1902 (House Document No. 2, Vol. 13, 57th Congress, 2nd Session, Serials 4452). Washington, D.C.: Government Printing Office, 1903.

SENATE DOCUMENTS

Affairs in the Philippine Islands. Hearings before the Senate Committee on the Philippines (Senate Document No. 331, 57th Congress, 1st Session, Serials 4242–4244). 3 parts in separate volumes. Washington, D.C.: Government Printing Office, 1902.

Articles in Reference to Philippines Printed in the Singapore Free Press (Senate Document No. 95, 55th Congress, 3rd Session, Serials 3731). Washington, D.C.: Government Printing Office, 1899.

Charges of Cruelty, etc. to the Natives of the Philippines (Senate Document No. 205, 57th Congress, 1st Session, Serials 4233). Washington, D.C.: Government Printing Office, 1902.

Communications Between the Executive Departments of the Government and Aguinaldo, etc. (Senate Document No. 208, 56th Congress, 1st Session, Serials 3854). Washington, D.C.: Government Printing Office, 1900.

Conduct of War Department in the War with Spain (Senate Document No. 221, 56th Congress, 1st Session, Serials 3859–3866). 8 vols. Washington, D.C.: Government Printing Office, 1900.

Correspondence Relating to the Treaty with Spain (Senate Document No. 148, 56th Congress, 2nd Session, Serials 4039). Washington, D.C.: Government Printing Office, 1901.

Disposition of Church Lands in Porto Rico (Senate Report No. 2977, 57th Congress, 2nd Session, Serials 4412). Washington, D.C.: Government Printing Office, 1903.

Education in the Philippine Islands (Senate Document No. 129, 56th Congress, 2nd Session, Serials 4039). Washington, D.C.: Government Printing Office, 1901.

First Annual Report of the Governor of Porto Rico (Senate Document No. 79, 57th Congress, 1st Session, Serials 4228). Washington, D.C.: Government Printing Office, 1901.

First Philippine Commission (Schurman) Report (Senate Document No. 138, 56th Congress, 1st Session, Serials 3885). Washington, D.C.: Government Printing Office, 1900.

Government for the Island of Porto Rico. Hearings before the Senate Committee on Pacific Islands and Porto Rico (Senate Document No. 147, 56th Congress, 1st Session, Serials 3851). Washington, D.C.: Government Printing Office, 1900.

Lands Held for Ecclesiastical or Religious Uses in the Philippine Islands (Senate Document No. 190, 56th Congress, 2nd Session, Serials 4040). Washington, D.C.: Government Printing Office, 1901.

Political Affairs in the Philippine Islands (Senate Document No. 259, 57th Congress, 1st Session, Serials 4235). Washington, D.C.: Government Printing Office, 1902.

Reports of the Taft Philippine Commission (Senate Document No. 112, 56th Congress, 2nd Session, Serials 4040). Washington, D.C.: Government Printing Office, 1901.

Treaty of Peace between the United States and Spain and Accompanying Papers (Senate Document No. 62, 55th Congress, 3rd Session, Serials 3732). Washington, D.C.: Government Printing Office, 1899.

The Department of State

Foreign Relations of the United States, 1898, 1899, 1901, 1902, 1903, 1904. Washington, D.C.: Government Printing Office, 1901, 1902, 1903, 1904, 1905, 1906, 1907.

The Department of War

Adjutant General of the Army, ed. *Correspondence Relating to the War with Spain. April 15, 1898 to July 30, 1902*. 2 vols. Washington, D.C.: Government Printing Office, 1902.

United States Insular Commission. *Report of the U.S. Insular Commission to the Secretary of War upon Investigations Made into the Civil Affairs of the Island of Porto Rico*. Washington, D.C.: Government Printing Office, 1899.

Wood, Major General Leonard, *Civil Report of Major-General Leonard Wood, Military Governor of Cuba, 1900*. 12 vols. Washington, D.C.: Government Printing Office, 1901.

Contemporary Periodicals

American Catholic Quarterly Review, 1895–1905.
Ave Maria, 1898, 1904.
Boston *Pilot*, 1895–1905.
Catholic Citizen, The, 1902.
Catholic World, 1895–1905.
Christian Advocate, The, 1896–1904.
Churchman, The, 1896–1904.
Collier's Weekly, 1898–1902.
Forum, 1898–1902.
Home Mission Monthly, 1898–1902.
Independent, The, 1896–1904.
Living Church, The, 1898–1902.
Methodist Review, 1898–1902.
Missionary Review of the World, 1898–1902.
New Century, The, 1902.
New York *Evening Post*, 1898–1903.
New York Freeman's Journal, 1895–1905.
New York Herald, 1898–1902.
New York Sun, 1898.
New York Times, 1898–1904.
North American Review, 1898–1905.
Outlook, 1895–1905.
San Francisco *Monitor*, 1898–1905.

Contemporary Articles

Alonso-Alonso, The Reverend A. "Religious Progress in Porto Rico," *Catholic World*, LXXVI (January, 1903), 445–452.

Atkinson, Fred W. "Education in the Philippines," *Atlantic Monthly*, LXXXIX (March, 1902), 360–365.

Bacon, Leonard Woolsey. "A Flaw in the Title?" *Outlook*, LXIII (November 18, 1899), 689–691.

Baldwin, Simeon E. "The Mission of Governor Taft to the Vatican," *Yale Law Journal,* XII (November, 1902), 1–7.

Baxter, Sylvester. "Cuban Teachers at Harvard University," *Outlook,* LXV (August 4, 1900), 773–782.

Bellessort, André. "A Week in the Philippines," *The Living Age,* CCXXI (May 20, 1899), 469–480.

Bonsal, Stephen. "The Work of the Friars," *North American Review,* CLXXV (October, 1902), 449–460.

Brent, Bishop C. H. "Bishop Brent on Religious Conditions in the Philippines," *Outlook,* LXXIV (August 22, 1903), 1004–1006.

———. "Religious Conditions in the Philippine Islands," *Missionary Review* of the World, XXVIII (January, 1905), 49–56.

Cantwell, Rev. William P. "Is the National Federation of Catholic Societies Desirable?" *Catholic World,* LXXV (May, 1902), 175–179.

Carroll, H. K. "Puerto Rico as a Mission Field," *Missionary Review of the World,* XXIII (August, 1900), 583–591.

Carter, D. W. "Cuba and Its Evangelization," *Missionary Review of the World,* XXV (April, 1902), 253–261.

Cassidy, Patrick S. "The Nicaragua Canal Project," *Catholic World,* LXII (January, 1896), 507.

Chandler, W. A. "The Land Question in Cuba," *The Independent,* LIII (July 25, 1901), 1736–1737.

Clinch, Bryan J. "Anglo-Saxon Missionary Methods," *American Catholic Quarterly Review,* XXVII (April, 1901), 243–265.

———. "Imperialism as a Policy for America," *American Catholic Quarterly Review,* XXIV (January, 1899), 150–161.

———. "Imperialism in the Philippines," *American Catholic Quarterly Review,* XXV (April, 1900), 219–226.

———. "The Language Despotism in the Philippines," *American Catholic Quarterly Review,* XXVII (April, 1902), 369–388.

———. "Spain and Cuba," *American Catholic Quarterly Review,* XXII (October, 1897), 809–819.

———. "The Story of the Philippines," *American Catholic Quarterly Review,* XXIV (April, 1899), 1–17.

———. "The Work of the Philippine Commission," *American Catholic Quarterly Review,* XXVI (October, 1901), 625–643.

Coleman, Ambrose. "Do the Filipinos Really Hate the Spanish Friars?" *American Catholic Quarterly Review,* XXX (July, 1905), 449–461.

———. "The Friars' Estates in the Philippines," *American Catholic Quarterly Review,* XXX (January, 1905), 57–59.

Cortesi, Salvatore, "First American Mission to the Vatican," *The Independent,* LIX (August 14, 1902), 1942–1945.

Coudert, Frederic R. "The American Protective Association," *Forum,* XVII (July, 1894), 513–523.

Creagh, John T. "Report of the Taft Philippine Commission," *Catholic World,* LXXIII (April, 1901), 6–16.

Doyle, A. P. "Religious Problem of the Philippines," *Catholic World,* LXVIII (October, 1898), 119–124.

Gibbons, James Cardinal. "President McKinley," *The Independent,* LIII (September 26, 1901), 2271–2272.

Harty, Bishop J. J. "The Church in the Philippines," *The Independent,* LV (October 8, 1903), 2402–2404.

Hendrick, Bishop Thomas T. "The Cebu Diocese in Prospect," *The Independent,* LVI (February 4, 1904), 238–239.

Hughes, Thomas A. "Catholic Spain—Its Policies and Liberalism," *American Catholic Quarterly Review,* XXII (July, 1897), 493–517.

Ireland, Archbishop John. "The Religions Conditions in our New Island Territory," *Outlook,* LXII (August 26, 1899), 933–934.

Jenkins, T. J. "A.P.A. Conspirators," *Catholic World,* LVII (August, 1893), 685.

Jones, W. A. "The Religious Orders in the Philippines," *Catholic World,* LXVIII (February, 1899), 579–593.

Kennan, George. "Governor Taft's Testimony," *Outlook,* LXX (February 15, 1902), 417–419.

Leo XIII. "The Church in the Philippines," *American Catholic Quarterly Review,* XXVIII (April, 1903), 372–379.

LeRoy, J. A. "Friars in the Philippines," *Political Science Quarterly,* XVIII (December, 1903), 657–680.

Lola, Ramon Reyes. "The Philippines and the Filipinos," *Collier's Weekly,* XXIII, 6 (May 13, 1899), 3–5.

Marshall, Edward. "Talk with General Wood," *Outlook,* LXVIII (July 20, 1901), 669–673.

McFaul, James A. "Catholics and American Citizenship," *North American Review,* CLXXI (September, 1900), 320–332.

O'Keeffe, Henry O. "A Word on the Church and the New Possessions," *Catholic World,* LXVIII (December, 1898), 319–322.

Reeves, Robert N. "Religious Conditions in the Philippine Islands," *Outlook,* LXIII (September 16, 1899), 158–160.

Regidor, Antonio. "The Filipino Case Against the Friars," *The Independent,* LII (February 7, 1901), 317–320.

Rodriguez, J. I. "The Church and Church Property in the Island of Cuba," *American Catholic Quarterly Review,* XXV (April, 1900), 366–390.

Runcie, Major James E. "American Misgovernment of Cuba," *North American Review,* CLXX (February, 1900), 284–294.

Shane, Charleson. "A Sketch of Catholicity in the Philippines," *Catholic World,* LXVII (August, 1898), 695–698.

Stuntz, Homer C. "Catholic Church Titles in the Philippines," *The Independent,* LIII (October 17, 1901), 2469–2470.

Taft, William Howard. "Civil Government in the Philippines," *Outlook,* LXXI (May 31, 1902), 305–321.

———. "The Philippines," *National Geographic Magazine,* XVI (August, 1905), 361–375.

Traynor, W. H. J. "Policy and Power of A.P.A.," *North American Review,* CLXII (June, 1896), 650–671.

Wallace, Lew, Jr. "Church Property in our Recent Acquisitions," *Outlook,* LXIV (February 17, 1900), 402–404.

Winthrop, Colonel W. "The Problem of the Philippines," *Outlook,* LIX (June 11, 1898), 377–383.

Wood, Leonard. "The Military Government of Cuba," *Annals of the American Academy of Political and Social Sciences,* XXI (March, 1903), 1–30.

Worcester, Dean C. "Knotty Problems of the Philippines," *The Century Magazine,* LVI (October, 1898), 873–879.

SECONDARY SOURCES

Books

Achutegui, Pedro S. and Miguel A. Bernard. *Religious Revolution in the Philippines: The Life and Church of Gregario Aglipay, 1860–1960.* Manila: Ateneo de Manila, 1960.

Ahern, Patrick H. *The Life of John J. Keane, Educator and Archbishop, 1839–1918.* Milwaukee: Bruce Publishing Company, 1955.

Barry, Colman J. *The Catholic Church and German Americans.* Milwaukee: Bruce Publishing Company, 1953.

Baumgartner, Apollinaris W. *Catholic Journalism: A Study of Its Development in the U.S. 1789–1930.* New York: Columbia University Press, 1931.

Beers, Henry P. *American Naval Occupation and Government of Guam, 1898–1902.* Washington, D.C.: Office of Records, Navy Department, 1944.

Billington, Ray A. *The Protestant Crusade, 1800–1860.* New York: Macmillan Company, 1938.

Blount, James H. *The American Occupation of the Philippines, 1898–1912.* New York: Putnam, 1912.

Brown, I. V. *Lyman Abbott, Christian Evolutionist.* Cambridge, Massachusetts: Harvard University Press, 1953.

Browne, Henry J. *The Catholic Church and the Knights of Labor*. Washington, D.C.: Catholic University Press, 1949.

Chamberlin, Frederick Carleton. *The Philippine Problem, 1898–1913*. Boston: Little, Brown and Company, 1913.

Cortissoz, Royal. *The Life of Whitelaw Reid*. 2 vols. New York: Scribner's, 1921.

Cronin, Bernard C. *Father Yorke and the Labor Movement in San Francisco, 1900–1910*. Washington, D.C.: Catholic University Press, 1943.

Desmond, Humphrey J. *The A.P.A. Movement*. Washington, D.C.: New Century Press, 1912.

Elliott, Charles B. *The Philippines*. 2 vols. Indianapolis: Bobbs-Merrill, 1917.

Ellis, John Tracy. *American Catholicism*. Chicago: University of Chicago Press, 1958.

———. *The Life of James Cardinal Gibbons, Archbishop of Baltimore, 1838–1921*. Milwaukee: Bruce Publishing Company, 1952.

Ferrara, Orestes. *The Last Spanish War*. New York: Paisley Press, 1937.

Forbes, William Cameron. *The Philippine Islands*. Boston: Houghton Mifflin, 1913.

Freidel, Frank. *The Splendid Little War*. Boston: Little, Brown and Company, 1958.

Goldman, Eric F. *Charles J. Bonaparte, Patrician Reformer, His Early Career*. Baltimore: Johns Hopkins University Press, 1943.

Guilday, Peter, *The National Pastorals of the American Hierarchy*. Westminster, Maryland: Newman Press, 1954.

Hagedorn, Herman. *Leonard Wood: A Biography*. 2 vols. New York: Harpers, 1931.

Healy, David F. *The United States in Cuba, 1898–1902*. Madison: University of Wisconsin Press, 1963.

Higham, John. *Strangers in the Land: Patterns of American Nativism, 1860–1925*. New Brunswick, New Jersey: Rutgers University Press, 1955.

Holden, Vincent J. *The Yankee Paul: Isaac Thomas Hecker*. Milwaukee: Bruce Publishing Company, 1958.

Kalaw, Maximo M. *Self-Government in the Philippines*. New York: Century Company, 1919.

Kane, John J. *Catholic-Protestant Conflicts in America*. Chicago: Henry Regnery Company, 1955.

Kinzer, Donald L. *An Episode in Anti-Catholicism: The American Protective Association*. Seattle: University of Washington Press, 1964.

Klinkhamer, Sister Marie Carolyn. *Edward Douglas White, Chief Justice of the United States*. Washington, D.C.: Catholic University Press, 1943.

Leech, Margaret. *In the Days of McKinley*. New York: Harpers, 1959.

LeRoy, James A. *The Americans in the Philippines: A History of the Conquest and First Years of Occupation*. 2 vols. Boston: Houghton Mifflin, 1914.

McAvoy, Thomas T. *The Great Crisis in American Catholic History, 1895–1900*. Chicago: Henry Regnery Company, 1958.

May, Ernest R. *Imperial Democracy: The Emergence of America as a Great Power*. New York: Harcourt, Brace and World, 1961.

Mecham, J. Lloyd. *Church and State in Latin America*. Chapel Hill: University of North Carolina Press, 1934.

Millis, Walter. *The Martial Spirit*. Cambridge, Massachusetts: Riverside Press, 1931.

Morgan, H. Wayne. *William McKinley and His America*. Syracuse, New York: Syracuse University Press, 1963.

Moses, Bernard. *Spain Overseas*. New York: privately printed, 1929.

Moynihan, James H. *The Life of Archbishop Ireland*. New York: Harpers, 1953.

Phelan, John Leddy. *The Hispanization of the Philippines*. Madison: University of Wisconsin Press, 1959.

Pratt, Julius W. *America's Colonial Experiment*. New York: Prentice-Hall, 1950.

———. *Expansionists of 1898*. Baltimore: Johns Hopkins University Press, 1936.

Rhodes, James Ford. *The McKinley and Roosevelt Administrations*. New York: Macmillan Company, 1922.

Roosevelt, Theodore Jr. *Colonial Policies of the United States*. New York: Doubleday Company, 1937.

Schroll, Sister Agnes Claire. *The Social Thought of John Lancaster Spalding*. Washington, D.C.: Catholic University Press, 1944.

Shaugnessy, G. M. *Has the Immigrant Kept the Faith?* New York: Macmillan Company, 1925.

Stokes, Anson Phelps. *Church and State in the United States*. New York: Harpers, 1950.

Storey, Moorfield, and M. P. Lichanco. *The Conquest of the Philippines by the United States, 1898–1925*. New York: Putnam, 1926.

Vollmar, Edward. *The Catholic Church in America: A Bibliography*. New Brunswick, New Jersey: Scarecrow Press, 1963.

Wilkerson, M. M. *Public Opinion and the Spanish-American War*. Baton Rouge: Louisiana State University Press, 1932.

Willoughby, William Franklin. *Territories and Dependencies of the United States. Their Government and Administration*. New York: Century Company, 1905.

Zwierlein, Frederick. *The Life and Letters of Bishop McQuaid.* 3 vols. Rochester, New York: The Art Print Shop, 1925–1927.

———. *Theodore Roosevelt and Catholics.* St. Louis: V. T. Suren, 1956.

ARTICLES

Auxier, George W. "Middle Western Newspapers and the Spanish American War," *Mississippi Valley Historical Review,* XXVI (March, 1940), 523–534.

Barton, George. "A Story of Self-Sacrifice. Being a Record of the Labors of the Catholic Sisterhoods in the Spanish-American War," *American Catholic Historical Society Records,* XXXVII (September, 1926), 104–192.

Blied, Benjamin J. "Catholic Aspects of the Spanish-American War," *Social Justice Review,* XVIII (August, 1933), 492, 513.

Byrne, Edward J. "The Religious Issue in National Politics," *Catholic Historical Review,* XIV (June, 1928), 329–369.

Farrell, John T. "Archbishop Ireland and Manifest Destiny," *Catholic Historical Review,* XXXIII (October, 1947), 269–301.

Goss, Edward F. "The Taft Commission to the Vatican, 1902," *American Catholic Historical Society Records,* XLVI (September, 1935), 183–201.

Harrington, Fred H. "The Anti-Imperialist Movement in the United States, 1898–1900," *Mississippi Valley Historical Review,* XXII (June, 1935), 211–230.

Kinzer, Donald L. "The Political Uses of Anti-Catholicism: Michigan and Wisconsin, 1890–1894," *Michigan History,* XXXIX (September, 1953), 312–326.

McAvoy, Thomas T. "The Formation of the Catholic Minority in the United States, 1820–1860," *The Review of Politics,* X (January, 1948), 13–34.

Pratt, Julius W. "The Large Policy of 1898," *Mississippi Valley Historical Review,* XIX (September, 1932), 219–242.

Reuter, Frank T. "American Catholics and the Establishment of the Philippine Public School System," *Catholic Historical Review,* XLIX (October, 1963), 365–381.

Robertson, James A. "The Aglipay Schism in the Philippine Islands," *Catholic Historical Review,* IV (October, 1918), 315–344.

———. "Catholicism in the Philippine Islands," *Catholic Historical Review,* III (January, 1918), 375–391.

Roohan, James E. "American Catholics and the Social Question, 1865–1900," *United States Catholic Historical Society Records,* XLIII (1951), 3–26.

Dissertations

Karraker, William A. "The American Churches and the Spanish-American War" (Ph.D. Dissertation, University of Chicago, 1940).

Parker, Donald D. "Church and State in the Philippines, 1896–1906" (Ph.D. Dissertation, University of Chicago, 1937).

INDEX

At the close of the Spanish-American War the United States found itself in possession of a colonial empire. The role played by the American Catholic Church in influencing administrative policy for the new, and predominately Catholic, dependencies is the subject of this incisive study by Frank T. Reuter.

Mr. Reuter discusses the centuries-old intricate involvement of the Spanish crown and the native Roman Catholic Church in the civil, social, and charitable institutions of Cuba, Puerto Rico, Guam, and the Philippines. He explores the attempts of United States officials to apply the traditional doctrine of separation of church and state in resolving the problems of a Church-run school system, the alleged desecration of native Catholic churches by American forces in the Philippines, the native antagonism toward the Spanish friars, and the disposition of Church property in dependencies with a deeply rooted correlation between the Catholic Church and the state.

Recounting the development of the Catholic Church in America, which felt responsible for maintaining the islands' religious structure after Spanish control was removed, Mr. Reuter sees the reaction of the Church to the war with Spain and to colonial policy in the early post-war period as voiced not by a monolithic political force, but by diverse spokesmen—in particular the unofficial voice of the Catholic press. He traces the growth of the Church in the United States from a disparate group of dioceses clinging to European backgrounds, disunited by a divided hierarchy, and attacked by the wave of the anti-Catholic, nativistic sentiments of the last two decades of the nineteenth century, to a church body unified by the problems in the colonies. Catholic opinion, although not utilized to its full political potential, achieved a common focus through the formation of the Federation of American Catholic Societies and the debate in Congress over the Philippine Government Bill.

This study of American and native Catholic attitudes toward the formulation of United States policy in the insular dependencies and the attitude of the United States government toward the Catholic interests in the dependencies details the interplay of personalities and organizations: Presidents William McKinley and Theodore Roosevelt; William Howard Taft, civil governor of the Philippines; James Cardinal Gibbons, moderator between